Conflict of Light
and Wind

Also by C. Christopher Soufas

*En torno al hombre y a los monstruos: Ensayos
críticos sobre la novelística de Carlos Rojas*
(edited with Cecilia Castro Lee)

C. Christopher Soufas

Conflict of Light and Wind

The Spanish Generation of 1927
and the Ideology of Poetic Form

Wesleyan University Press
Middletown, Connecticut

Copyright © 1989 by C. Christopher Soufas

This book is supported by a grant from The Program for Cultural Cooperation Between Spain's Ministry of Culture and United States' Universities.

All inquiries and permissions requests should be addressed to the Publisher, Wesleyan University Press, 110 Mt. Vernon Street, Middletown, Connecticut 06457.

Library of Congress Cataloging-in-Publication Data

Soufas, C. Christopher
Conflict of light and wind : the Spanish generation of 1927 and the ideology of poetic form / C. Christopher Soufas.—1st ed.
p.   cm.
Includes index.
ISBN 0-8195-5219-4
1. Spanish poetry—20th century—History and criticism.
2. Politics and literature.   I. Title.
PQ6085.S65   1989
861'.62'09—dc19   89-5533
                                                                      CIP

Manufactured in the United States of America

First Edition

For Teresa

Contents

Illustrations

Preface

Literary criticism is the product of a point of view rooted in certain historical and ideological assumptions about literature. The critical model I embrace recognizes both the need for a concept of representation—that literature, and especially poetry, is engaged in the production of a form or structure that demands that it be understood both verbally and visually—and the equal need to ground the words and images that constitute form in the historical-ideological medium that constitutes them. The radical rejection of mimesis in postmodern critical theory— even to the point of characterizing consciousness as simply a process of writing scrupulously independent of the empirical tradition that conceives human understanding in terms of an idea or image's being imprinted on the etching plate of the mind—is certainly not original, only perhaps the most severe case imaginable. Indeed, it is the severity of the rejection of the image and of the notion that the human mind needs to make clear and distinct ideas and pictures about things (especially by Paul de Man, who has found in language a hopeless ambiguity that in turn suggests the human mind's incapacity for decision) that makes recent critical assertions seem less than objective. All contemporary art, however, is premised on critiquing the empirical model of the image. Long before Jacques Derrida and de Man, innumerable artists, but most significantly Spanish artists such as Francisco de Goya and Pablo Picasso, affirmed the insufficiency of mimetic theories of art, the empirical mind model, and its requirement that images be considered an exact, translatable

equivalent of ideas or things existing in nature. Yet these critiques have never posited the complete elimination of image-
making in art and what is, at least from the Renaissance onward,
the decisive feature of Western artistic values.

Goya's affirmation in *Los Caprichos (The Caprices)* at the turn
of the nineteenth century that "El sueño de la razón produce monstruos" ("The dream of reason produces monsters")—the human
mind is capable of producing strange and grotesque images for
which empirical theories do not account—marked a turning point
in Western art and thinking about the status of images and how
they come into being. What Goya discovered was that images do
not have to originate in nature as part of a passive, objective process of sensory perception but can also be the products of "original
ideas" (see Locke), in the imagination and elsewhere, for which
empirical-sensationalist philosophy cannot account. Goya's profound discovery was that images can also be the products of an
inner, subjective experience that does not reflect what normally
exists in nature but rather in a single "fevered" imagination. Departing only slightly from these insights, Marx wrote, half a century later, in *The German Ideology* that entire social classes and
nations also produce biased and partial images, likened to the up-
side-down image that the photographic camera obscura produces, which have no objective status in nature but rather reflect
a much narrower national or class agenda. To this subjective,
biased, partial image, which parades as the complete and objective
truth, Marx assigned the name "ideology."

In his seminal study on the rhetoric of iconoclasm in contemporary thought and criticism, W. J. T. Mitchell relates Marx's
concept of ideology to artistic and literary works in his observation that

the concept of ideology is grounded, as the word suggests, in the
notion of mental entities or "ideas" that provide the materials of
thought. Insofar as these ideas are understood as images—as pictorial,
graphic signs imprinted or projected on the medium of consciousness—then ideology, the science of ideas, is really an iconology, a
theory of imagery. (164)

In relation to its earliest application, therefore, the term "ideology" refers to the process by which a particular group in society

creates a false image or set of images by which to live and even to worship. Ideology for Marx carries negative connotations about the way one class of society, the middle class, creates its idols at the expense of the larger underclass. Significantly, Marx's concept of ideology is applied to an entire process of valuation, not simply the political aspects, by which a set of false images is given excessive valuation at the expense of other possibilities.

What is also suggested in this very broad definition of ideology, by which an ongoing process of image production on a class and societal scale elevates one group above another, is not only the inescapability of the concept but also the ideological status of ideology itself. What Marx expresses along with his distrust of the bourgeoisie is his equal distrust of images, which is suggested by the fact that he chooses the inverted image of the camera obscura, today's metaphor for faithful representation, as his metaphor for false representation. In this book, which concerns itself with the critical image of and the poetic images produced by the Generation of 1927 (from about 1920 to 1936), I have chosen to use Mitchell's refinement of Marx and to regard ideology in an even broader but more positive sense, as a principle of differentiation. Since I am skeptical of criticism that makes all-encompassing claims, my reading of the work of the Generation of 1927 offers simply a valid if unorthodox point of view. Ideology must not be limited only to political considerations but understood to reflect all factors constituting an artist's attitudes toward reality and art. In this sense it is possible to say that ideology constitutes the formal possibilities of the literary work. In recent years Louis Althusser, Pierre Macherey, Terry Eagleton, and especially Fredric Jameson, in *Fables of Aggression: Wyndham Lewis, the Modernist As Fascist,* have held that it is possible to speak about intimate interconnections between formal and ideological dimensions of a work of art if it is understood that "the ideological achieves objective figuration" by means of "an intrinsically negative and critical 'distantiation' of its ideological starting point, rather than its simple replication" (Jameson 22). Further, Jameson writes,

great art distances ideology by the way in which, endowing the latter with figuration and with narrative articulation, the text frees its ideolog-

ical contents . . . by the sheer formal immanence with which an ideological system exhausts its permutations and ends up projecting its own
ultimate structural closure. (22–23)

Wyndham Lewis, a contemporary of the poets of the Generation of 1927, has been traditionally considered nonideological
because his writing does not overtly articulate a political
position. Jameson's choice of Lewis as a model for exploring
the ways in which ideology represents itself in, and as, form
is germane to a study of the poets of the Generation of 1927;
these poets created a body of work that for half a century has
been studied primarily in terms of its separation from historical
events: political developments, which culminated in the Spanish Civil War, but also broader philosophical and artistic
debates in Spain and the rest of Europe during the early
decades of this century. Critical approaches to the Generation
of 1927 have consistently advocated a strict separation between the formal aspects of this poetry, defined in a narrow
and limiting sense, and literally everything else. Ever since the
concept of a Generation of 1927 arose, the critical premise
has been that this poetry has nothing to do with ideology,
that the poetry written during the 1920s and '30s should be
considered, much as the American and English New Criticism
for so long conceived literary works, as exemplary instances
of the production of "verbal icons" (see Wimsatt). From
Dámaso Alonso's earliest opinions about the literary history of
a "generación [que] no se alza contra nada" ("generation [that]
revolts against nothing") (172) to present thinking that "the
years during which the generation ... reached its creative
maturity (1924–31) left no significant ideological traces in
their work" (Jiménez-Fajardo 21), opinion has been nearly
unanimous that this group of poets, and its poetry, was almost
untouched by the fervor of position-taking that so obsessed
Europe and Spain during the years that these poets produced
their most acclaimed work. My reading suggests that such
opinions are distortions of literary history, products of an
undemocratic critical ideology that has discounted the interre-
lation between form and ideology, between the words and
images of apolitical poetic texts and the production of those
images in a historical milieu.

Critical opinion about the poetry of the Generation of 1927—
and, indeed, the very concept of a Generation of 1927—has
been dominated by an ideology premised on the notion that the
production of this poetry is a phenomenon separable from the
political, psychological, and moral forces of history. Such an
idea has restricted this field of study, has underemphasized this
group's commonality with other poetic developments in modernist Europe, and has served to propagate the idea that this
poetry is interesting only for rather limited aesthetic reasons.
By reading the poetry of Jorge Guillén, Pedro Salinas, Vicente
Aleixandre, Luis Cernuda, Federico García Lorca, and Rafael
Alberti in the context of ideology, including all relevant factors
in these poets' belief system—that is, how they come to produce
the images that constitute their poetry—this study chooses to
understand the words and images of the Generation of 1927 as
products not exclusively of a creative will but also of a dialectical
engagement with its historical circumstance.

The study of the poetry of individual poets has been fundamentally influenced by an especially ungenerous idea of literary
history that became consolidated during the forties, simultaneous with, and ultimately complementary to, Francisco Franco's
attempt to establish political hegemony, and that steadfastly
dedicates itself to the notion that there is an objective entity
identifiable by the name Generation of 1927, "grupo poético"
("poetic group"), or a similar term. This idea, which I characterize as an interested ideological concept, has fundamentally determined the conditions under which this poetry has been studied
during the last half century. The critical paradigm that emerges
from the literary criticism of members of this group—specifically
that written by Pedro Salinas and Dámaso Alonso—has influenced the critical consciousness of this era and has prevented
the emergence of a more generously conceived critical agenda
in post-Franco Spain. Before offering my reading of these poets,
therefore, it is necessary to address the issue of the Generation
of 1927 as an ideological construct and an inadequate reflection
of the conditions of literary production, and to propose in the
process an alternative, more historically sensitive methodology
presented simply as a viable image through which to understand
this body of poetry.

Acknowledgments

I should like to thank the National Endowment for the Humanities for providing research funding for the investigation phase of this project in the form of an NEH Summer Seminar (1984) and an NEH Summer Stipend (1985). For support during the writing phase, I wish to thank the Research and Publications Committee at West Chester University, West Chester, Pennsylvania, for a summer research grant (1986) and the Council on Research at Louisiana State University for a summer research stipend (1987). All of this assistance has greatly facilitated the completion of this study. I should also like to thank Madelyn Gutwirth, of West Chester University, for many valuable insights about the proper scope of literary criticism, W. J. T. Mitchell, of the University of Chicago, and Wendy Steiner, of the University of Pennsylvania, for the theoretical grounding they have provided in the field of iconology, and Carlos Rojas, of Emory University, for his careful reading and critique of this manuscript at various stages. The translations, entirely my own, are intended only to assist nonreaders of Spanish in following the text.

"... el conflicto de luz y viento"

Federico García Lorca
"Norma y paraíso de los negros"
Poeta en Nueva York

Conflict of Light
and Wind

Introduction

The Generation of 1927
As an Ideological Concept

Although Spanish criticism has been dominated by the idea of the literary generation as a critical concept for almost the last fifty years and has witnessed the naming of at least six principal generations of Spanish writers—the Generations of '98, '14, '27, '36, '50, and, most recently, '68—there have been surprisingly few theoretical statements or subsequent substantive debate about the suitability of the concept in describing Spanish literary history of the twentieth century. Such a concept originates largely from applications of models provided by German philology and literary history, especially the work of Julius Petersen. Petersen's ideas—via Pedro Salinas and, later, Dámaso Alonso—provide the decisive theoretical model for the Spanish "generación literaria" in its more critically rigorous form, which today remains the fundamental organizing principle of contemporary Spanish literary history. In many countries contemporary literary history has been organized into all-inclusive yet very loosely unified categories, such as modernism and postmodernism, whose duration is usually much longer than a generation. In Spain, on the other hand, critics have tended to identify generations of writers. These generations necessarily do not include all aspects of the literary production of a given period; rather, the name is applied to more specific, yet often fragmented, literary phenomena within a certain period. The unfortunate consequence is a literary history in which the part stands for, and becomes, the whole.

This is certainly the case of the Generation of 1898, which emerged early in the century as a very loose and flexible concept without any pretense of its being used as a model for literary history. The term quickly came to describe the phenomenon of a group of Spanish writers who had apparently dedicated their literary energies to an examination of Spanish problems. Members of the group did little to encourage the idea that such a generation existed; their pronouncements on the subject were, with the notable exception of Azorín, somewhat contradictory. Azorín challenged the use of the term as a means to identify a group of contemporary writers rebelling against the values of what was commonly perceived to be a conformist and acquiescent earlier generation. In his 1910 essay "La generación de 1898," Azorín takes great care to deemphasize rebelliousness and to stress the many specific ideological continuities between the Generation of 1898 and the previous group of writers of importance, which he labels the Generation of 1870: "La generación de 1898, en suma, no ha hecho sino continuar el movimiento ideológico de la generación anterior" ("The generation of 1898, in short, simply continued the ideological movement of the previous genera- tion") (255).

Azorín maintains that there had been a much longer tradition of "crítica social" ("social criticism") in Spain than popular coin- ers of the term Generation of 1898 were willing to admit. With- out such a tradition the Generation of 1898 would not have been able to develop.

La gran corriente ideológica de 1870 a 1898 ... concluye lógica- mente—avivada por el Desastre—a la crítica social que florece desde 1898 hasta algunos años después. ... Cuando hayáis considerado tal hecho histórico comprenderéis de qué manera ha podido moldearse la mentalidad de la generación de 1898, y cómo ese vasto y acre espíritu de crítica social ... ha llegado a encarnarse hoy sólido, fuerte, profundamente en la muchedumbre.

The great ideological current between 1870 and 1898 ... concludes logically—inflamed by the Disaster—at the social criticism that flour- ishes from 1898 to a few years later. ... When you consider such a historical fact you will understand how the mentality of the generation of 1898 has been able to mold itself, and how this vast and biting spirit of social criticism ... has embodied itself solidly, strongly, deeply in the masses.   (247–48)

Azorín subtly denies an essential difference between the ways the Generation of 1898 interpreted Spanish reality and the ways of the preceding era. According to Azorín, a spirit of cooperation and conformity with an earlier ideological line informed the development of the present group. Thus what seemed to be a sharp break with the past was, in Azorín's view, a profoundly felt spiritual communion with the past; what seemed to be the emergence of distinctive ways of liberated thinking was really an inheritance from the previous generation. The logical conclusion to be drawn from Azorín's essay, therefore, is that there was nothing fundamentally new about the ideological position of the Generation of 1898 since its thinking did not differ in essence from that of José Echegaray, Ramón de Campoamor, and Benito Pérez Galdós.

Azorín undermines the notion of a Generation of 1898, at least as popular opinion conceived of it, at the very moment he affirms its existence. The Generation of 1898 is represented as a natural and logical consequence of historical developments that upheld, rather than opposed, an ideological line. Individual differences, distinctive characteristics, manifestations of nonconformity and rebellion are less important than the understanding that the writers in this group were of one mind about the issues they faced and, further, that such issues were prefigured for them by the ideological agenda of the earlier generation. For Azorín, therefore, the Generation of 1898 existed primarily to give greater direction to preexisting ideas in the aftermath of the national crisis of Spain's war with the United States, not to reject them. Azorín's attitude reflects a realization common to members of this group: after initially flirting with radicalism, they concluded that a political solution to Spain's problems was impossible. The solution they favored was to redefine the problem of Spain, to advocate change through nonpolitical means (see Blanco Aguinaga). It was desirable, therefore, for Azorín to situate himself in the ideological mainstream rather than to uphold an image of his generation at the critical fringe. His strategy was to use the concept Generation of 1898 to voice his concerns in a more universal and less overtly political context, to suggest that the ideological program of the Generation of 1898 was not essentially different from that advocated by others who had already achieved a high valuation in critical and public opinion. The first serious statement about the nature and constitution of the literary generation in twentieth-century Spanish literature was, therefore, a conservative political maneuver intended to emphasize that the concept Generation of 1898 referred to a mainstream literary-philosophical movement. Azorín's essay undermines the distinctiveness of the concept of a Generation of 1898 since he clearly wishes to suggest that this idea started much earlier. Interestingly, José Ortega y Gasset's important and extensive philosophical ideas on the generation (discussed later) were overlooked when, some twenty-five years later, Salinas invoked Azorín's model to provide his own, and now Spain's, borrowed directly from Petersen.

Salinas provides the first rigorous theoretical statement on the constitution of the Generation of 1898, but, more important, the first and final model of the literary generation in general in "El concepto de generación literaria aplicado a la del 98" ("The Concept of the Literary Generation Applied to the Generation of '98") in *Literatura española: Siglo XX*. Azorín's and Salinas's essays are quite similar in many ways, especially in the idea of the ideological unity of the literary generation. They differ, however, in their conception of the historical mechanisms by which the agenda of a generation comes into being. Salinas's essay is offered, in fact, as a more critically rigorous confirmation of what he considers mere intuitions "para ver si aquello que Azorín llamaba 'generación,' por una buena ventura o por una opinión puramente personal, podía corresponder a lo que llama generación la historiografía literaria alemana" ("to see if what Azorín called 'generation,' by a stroke of good luck or a purely personal opinion, could correspond to what German literary historiography calls a generation") (47). The literary generation—and the Generation of 1898 in particular—for Salinas, like Azorín, operates on a principle of group conformity and similarity. Yet whereas Azorín's notion of similarity responds to a desire to answer what he considers common misconceptions,

Salinas claims that certain objectively verifiable historical conditions must exist before there can be a literary generation. Salinas in fact does bring much greater rigor to Azorín's loose idea of an ideological compatibility among members of the Generation of 1898—which, according to Azorín, was a consequence of their fraternal association and ideological compatibility with the previous generation of authors—by defining the group as a consequence of their fraternal association and ideological compatibility with themselves. Basing his analysis exclusively on the theoretical model of Petersen, Salinas develops the thesis that personal characteristics in common among the members of the literary generation directly reflect artistic and ideological similarities in the art that the group produces.

No generation can exist unless certain fundamental conditions are met. The first of these is a coincidence of birth; the members of a literary generation must be born within a certain range of years. Even more important is a homogeneity of educational experiences that will lead to "la especial modelación mental del individuo . . . en que se desarrolla un grupo nacido en los mismos años" ("the special mental molding of the individual . . . in which a group born in the same years develops") (49). Strongly implied but not stated is that generation members will almost necessarily be from the same social class. Opportunities for frequent personal contact among the members of the group are also important. Among the types of contact Salinas mentions is the exposure to fellow generationalists' ideas—by direct personal contact or, lacking that, by means of literary and other reviews: "Las revistas son, para mí, uno de los índices más claros para estudiar lo vivo de la preparación de un nuevo estado espiritual" ("The literary magazines are, for me, one of the clearest indices to study the intensity of preparation of a new spiritual state") (51). This suggestion is, I suspect, also motivated by Salinas's personal experience with his own circle of friends, many of whom were actively engaged in publishing literary reviews during the twenties and thirties. Also indispensable is a common generational experience, as, for example, the national catastrophe of 1898, or corrolary to that, the awareness that the previous generation had run its course and offered nothing new to emulate. Here lies the real discrepancy with Azorín, who wants to diminish the idea of distance between the Generation of 1898 and its predecessors.

More controversial, however, are the most distinctive features of the membership requirements. What Petersen terms *Führer-tur* and Salinas translates as *caudillaje,* a generational leadership, is also an essential feature of the literary generation since it ensures that there is a willful unifying impetus toward ideological unity within the group. Although he concedes that it would be difficult to name a flesh-and-blood spokesman for the Generation of 1898, Salinas maintains that "sería difícil negar también que ideológicamente había una guía de esta generación" ("it would also be difficult to deny that ideologically there was a guide to this generation"), the fatherly figure of Friedrich Nietzsche, whose presence is all the more powerful in the case of the Generation of 1898 because of his absence: "yo me atrevería a decir que en todo el ambiente ... de la época se advierte en-tonces la apetencia del caudillo, que el *führer* está presente precisamente por su ausencia" ("I would dare to say that in the entire atmosphere ... of this time one senses an appetite for the strong leader, that the *führer* is present precisely because of his absence") (55). The leader does not have to be a person: a guiding, unifying idea is sufficient. Most interestingly, Salinas defines the *Führer* of the Generation of 1898 as the desire to be led even in the absence of a leader. What this demonstrates is not necessarily Salinas's desire to make the concept fit the reality but rather his wholehearted acceptance of the model and thus his desire to understand groups of writers unified ideologically rather than ideologically disunited. The requirement of ideologi-cal uniformity brings with it a companion requirement, the development of a generational language, which in the case of the Generation of 1898 Salinas associates with the "*modernismo*" of Rubén Darío: "Se ha intentado dar como equivalente a la generación del 98 la del modernismo. Me parece erróneo: el modernismo, a mi entender, no es otra cosa que el lenguaje generacional del 98" ("There has been an attempt to make the generation of '98 equivalent to *modernismo*. This seems errone-ous: *modernismo,* to my way of thinking, is nothing other than the generational language of the generation of '98") (56). Such a maneuver, a convenient means of devaluing a competing literary phenomenon defined in terms of its stylistic innovations rather than its ideas, is also a means of underscoring that a generational language is at the service, if not of revolution, of the "absent father" of a common ideology. Thus Azorín's weak concept of a loosely unified group of like-minded writers defined by the past is redefined in Salinas's criticism by a rigorous and disciplined method of analysis that appeals to historical facts and phenomena in relation to an ideological program that fellow generationalists, or their *Führer,* decide. Underlying Salinas's "objective" methodology is the idea that the forces of history are moving toward unity, that history provides the means for the expression, not of a plurality of opinions and positions in art, but of just one will, as Petersen says, "una unidad de ser debida a la comunidad de destino" ("a unity of being owing to a commonality of destiny") (188), whose artistic product is an art that springs from a common consciousness.

It is evident that this method of analysis, understood by Salinas as a much more objective and historically rigorous approach to literary history, applies to other groups of writers, including his own. New literary generations also emerge through acts of will to fill an aesthetic vacuum, the consequence of "el anquilosamiento o parálisis de la generación anterior" ("the immobility of the previous generation") (56), and to fulfill a destiny that the past is acknowledged as having only a minimal role in shaping. Salinas's essay profoundly legitimizes the vague concept Generation of 1898 as it also, and more importantly, lays the foundation for the study of contemporary literary history in Spain by means of the methodological vehicle of the literary generation. This seminal essay provides the theoretical and practical justification for other studies on the question of the literary generation immediately following the Spanish Civil War. Among the most noteworthy, in whole or in part, on this question are studies by José Gaos, María Luisa Caturla, and especially Pedro Laín Entralgo that serve to enhance and solidify this concept in the Spanish literary-critical consciousness.

An almost identical process occurs with regard to the emergence of the concept of a Generation of 1927. Dámaso Alonso coined the term in his highly influential semicritical, semitestimonial account in "Una generación poética (1920–36)" of the primordial event in the life of Spain's second literary generation of the century—the gathering in 1927 in Sevilla of most of the members associated with this group to pay homage to Luis de Góngora on the occasion of the tercentenary of his death. This essay has proven decisive in establishing both the notion that there is a Generation of 1927 and that the literary production of the group should be studied in such a context. Alonso's criteria for classification come exclusively from Salinas and Petersen: "esos escritores no formaban un mero grupo, sino que en ellos se daban las condiciones mínimas de lo que entiendo por generación: coetaneidad, compañerismo, intercambio, reacción similar ante excitantes externos" ("these writers did not form a mere group, but rather in them were to be found the minimal conditions for what I understand as a generation: contemporaneity, comradeship, intellectual exchange, similar reaction in the face of external stimulants") (667). At another point Alonso also expresses the idea that the poets of this generation are of a like mind about their poetry: "Magnífico coro, donde cada voz tiene su timbre, pero que, conjunto, se ofrece ante el altar, con un pureza de intención como seguramente no ha conocido nunca la literatura española" ("Magnificent choir, where each voice has its timbre, but which, together, offers itself before the altar, with a purity of purpose that surely has never been known before in Spanish literature") (675).

Most noteworthy about Alonso's essay is that by the time he was writing (1948) he did not feel compelled to justify the theoretical category literary generation. The justification was by then already present in the critical consciousness, and thus it is not necessary for Alonso to establish formal categories or criteria for this new generation. He has only to invoke an already popular notion and thus to adduce, through his evocation of their association and friendship, the objective evidence of the existence of such a generation. From here, however, Alonso leaps to the conclusion that their friendships, collaborations, and so forth also mean that these poets think alike. As in Azorín, Salinas, Laín

Entralgo, and others, Alonso's idea of both the literary generation in general and the Generation of 1927 in particular includes the notion of like-mindedness among the generation members. Unlike Salinas, however, who invokes the concept of ideology, Alonso makes the poets ideologically neutral in both a political and artistic sense:

No, no hubo un sentido conjunto de protesta política, ni aun de preocupación política en esa generación. ... Pero es el caso que tampoco literariamente se rompía con nada, se protestaba de nada ... no hay ninguna discontinuidad, ningún rompimiento en la tradición poética. Puedo decir más: no hay quiebra fundamental alguna ... entre la revolución modernista y la poesía de hoy, de 1948.

No, there was not a united feeling of political protest, nor even of political concern in that generation. ... But it is the case that neither did it break literarily with anything nor did it protest against anything ... there is no discontinuity, no breaking with the poetic tradition. I can go further: there is no fundamental break whatsoever ... between the *modernista* revolution and the poetry of today, 1948. (659)

As for Azorín and Salinas before him, literary history for Alonso is premised on the idea that it produces conformity and continuity but not difference. Alonso takes pains to make his generation seem apolitical, like-minded continuers of a literary tradition "profundamente arraigada en la entraña nacional y española" ("profoundly rooted in the national and Spanish essence") and decidedly unlike "otros movimientos estéticos que pasan las fronteras por esos años inmediatamente anterior al cuajar de nuestra generación" ("other aesthetic movements that cross the national borders during the years immediately before the congealing of our generation") (661). In other words, the Generation of 1927 was also motivated by nationalist sentiments similar to those that were, in 1948, the policy of the Franco government. An idea of a literary generation based on a paradigm of similarity and uniformity is supplemented with the corollary that the Generation of 1927 was also a particularly Spanish generation whose poetry was grounded in a profound respect for literary tradition and for the national, and even nationalistic, genius of Spanish literary expression. The generational concept as it evolved was entirely compatible with the state ideology that emerged after

the Civil War. The Francoist state was an ideologically impover-
ished regime whose ability to maintain power depended primarily on its appeals to uphold national unity and separation from a
disapproving European mainstream rather than on any elaborate
ideological program. The literary generation, premised on a
principle of unity and similarity of purpose, fitted well into the
larger political agenda during the Franco years. Indeed, the term
generation referred specifically to a national grouping of writers.
In other words, the literary generation stopped at the Spanish
border. Like Francoism, the literary generation was seen to uphold a principle of national unity at an artistic level as its highest
value.

An examination of representative critical studies of the Generation of 1927 during subsequent decades reveals a largely un-
questioning acceptance of both Salinas's theoretical notion of
the literary generation and Alonso's view that there existed a
unified, sympathetic, friendly group of poets who began their
poetic production in earnest during the middle 1920s and about
whom the name Generation of 1927 carries great validity. The
most zealous upholder of this idea is José Luis Cano, whose label
for the group, "La generación de la amistad" ("The generation of
friendship"), affirms Alonso's thesis that these poets are characterized both by an "afinidad de gustos estéticos" ("affinity of
aesthetic tastes") and by "la amistad que unía a todos los poetas
del grupo" ("the friendship that linked all the poets of the group")
(14). As a practical phenomenon, the most distinguishing characteristic of this generation is friendship that reaffirms at an inter-
personal level the idea of like-mindedness and unity of artistic
purpose. Andrew Debicki, to whose ideas I shall refer in greater
detail later in this introduction, adopts a slightly different temporal label, the "Generación de 1924–25," to denote the specific
time the work of this group began in earnest. Debicki advances
and refines Alonso's and Salinas's theses. While certainly more
sophisticated than those of his critical predecessors, his ideas
about the group are nevertheless premised on the assumption
that there is a unifying "elemento clave de la poética de todo
este grupo" ("key element to the poetics of this whole group")
(29), which he uses to redefine, in the formalist rhetoric of the

New Criticism, Salinas's idea of a unifying ideological orientation as a common poetics. C. B. Morris, in a study entitled *A Generation of Spanish Poets: 1920–36,* also proceeds on the assumption that there is a fundamental unity of artistic purpose within the group, affirming at a thematic level the like-mindedness that both Salinas and Alonso maintain is the most significant feature of groups like the Generation of 1927.

Although there has emerged a much wider range of opinions regarding the Generation of 1927 over the last decade and a half, including a number of attempts to reformulate the generational concept as applied to the Generation of 1927, the fundamental attitudes remain largely intact. Indeed, the one Spanish critic who has earned something of a reputation for resisting the idea that there is an all-inclusive notion of a Generation of 1927 (or Generation of 1925), Ricardo Gullón, in fact uses and affirms all of Petersen's categories in "La generación poética de 1925" ("The Poetic Generation of 1925") to lament the difficulties of including all significant figures of the period in a generational grouping. At the same time, however, he declares that differences among the poets traditionally associated with the Generation of 1927 (or 1925) "son normales y no estorban el concepto de unidad" ("are normal and do not disrupt the concept of unity") (3). In a recent essay, "Recuerdo de los poetas" ("Remembrance of the Poets"), Gullón repeats his objections only to affirm, in nongenerational terms, conditions identical to those established by Alonso nearly forty years earlier. While denying the category, Gullón makes essentially identical affirmation about these poets. This critical slipperiness characterizes, in fact, the bulk of commentary aimed at refining the concept.

In a study of surrealism and the Generation of 1927, Carlos Marcial de Onís considers that the avant-garde aspect of some of these poets, the surrealism with which some of the poets of this group experimented briefly, is sufficient cause to proclaim, in effect, a surrealist generation and to consider Salinas and Guillén more as precursors and others (Alonso, Manuel Altolaguirre, Emilio Prados, and Gerardo Diego) as only marginally associated with the smaller central core of poets who constitute, according to Onís, the real mainstream: Alberti, Aleixandre, Cernuda, and Lorca. Onís borrows heavily from Cernuda's account of a "Generación de 1925," and his position is ultimately less inclusive than Cernuda's (discussed later). Onís does not account for even the avant-garde contribution of this group, which is certainly more extensive than surrealism and was practiced, as I shall demonstrate, even by Guillén and Salinas in their own particular fashion. An alternative approach along these lines is provided by Juan Manuel Rozas, who maintains that since the avant-garde characterizes this period in general it is possible to speak of a "Generacíon de la vanguardia" ("Generation of the avant-garde"). In the same breath, however, Rozas concedes that an equally good case can be made for a "Generación de la tradición" ("Generation of tradition") since a significant aspect of this poetry was inspired by the Spanish classical and popular tradition. He concludes by suggesting that all the tendencies of twentieth-century art coincide in the Generation of 1927 and, therefore, that the term Generation of 1927 offers a poetic model similar to developments in other genres. Rozas seems to suggest that the term be expanded to include other genres. Although Onís invokes the avant-garde to exclude and diminish the scope of the Generation of 1927, Rozas uses the same criteria to extend the concept to other genres.

Another tendency in recent years, an off-shoot of a certain uneasiness with the generational concept, is to adopt the terminology "grupo poético de 1927" ("poetic group of 1927"), first advocated by Vicente Gaos and later by Angel González, as an alternative designation. Although the concept of a group rather than a generation responds to the objections that "generation" refers only to a circle of poets, the concept actually serves to validate the notions earlier associated with the concept of a Generation of 1927. The "grupo poético" concept challenges none of the assumptions of the original concept and effectively reaffirms, or even reifies, the principle of like-mindedness that lies at the heart of the meaning of this term in the Spanish literary-critical consciousness. Indeed, there is nothing of a conceptual nature to differentiate a "grupo poético" from a "generación" except possibly the number of writers to which the term is intended to refer, as Rozas (with Torres Nebrera) demonstrates in a more recent book entitled *El grupo poético del 27*. He uses the term "Generación de 1927" interchangeably with "Grupo poético de 1927," at one point writing "grupo y generación del 27" ("group and generation of '27") (9). Whether to affirm, in whatever variant manner, the existence of a Generation of 1927 (or equivalent designation) or to redefine the same concept as a "grupo," the result is the same: a further validation and reification of the original concept.

The problem with the generational concept and the "grupo poético" alternative is that both are premised on a very narrow conception of historical dynamism. Both uphold an idea of poetic production in which the poet, or the group, is seen to be in exclusive control of such activity, and the poetry is seen as a response to an agenda that the group alone determines. In other words, the poetry of a generation or group of poets such as the Generation of 1927 is a completely willful production that originates in a shared set of values, a common ideology that is called by a different name. As conceived by Salinas and Alonso—but also a surprising number of their critics—literary generations seem to arise in a historical vacuum. Especially in comparison with other possible historical models—namely moderate, pluralistic, non-Marxist models of history—that could have been adopted in the aftermath of the Civil War as a basis for historical categorization, the generational concept is more than simply conservative. It is an extreme position that carries with it many of the governing assumptions of the post–Civil War Francoist state. With Alonso, the generational concept becomes explicitly nationalistic. Indeed, there is no historical model more compatible with Francoism than the notion that there is a will in history that organizes literature into literary generations. Added to this, the hegemony of literary formalism in the New Criticism as the dominant critical mode after World War II and the New Critical insistence on the work of art as being separate from ideological considerations make it exceedingly easy to justify a theory of poetic production based exclusively on the artifact isolated from its context.

It is significant that Salinas does not acknowledge, and Alonso takes exception to, the contributions of Ortega y Gasset to the

generational concept, especially given that the idea of generations is central to Ortega's concept of history.[1] Ortega's generational model is qualitatively different from the one that became
dominant after the Civil War. While there is certainly the strongest notion in Ortega of the participation of the human will in
history, his concept of the generation is significantly different
from that of the generation in Spanish literary criticism. There is
much greater dialectical sense in Ortega, whose concept stresses
variation and difference:

*Las variaciones de la sensibilidad vital que son decisivas se presentan
bajo la forma de generación. . . . Una generación es una variedad
humana. . . . Dentro de ese marco de identidad pueden ser los indivi-
duos del más diverso temple, hasta el punto de que, habiendo de
vivir los unos junto a los otros, a fuer de contemporáneos, se sienten
a veces como antagonistas.*

The variations of vital sensibilities that are decisive present themselves
under the form of the generation. . . . A generation is a human
variety. . . . Within that frame of identity can be found individuals of
the most diverse temper, even to the point that, having to live together
with each other, as contemporaries, they consider themselves at times
antagonists.   (*Tema* 147–48)

The generation for Ortega is the very measure of change. And
unlike Salinas's and Alonso's model, his asserts, "El concepto de
generacion no implica . . . más que . . . tener la misma edad y
tener algún contacto" ("The concept of a generation does not
imply . . . more than . . . being of the same age and having some
contact") (*Galileo* 38). Whereas Salinas and Alonso see the
accidental forces of history leading toward unanimity of intention within the group, Ortega characterizes the generation as
pluralistic, with the interplay of many different positions collectively determining the generation's direction.[2]

Ortega's ideas about literary generations, specifically the Generation of 1898, are also different from Salinas's and Alonso's.
Although Ortega recognizes that fundamental similarities do
exist within a given generation, that members of a generation
tend to be "hombres de su tiempo" ("men of their time") who
"por mucho que se diferencian se parecen más todavía" ("however much they differ from each other they resemble each other

still more") (*Tema* 148), there is also a strong idea that the members of a given generation are aware that they are formulating new ideas and values that they may not necessarily share with other members of the group, as, for example, the Generation of 1898: "Los escritores de esa generación se diferencian tanto entre sí que apenas si se parecen en nada positivo. Su comunidad fue negativa" ("The writers of that generation differed so much among themselves that they hardly resembled each other in anything positive. Their commonality was negative") (*Ensayos* 149). And elsewhere: "No se parecían. . . . Eran no conformistas. Convergían sus heterogénicas tendencias en la inaceptación de la España constituida" ("They did not resemble each other. . . . They were nonconformists. Their heterogeneous tendencies converged in the nonacceptance of Spain as it was then constituted") (*Ensayos* 189). These statements clearly suggest that Ortega's more pluralistic, less confining ideas about generations, literary or otherwise, were roundly ignored as the new critical paradigm, based almost exclusively on German ideas, emerged forcefully in the first decade after the Spanish Civil War.

Historically, the literary generation has evolved to become the principal instrument of literary valuation in contemporary Spanish studies, especially for the pre–Civil War era. The literary generation is ultimately a selection from a given milieu of those few writers deemed to be the truest embodiments of the literary agenda of a specific period—in the case of the Generation of 1927, a period of nearly twenty years. The conferring of generational status has become the surest way for Spanish criticism to place value on a type of literary production. Authors and works that do not fit into such a category find themselves at a striking disadvantage. Indeed, the naming of a generation is actually a political process that parades as a literary-critical and historical exercise. That the generational concept has not been significantly challenged on these grounds is an indication of the undemocratic state of affairs still obtaining in contemporary Spanish literary studies. In comparison with other methods of literary history, the generational concept with its built-in exclusionary bias must be judged, at best, as ungenerous. The concept of the literary generation has evolved little and has remained fundamentally intact since the time of its inauguration. One of the poets physically absent from the 1927 homage to Góngora and relegated in Alonso's essay to a lesser role among this group is Luis Cernuda, the only poet to dissent publicly against Alonso's generational model, in his "Carta abierta a Dámaso Alonso" ("Open Letter to Dámaso Alonso") (1948), or to embrace what may be termed an Orteguian approach to the question of what constitutes a literary generation. The striking exception to the view of a "generation of friendship," Cernuda was Alonso's lifetime enemy. More significantly, Cernuda also had serious personal difficulties and differences with Guillén and Salinas. Salinas and Guillén do not merit full membership in Cernuda's account of a Generation of 1925 since they did not, according to him, participate in the avant-garde experimentation of the late twenties and thirties that characterizes his own poetry and that of Alberti, Aleixandre, and Lorca. Cernuda, in fact, considers Guillén and Salinas bourgeois poets with no real connection to the larger, and younger, group that outgrew its earlier mentors. While there is a certain amount of truth to Cernuda's position, his ideas about what constitutes a literary generation are more significant than his conclusions about specific poets. Cernuda's Generation of 1925 is based solely on the median date of publication of the members' first books of poetry. In other words, Ortega's uncomplicated criteria, a coincidence of age and some contact, informs Cernuda's concept at a purely literary level. Strongly implied here is the possibility of ideological diversity, which Cernuda considers differentiates the older and conservative Salinas and Guillén from the more like-minded and more radical younger poets who embraced the avant-garde shortly after 1927. Thus Cernuda considers the real core of the group to be Alberti, Aleixandre, Lorca, and himself. According to Cernuda, therefore, there are two ideological tendencies within the group originally identified by Alonso, the better and perhaps more interesting poets belonging to Cernuda's camp, and the less interesting bourgeois poets occupying a lesser role. In proposing his alternative generation, Cernuda makes a conscious ideological adjustment intended to counter the bias of the predominant model. Just as Alonso effectively excludes Cernuda and Altolaguirre from full membership in his constitution of the generation, so Cernuda excludes Alonso completely and Salinas and Guillén partially from the history of the generation that he proposes.

From this selective survey of exemplary positions, it seems evident that both the model of Alonso, Salinas, and Petersen and the Cernuda model (inspired vaguely in Ortega) beg many questions regarding the literary history of the 1920s and '30s. Both models limit to a great extent the areas of legitimate critical inquiry. While Cernuda may have taken exception to his (and Altolaguirre's) effective exclusion from the original list of full generation members, his own proposals are, in their own ways, just as elitist and exclusionary since he accepts a modified generational model in order to exclude those with whom he had personal quarrels. Cernuda is perhaps to be commended for having the honesty to exclude Salinas and Guillén on consciously ideological grounds. Essentially the same process has been at work in most of Spanish literary criticism, which has defined a critical discourse that, in comparison to other models, seems anything but an objective literary history. One need only consult the well-known and very popular *Poesía española: Antología (Spanish Poetry: Anthology)*, edited by Gerardo Diego, to encounter a then-contemporary model much more broadly conceived than that of the literary generation. Diego includes members of the Generation of 1898, the Generation of 1927, Juan Ramón Jiménez (often associated with a Generation of 1914), others who have not fared as well for not having "fit" within a specific generation such as Juan Larrea and Leon Felipe, and two female poets, Ernestina de Champourcín and Josefina de la Torre (likewise, in Azorín's essay, he includes as members of the Generation of 1898 writers such as Darío, Manuel Bueno, Jacinto Benavente, Vicente Blasco Ibañez, and others who have been subsequently eliminated largely because of the implementation of more rigorous criteria). The fact that Diego specifically includes a preliminary section where each poet supplies a "poética," a short manifesto of his or her poetic position, is illustrative of the greater freedom and ideological diversity enjoyed by these poets and encouraged in efforts such as this, during the years preceding the Spanish Civil War. The fact that fourteen of the

poets listed in the Diego anthology (Francisco Villaespesa, Edu-
ardo Marquina, Enrique de Mesa, Tomás Morales, José del Río
Sainz, José Moreno Villa, "Alonso Quesada," Mauricio Bacarisse,
Antonio Espina, Juan José Domenchina, Ramón de Basterra, Fer-
nando Villalón, Champourcín, and Torre) today are not studied
with great regularity, or at all, cannot be attributed to a paucity
of enduring talent. An exclusionary politics, a corollary aspect
of the literary generation concept as it has evolved, is at least
partly responsible for these poets' subsequent devaluation.

Given the need for precise methods of classification by literary
historians, the passage of time inevitably brings with it the need
to make more definitive selections and valuations among the
writers of a given period. Yet the existence of literary generations
adds additional value to the writing of those initially included
and devalues more severely the work of those not a part of the
mainstream as defined. It also makes more difficult the revalua-
tion of certain authors, since the literary generation has historically proven to be an instrument of exclusion rather than of later
inclusion. This has the effect of causing literary history to be
written sooner and more definitively than is healthy for the
canon and even for those so canonized. In the case of the early
establishment of a definitive Generation of 1927, the conditions
for the study of such a group so named are also established:
namely, that the members of this group think alike and thus
conceive of and write "aesthetic poetry" that is fundamentally
similar to that of all the others so designated. Critical conclusions
about the Generation of 1927 are, therefore, not conclusions so
much as preordained affirmations determined by the generational concept that emerged after the Spanish Civil War. The
result of this historical development in contemporary Spanish
criticism is, I believe, a distortion of the literary history of Spanish
poetry between 1920 and 1936.

A historically sensitive criticism must provide a framework by
which to approach a given writer's work not only in an individual
context but also for its points of commonality and discrepancy
with its contemporaries. Such a model conflicts with the genera-
tional-group idea in that it assumes an aesthetic and ideological
pluralism within a given period. More significant than the forma-

tion of self-enclosed, autonomously functioning literary groups or generations, Spanish writers of the first decades of the twentieth century were also unified by a common rejection, by various means, of the tenets of nineteenth-century realism-naturalism. If it is valid to speak of national contributions to a widespread or universal literary phenomenon, then the concept of the literary generation, with its built-in nationalistic bias, has impeded the higher valuation and harmed the international prestige of Spanish literature. If there is a common link among all the Spanish writers of the early twentieth century whose work has achieved significance in critical opinion, it is their willingness to embrace, each in his or her own way, an aesthetic position that has been described in other literary traditions as modernist.[3] Such a point of commonality implies that the real generation, if one wishes to call it that, is one that lasts from 1898 until 1936 and that parallels in significant detail developments in European modernist art.

That most critics of the Generation of 1927 have invoked a paradigm of similarity to describe a literary phenomenon that existed in a period in Spanish history characterized by ideological commitment of the fiercest sort and political position-taking of every imaginable variety suggests to me that such a criticism fulfills, in a negative sense, my working definition of ideology, a false image parading as an objective truth. My alternative begins with a reply to what I consider perhaps the most cogent theoretical statement to date regarding the Generation of 1927, Andrew Debicki's "Una generación poética" ("A Poetic Generation"), the introduction to his *Estudios sobre poesía española contemporánea (Studies of Spanish Contemporary Poetry),* which recalls Alonso's earlier essay. Paralleling Salinas's refinement of Azorín, the North American Debicki translates Alonso's rather vague ideas about the Generation of 1927 into sound formalist principles. Debicki proposes that the poets of the Generation of 1927 ('24–'25 in his terminology) embrace both of two fundamental attitudes that poets invariably adopt toward reality. In the first, the poet considers reality a means by which to communicate his or her own inner or private vision. The second attitude is more directly involved with reality in that it attempts to communicate

"ciertas realidades vitales del mundo" ("certain vital realities of
the world") (21). The first attitude leads to poetry's, and the
poet's, "elevación sobre lo ordinario" ("elevation above the ordinary") (22). The second possibility, while it diminishes the role
of the poet, "tiene la ventaja de relacionar la poesía con valores
importantes de nuestro mundo" ("has the advantage of relating
the poetry to important values of our world") (22). Debicki
concludes that these two perspectives converge to form a working definition of the poetry of this group "como modo de hallar
y de crear una visión de la realidad" ("as a way of finding and of
creating a vision of reality") (33). Indeed, it is "su concepto
transcendente de la poesía y . . . el fuerte deseo de cada uno de
lograr, a su manera, una obra a la vez perfecta, humana y universal" ("their concept of poetry and . . . the strong desire of each
one to develop, in his own way, a body of work at once perfect,
human, and universal") (48) that constitutes these poets as a
generation. While Debicki recognizes that there are differences
among them, he emphasizes that "la relación entre ellos obedece
a razones profundas y no a coincidencias externas o superfici-
ales" ("the relationship among them conforms to profound reasons and not to external or superficial coincidences") (48).
Attempting to be as generous as possible by suggesting that this
is not a dehumanized or formalized poetry but one whose "visión
. . . incluy[e] y combin[a] ambos conceptos, el de la poesía como
creación de algo nuevo a base de materiales reales trans-
formados, y el de la poesía como descubrimiento y comunicación de lo real" ("vision . . . includes and combines both con-
cepts, that of poetry as the creation of something new from
transformed materials, and that of poetry as discovery and communication of the real") (23), Debicki is nevertheless committed
to the rhetoric of the New Criticism and the verbal icon.

The New Critical affirmation of a formal unity within the
literary work weds itself nicely with the notion that, by virtue
of their sharing a common poetics, defined as a fundamentally
similar orientation toward reality, the poets of the Generation
of 1927 are involved, each in his own way, in affirming a similar
purpose of art. What is for Salinas, Petersen, and Alonso something of a sociological, and even biological, justification for like-

mindedness among the generation members becomes now an exclusively literary phenomenon. In other words, the similarity of purpose among these poets is to be found in the poetic text itself, capable of providing a "cuadro completo" ("complete picture") (21) that responds to the desire to "desarrollar una visión" ("develop a vision") (23). Form, the language and structure of the text that expresses itself through picturing, provides the sole means of understanding what and how a work communicates:

pudiera decirse que una obra poética se vale de todos sus recursos formales para comunicarnos aspectos de la realidad que nos tocan personalmente, y que se quedarían escondidos en una presentación lógica o fotográfica de las cosas. Mediante el empleo de la forma, de las imágenes y los símbolos, y de diversos otros recursos estilísticos y estructurales, el poeta encarna los múltiples aspectos conceptuales y afectivos de su realidad dentro de un cuadro completo; mediante estos procedimientos, logra también que este cuadro se torne una experiencia vital para el lector.

it could be said that a poetic work avails itself of all its formal means to communicate to us aspects of reality that touch us personally, and that would remain hidden in a logical or photographic presentation of things. By means of form, images and symbols, and other diverse stylistic and structural means, the poet embodies the multiple conceptual and affective aspects of his reality in a complete picture; through these procedures, he also makes this picture become a vital experience for the reader.   (21)

The mechanics of the camera obscura are thus invoked to suggest that poetry is capable of projecting or reproducing not only a full but a better picture of reality in the reader, a "visión esencial de la realidad" ("essential vision of reality") (31), a transcendent picture that exists in a purer state than does ordinary reality and that produces "algo nuevo" ("something new"). I am unconvinced that such insights constitute proof of a common poetics—an idea echoed less eloquently by a host of others—or a poetic vision dedicated to the affirmation of essences. If one chooses, as I do, to place these formal-essential categories and attitudes in an ideological context that understands pictures and images referring not so much to an essential vision of things, an autonomous picture with no need to refer to anything outside itself, as to historical forces that condition the vision, then a much different picture of the Generation of 1927 emerges.

It is possible, however, to situate the two attitudes to reality—one in which the poet affirms an inner vision of reality (reality as a means to an aesthetic end), another that affirms an image of the world via the poet's more direct involvement with reality (reality as an end)—in the ideological context of the 1920s and '30s in Spain and Europe, which can also be understood, as Debicki suggests, in terms of the productive principle of an artistic image, or a principle of image production. By the early years of this century, even rather conservative writers such as Miguel de Unamuno and Pío Baroja had moved beyond the formal tenets of realism-naturalism and its demands for the representation of a complete, omniscient, and objective vision free of irony. Such an illusion is destroyed, for example, in Unamuno's *Niebla (Fog)* in which the opposite idea—the impossibility of representing an autonomous or omniscient position in reality—becomes the central issue of the novel. The protagonist Augusto Pérez's discovery that he is a character in a novel by an author named Unamuno, whom he visits in Salamanca eventually to protest in the strongest of terms the mortal destiny that is revealed to him during his visit with his maker, represents as well Unamuno's awareness of his sense of absence from existence in the world, which is threatened with the same unjust destiny as his character. Baroja's *El árbol de la ciencia (The Tree of Knowledge)* parodies French naturalism in that its protagonist, a doctor named Andrés Hurtado, a Spanish version of a naturalist "objective observer" of societal conditions, succumbs to his own observations of reality. Baroja's novel is even more interesting because of the equal unwillingness of the narrator simply to observe a narrative situation. The narrator makes no pretense of objectivity or distance from events. He interprets reality rather than narrates it, interjecting himself frequently to make declarations of every sort and variety and thus disrupting the illusion that the novel is representing an objective picture. Just as the Spanish reality invades the existential space of the protagonist whose philosophical efforts to circumscribe it—to make it a tolerable picture—fail, so too the narrator undermines the distinction between his space and that of his characters. Similar, indeed stronger, statements can be made regarding Ramón del Valle-Inclán, Ramón Pérez de Ayala, Ramón Gómez de la Serna, and many others. Unamuno and Baroja, therefore, also exemplify the attitudes toward reality ascribed to the Generation of 1927 in that Unamuno certainly uses reality as a means while Baroja's protagonist comes to the despairing conclusion that there are no means by which to deal effectively with the oppressive end that is Spanish reality at the turn of the twentieth century.

Debicki's categories are of little value in differentiating the poetics of the Generation of 1927 from that of other groups since unless art is dedicated exclusively to representing abstractions it must confront reality in some way, as a means, end, or some variation. Placed within the ideological context of the 1920s and '30s, however, these categories acquire much greater relevancy as Spanish modernism achieves its plenitude in the poets of the Generation of 1927, who were even more consciously dedicated than earlier writers to the production of nonobjective images of reality. The tendency in art, just as in politics, after World War I was to affirm one, and not the other, attitude toward reality. That is to say, just as in realism-naturalism, modernist artists continued to see art in relation to reality. The significant difference, however, was that this reality was often not a universal one and not intended for the average person from a middle-class background, whose common-sense values—a realistic mode that represented by imitating what could be seen with the eyes via light—left the early twentieth-century artist unsatisfied. Art thus became progressively dedicated to the discovery of other realities invariably considered to provide better images than those available through the traditional modes of realistic representation.

Just as new political ideologies—primarily a leftist socialism-communism and anarchism (especially in Spain), and after World War I, varieties of a rightist position that today is frequently evoked under the name fascism—gained strength in Europe and Spain in the early decades of the century, so too literary movements strongly identified with rightist (futurism, imagism) and leftist (surrealism) political doctrines emerged to challenge bourgeois norms of social and artistic organization and expression. The bourgeois political system was the target, especially in Spain, of increasingly doctrinaire political movements whose goals were to implement an ideological program; at the same time there was less and less regard for the means employed to achieve such goals as the Spanish nation moved toward a tragic civil war. I do not wish to use the political lives of the poets of the Generation of 1927 to discuss the ideological dimensions of their poetry, although in my conclusion I suggest that the poetic values correlated rather well with the prevalent political attitudes in Spain and Europe during this period. I am more interested in suggesting that if it is possible to think of these poets in the context of a modernist aesthetic, it is also possible to ground their attitudes toward art in a more complete manner by also understanding form as an expression of ideology. Modernism provides a critique of bourgeois representational values as intense and unrelenting as the leftist and rightist political critiques of bourgeois democracy. Both critiques are premised on a rejection of the empirical value system that organizes and structures such a reality, as Marx and countless others suggest—an ideology that has achieved an almost unquestioned "natural" status.

If capitalism's nearly five-hundred-year ascent and hegemony as an organizing model for European society parallels the nearly five-hundred-year hegemony of a representational norm that emerged in the Renaissance, through the principles of one-point perspective (outlined as early as the fifteenth century in Leon Battista Alberti's *On Painting*), it should not come as a surprise that the rightist and leftist challenge to such an economic and political hegemony is also paralleled by aesthetic ideologies that question the common-sense approach to the production of images affirmed by realist-naturalist artists. Marx's distrust of the camera obscura reflects his deep distrust of the bourgeois means of the production of images. With the emergence of rightist doctrines after World War I, however, the empirical image and mode of picturing was assailed on yet another front. What seemed for centuries, especially in Locke (and the empiricists) and Voltaire, an appeal to nature—that the mind understands not only images of reality but also verbally expressed ideas in a process that can best be described as an imprinting and picturing upon the medium of consciousness the raw materials of experience—became by the early twentieth century an unreasonable restriction. The overturning of one-point perspectival representation that began with cubism and other artistic movements freed artists to embrace reality in a much more expanded context. Free of the constraints of a representational norm revealed irremediably to be a false image, European artists diverged in many directions in search of their alternative to ordinary reality.

Unquestionably the most extreme political doctrine to look upon reality as a means was the Nazi movement under Hilter, in which literally the control of the entire world, its subjection to the unquestioned will of one leader, was understood to be the destiny of the German people, a terrible fulfillment of Marx's notion of ideology as a false image. The image in question was the necessarily superior vision of the leader communicated to the "superior race" capable of imposing such a vision on the necessarily "blind" and "inferior" races of the rest of the world. Whereas such an attitude to reality could not seem evil during the early thirties, when it prevailed more in rhetoric than in action, there are certainly artistic parallels that express a similar attitude. Jameson outlines the aggressive, action-oriented qualities of Wyndham Lewis's writing as indicative of a protofascist attitude in the writing of an "apolitical" modernist. A better example, however, is that of Ezra Pound, the founder of imagism and vorticism. Pound's ideological interest in the image is exemplified in his obsession with Chinese writing and his mistaken assumption that it is not an entirely verbal phenomenon but that its ideographic writing is indicative of the iconic nature of all language. Chinese writing, Pound felt, represented an earlier moment in Western writing when language was more immediate and characterized by much more activity. According to this line of reasoning, for example, verbs were the originators of nouns, which means that there is an active, vitalistic structure to the evolution of language, a reflection in language of a vision of reality in which things are "working out their fate" in an active mode. The postulation of the iconicity of language (and the corollary denial of the possibility of what is now called the semiotic sign) is an affirmation of the image as the highest of literary values, a "primary apparition," the full and direct presence of what is there. For Pound, therefore, a metaphor is not only always an image, it is an image that expresses an "objective relationship" between things and ideas. What is a passive process under empirical models becomes in Pound an activity, the effective transferal of the etching plate of empiricism from the mind to the work of art. For Pound, the image is not a representation; it is a thing in itself. Language and art are activity just as life is activity and a call to action. It is not difficult to understand why Pound would be influenced politically by fascism and its action-oriented agenda.[4]

Likewise, left-wing political movements, epitomized in communism, which assigns the highest value to the impersonal forces of history—understood to be moving inexorably to bring power to the collectivity and an end to private control of the means of economic production—share a common bond with certain iconoclastic literary movements that also harbor Marx's distrust of the bourgeois mode of image production, the most noteworthy being surrealism. If Pound believes that an image is an actual presence, a thing in itself that embodies the highest value, most surrealists, especially those under the *caudillaje* of André Breton, who for a time placed surrealism at the service of Communist revolution, believe largely the opposite. The images produced as a consequence of automatic writing and other surrealistic means of making contact with the hidden and uncontrollable aspects of reality—defined in terms of a more valuable aspect of being, which it is desirable to know—become confirming evidence that the phenomenon of being is something much more extensive, unexplainable by rational-empirical or "putrefied" (to use the term of Dalí and Lorca) means, middle-class philosophies and art forms. If the imagist, fascist, modernist Pound and others claim an objective status for the literary image, that it is actually an image that "sees for itself," the surrealist, Marxist, modernist Breton and others understand the poetic image primarily as the by-product of a process that can be likened to listening to the distant voice of being that lies in a realm beyond traditional representation. Rosalind Krauss has gone further in considering that automatic writing "is not, like the rest of the written signs of Western culture, representation" but actually equivalent to a kind of psychic photography. Like the image of the camera obscura that many have chosen to consider an unmediated, indexical equivalent of the slice of visual reality it captures, the surrealist image, Krauss believes, is "a kind of presence, the direct presence of the artist's inner self" (12). It would be more correct to say, however, that the surrealist image offers only a partial view of the totality or presence of being, which is larger in fact than any combination of "psychic photographs" can convey. The surrealist certainly believes in the superiority of his or her images, but they are superior because they come from a more powerful force in charge of the means of production. Dalí is perhaps closest in actual practice to this ideal; for him, each painting is a "critical paranoid" response to an aspect of the artist's being revealed to him through the truest medium of image production available, Salvador Dalí.

These positions, illustrative of the ideological polarities within the avant-garde schools constituting modernism, correspond to the same attitudes outlined by Debicki in apolitical terms in support of the idea of a common poetics among the members of a Generation of 1927. Jameson characterizes the attitudes quite differently, as proof of the wide variety of ideological possibilities within the historical milieu of the early twentieth century, unified only in their opposition to middle-class representational values:

The most influential formal impulses of canonical modernism have been strategies of inwardness, which set out to reappropriate an alienated universe by transforming it into personal styles and private languages: such wills to style have seemed in retrospect to reconfirm the very privatization and fragmentation of social life against which they mean to protest.   (2)

Concerned exclusively with understanding rightist positions within modernism, Jameson's characterization of this tendency as an attempt to reappropriate the world through the adoption of a willful style, or a style that exalts the creative will, is, nevertheless, a cogent one. The will's inner vision is confirmed on the site of reality. Some realities and some forms—for Pound

the short poem-image—are more amenable than others to facilitating the presence of the will, and thus the poet's being, in the
act of representation. It also implies that the act of reappropriat-
ing the reality from which membership in middle-class existence
alienates him can be an active, forceful phenomenon in which
the inner and outer visions of reality are willed into unity. Although Jameson chooses not to examine leftist manifestations of
modernism, it is possible to complement his partial image by
suggesting that by virtue of the belief in larger historical forces
that shape individual existence, leftist positions tend to affirm a
guiding force that has determined, and is determining, them but
that cannot be contained within a single personality. Thus the
surrealist techniques dedicated to establishing "existential soli-
darity" with the hidden aspects of being, are not incompatible,
if one wishes (like Breton and his colleagues for a time) to
make such a connection, with the Marxist version of reality and
existence and make it possible to understand the determinism
of history as a cosmic version of automatic writing.

These artistic positions, in addition to their compatibility with
political positions, also parallel other doctrines, for example,
philosophy, and specifically Heideggerian existentialism, also
obsessed with the issue of being and its division into more and
less valuable, authentic and inauthentic spheres. Again, bourgeois, clock-bound ideas about temporality affirm an inauthentic
existence, a false image or model of how one should conduct
one's life, while authentic existence is reserved for those brave
enough to understand existence defined by the definitive nothingness toward which all life is inexorably moving. It is impossible, therefore, to understand the objective categories of the
Petersen model for literary history, which maintains that history
provides the conditions favorable for the emergence of an ideologically uniform literature dominated by the strongest literary
wills and united by "una unidad de ser debida a la comunidad
de destino" ("a unity of being owing to a commonality of destiny") other than in terms of other "ideologies of the will" that
gained prominence in the 1930s. Although literary ideologies of
this period now seem particularly suspect after the defeat of the
political doctrines from which they gained strength, such ideas

have yet to be fully overthrown in Spanish literary criticism. If Spanish criticism is lucky in a sense that the ideological impoverishment of Francoism did not require extensive theoretical justification for cultural and literary expression, this situation also ensured the absence of challenges to this system of literary history, which has survived largely unmodified as one of the last vestiges of a certain image of the world. Although very few Hispanists ever concern themselves with the ideological implications of literary generations, the fact is that a very marginal concept, especially in comparison with existing literary-historical models, has molded the parameters of critical thinking about contemporary Spanish literature for the past half-century. Whether or not the literary generation is invoked in a given critical discussion about a poet of this period, its assumptions about like-mindedness and uniformity of approach to the task of poetry among these poets—in whatever more or less profound sense—have informed the guiding assumptions about the content of that poetry.

The readings that follow attempt to situate six significant poets, all associated with the Generation of 1927, in an ideological milieu that places each poet's specific nonobjective attitudes to reality in as broad a context as possible. Such an attempt is understood as a necessary preliminary to the affirmation of a more generous idea and image of Spanish literary history. All the major tendencies in European modernist art are present in the poets of the Generation of 1927. The difference between this and other approaches is that it attempts to ground the poetic images in a milieu of competing modes of image production, which I have chosen to interpret as a competition among nonobjective images of reality. To be sensitive to historical developments, I have based these readings on the chronological production of the poetry whenever possible. This is especially significant for Cernuda's *La realidad y el deseo* (the first edition, published in 1936), which is intended as a chronological account, a poetic autobiography. This is impossible, however, for Guillén's *Cántico* (the second edition, published in 1936), a collection of special moments and the subject of the initial reading.

CHAPTER 1

Jorge Guillén

For Luis Cernuda, one of the few critics to characterize Jorge Guillén's poetry ideologically, *Cántico* (*Canticle*; this study examines the poetry through the second edition, published in 1936) epitomizes a bourgeois attitude; that is, it affirms an outmoded representational value system. The notion of a bourgeois poet suggests an affirmative, accepting attitude toward a world that, according to an oft-cited verse of Guillén's, is "bien hecho" ("well made"). Cernuda's negative view, however, is different in substance only in its conclusions from the views of other critics who have ascribed a very positive value to what is consistently characterized as the affirmative assumptions of this poetry. Both sets of opinions render a disservice to Guillén's early poetry in that they tend to overlook the processes by which the poet affirms his vision of the world, through well-made, indeed, "better images" of the things he most values. Although Guillén rejects the surrealism that Cernuda and others turned to during the late twenties and thirties, his poetry demonstrates an attitude toward art and reality that, to my view, is not bourgeois but modernist in the important sense that it provides a decisive critique of traditional modes of image production and offers an alternative vision of a better way to be, consciously premised on the inadequacy of bourgeois models of existence. Only Joaquín Casalduero's pioneering study of *Cántico* aligns Guillén's poetry with a truly avant-garde school, cubism (137– 38). The great majority of critics cite as Guillén's aesthetic point of departure Paul Valéry and French symbolism (Blanch; Macrí

14–20; MacCurdy 20–22; Xirau 130–32; Zardoya). It is more productive, however, to understand the Guillénian aesthetic of the twenties and thirties in terms of its opposition to the values of cubism. Guillén himself identifies imagism as the avant-garde school he most associates with his generation ("El nombre ameri-cano *imagists* podría aplicarse a cuantos escritores de alguna imaginación escribían acá o allá por los años 20" ["The American name *imagists* can be applied to any writer of some imagination who wrote here or there during the twenties"] ["Generación" 20]). It is through the production of a different kind of image, not simply a copy of reality but a new and altogether different reality, that poetry proceeds during these years ("la realidad no ... reduplicada en copias sino recreada de manera libérrima" ["reality not ... duplicated in copies but re-created in the freest manner possible"] [20]).

The initial, multisection poem of the first section of *Cántico,* "Más allá" ("Farther Away"), provides the most systematic ac-count of Guillén's attitude to the production of images taken from reality.[1] The poem begins by invoking a "más allá," exterior empirical reality, to which the poet immediately ascribes agency for his very being. As it communicates its presence at daybreak, the sun's light seems also to assimilate the recently awakened poet into the day's incipient glory, almost to appropriate him as one of its creatures:

> *Soy, más, estoy. Respiro.*
> *Lo profundo es el aire.*
> *La realidad me inventa,*
> *Soy su leyenda. ¡Salve!*

> I am, more, I am here. I breathe.
> The air is the profound thing.
> Reality invents me,
> I am its legend. Glory!   (19)

The light that "invade / Todo mi ser" ("invades / My whole being") (14) is preceded, however, by a much more active presence, centered in the eyes ("(El alma vuelve al cuerpo, / Se dirige a los ojos / Y choca.)—¡Luz!" ["(The soul returns to the body, / It makes its way to the eyes / And collides.)—Light!"]

[14]). This is the poet's sentience and consciousness, which emerges to affirm a very different interpretation of the meaning of the light. The things that emerge from the light, but not the light itself, are understood to affirm another purpose, that of orienting and centering the poet's being:

> ... *van presentándose*
> *Todas las consistencias*
> *Que al disponerse en cosas*
> *Me limitan, me centran.*

> ... making their appearance
> Are all the consistencies
> That upon ordering themselves in things
> Limit me, center me.   (15)

With the presence of things, the light fragments into component particles, "things" understood to have traveled great distances over time in order collectively to produce the image of the day:

> *¿Hubo un caos? Muy lejos*
> *De su origen, me brinda*
> *Por entre hervor de luz*
> *Frescura en chispas. ¡Día!*

> Was there a chaos? Very far
> From its origin, it offers me
> Through a seething of light
> Freshness in sparks. Day!   (15)

Whereas the accumulation of light particles produces a temporal image of the day, it is not the exclusive, or even primary, medium operating in the poem. It is incapable of effecting the significant transformation that now proceeds under the auspices of a more powerful agent: "mis ojos / Que volverán a ver / Lo extraordinario: todo" ("my eyes / That will see again / The extraordinary: everything") (16). The day's temporality is suspended by the awakened activity of consciousness that reconstitutes its diachronic progression in an atemporal context. A second "más allá" now begins to assert itself, for itself:

> *Todo está concentrado*
> *Por siglos de raíz*

Dentro de este minuto,
Eterno y para mí.

Y sobre los instantes
Que pasan de continuo,
Voy salvando el presente:
Eternidad en vilo.

All is concentrated
For ages entirely
Within this minute,
Eternal and for me.

And above the moments
That continually pass,
I am saving the present:
Eternity suspended.   (16–17)

The "más allá" that provides the image of the day, the landscape and its objects, elicits an active response from a will desirous of affirming its presence against such a visual background:

Ser, nada más. Y basta.
Es la absoluta dicha.
¡Con la esencia en silencio
Tanto se identifica!

¡Al azar de las suertes
Unicas de un tropel
Surgir entre los siglos,
Alzarse con el ser,

Y a la fuerza fundirse
Con la sonoridad
Más tenaz: sí, sí, sí,
La palabra del mar!

To be, nothing more. And that's enough.
It is absolute bliss.
When being is in silence
So much is recognized!

At random from the unique destinies
Of a throng
To emerge from among the ages,
To rise with being,

And by force to unite
With the most tenacious

Sonority: yes, yes, yes,
The word of the sea!   (17–18)

This desire to be is understood as an activity, a force of will ("a la fuerza") that can accept no other interpretation of the landscape but an affirmative one. The external reality also seems to become infected with the same desire to attain an absolute status. While singing to empirical reality and ascribing agency to it, the landscape has become transformed into a projection of the poet's will to affirm the presence of being in the world:

> *Todo me comunica,*
> *Vencedor, hecho mundo,*
> *Su brío para ser*
> *De veras real, en triunfo.*
>
> All communicates to me,
> Victorious, made world,
> Its daring to be
> Truly real, in triumph.   (18)

Guillén's conclusion that "La realidad me inventa" ("Reality invents me") (19) is true only in the special sense that the empirical realm has provided the raw material, but nothing else, for an activity of self-invention. Nature provides necessary but fragmented and empty images (including the light particles) that attain their plenitude only by virtue of their transformation and incorporation into a greater unity, which centers in the consciousness.

The evidence for such an interpretation is provided explicitly in the second section, which represents "este / Ser, avasallador / Universal" ("this / Being, universal / Dominator") (21), the desire to be, which manifests itself poetically as a will to form ("vaguedad / Resolviéndose en forma" ["vagueness / Transforming itself into form"] [20]). In the darkness of the inner realm of consciousness, the empirical light of the first section plays no role in the "Vigor / De creación" ("Vigor / Of creation") (20) recounted here. This ever-vigilant center resides "En lo desconocido" ("In the unknown"), in "Un más allá de veras / Misterioso, realísimo" ("A beyond truly / Mysterious and most real") (21), a more real and valuable

realm than light-bound empirical reality. Represented, therefore, is an inner reality that lies beyond representation but
that nevertheless embodies a principle of artifice more significant than the sensually available outer realm. It is through the
activity of this interior "más allá" that the empirically available
"más allá" is appropriated to fulfill a more valuable function:
to provide the formal building blocks for being, the "más allá
. . . realísimo." The empirical three-dimensionality of nature,
whose form depends on light, is not an end but rather a means
to a more significant agenda. In formal terms, this devaluation
of the empirical experience is expressed as a transference of
the representational locus from nature to the consciousness
upon which such a form acquires a new meaning in a plane
or two-dimensional medium. An image from nature is reappro-
priated to an active medium understood metaphorically as a
white canvas.

The available means of transference is examined further in the
third section, which also deals with things unexplainable, this
time "Largos, anchos, profundos / Enigmas—en sus masas"
("Long, wide, deep / Enigmas—in their masses") (22). Like raw
experiences, enigmas—unsettling ideas and philosophical con-
cepts beyond the poet's understanding, impediments to the affirmation of the fullness of being—also become part of the
agenda of the higher reality. Here, however, their negative potential is circumvented by means of a process of naming:

> *Hacia mi compañía*
> *La habitación converge.*
> *¡Qué de objetos! Nombrados,*
> *Se allanan a la mente.*

> Toward my company
> The room converges.
> What a lot of objects! Named,
> They conform to the mind.   (23)

Guillén assigns them the name "enigma" and leaves it at that.
The things he cannot understand are consigned to a mental
realm where they assume a beneficial function even in their
negativity:

Enigmas son y aquí
Viven para mi ayuda,
Amables a través
De cuanto me circunda

Sin cesar con la móvil
Trabazón de unos vínculos
Que a cada instante acaban
De cerrar su equilibrio.

They are enigmas and here
They live for my benefit,
Kind through
All that surrounds me

Without stopping with the movable
Connection of some bonds
That at every instant have just
Sealed their equilibrium.   (23)

The attitude toward these mental mysteries demonstrates a concept of language quite different from that of the empirical tradition, which views words largely as faithful mirrors of the images
and ideas of experience. Guillén's response to the mass of enigma
that surrounds him is not to engage it philosophically but to
overwhelm it through the activity of the intellect.[2] The poet's
idea of naming is not the faithful translation of an experience,
image, or idea into a verbal response that reproduces it. Rather,
he understands it as an activity of consciousness aimed at redefining the enigmas as an essential category and thus part of the
true "más allá." Words are not symbolic equivalents of images
and ideas but rather counter-images by which to reassign images
and ideas both a name and a place. The naming process is an
activity that transforms potentially disruptive enigmas into their
opposite, principles of continuity and of distance from enigmas.

Such an "active principle" fuses the traditionally separate functions of will and intellect (MacCurdy 44). The memorative component of consciousness is concomitantly devalued since, more
than an accumulated record of experiences, the values of being
to which such an epistemology responds require a present unen-
cumbered by "enigmas" that impede "la energía / De plenitud"
("the energy / Of plenitude") (25), among the most formidable

of which is time but also the enigma "being" as an intellectual concept. Such energy also requires the more intimate association of inner and outer realms, correlatives for which are rendered, in the fifth section, as the presence of the sunlight on the plane surface of a white wall of an edifice understood as "¡Gozosa / Materia en relación!" ("Joyful / Matter in relation!") (26), and the contact between the sunlight and the treetop leaves that also "me enamora" ("enamors me") (27). These activities exemplify image production as an epistemological but also as a value phenomenon. While there is undeniably a positive value to the empirical dimension embodied in the presence of light on the plane surface of the wall that gives it a golden hue, a much higher value is assigned the active, transforming response to the sun's presence by the leaves that use the light to generate their own energy. Thus in the final section, when Guillén declares that "dependo / Del total más allá" ("I depend / On the total beyond") (28), it is clear that "total" includes the presence of an active, totalizing principle of consciousness that, somewhat as leaves with the sun's raw energy, is able to transform light-bound, visual experience into something different: "Un rayo de sol más" ("An extra ray of sun") (32). An alternative epistemology only minimally dependent on images taken from empirical reality is responsible for the constituting images of this poem (and those that follow). A willed intensification of the understanding redefines the outside medium, the sunlight "Muy lejos / De su origen" ("Very far / From its origin"), in order to affirm itself as something completely new.

The poem's final strophes affirm the ascendancy of an alternative principle of image production as the inner principle affirms its domination of the visual field of creation:

> ... *Y con empuje henchido*
> *De afluencias amantes*
> *Se ahinca en el sagrado*
> *Presente perdurable*
>
> *Toda la creación,*
> *Que al despertarse un hombre*
> *Lanza la soledad*
> *A un tumulto de acordes.*

... And with swelled force
From loving influxes
There hurries in the sacred
Everlasting present

All of creation,
Which upon awakening a man
Casts off solitude
To a tumult of harmonies.   (32–33)

The awakening is a double one: the first occurs in a physical sense as Guillén receives visual reality; the second is the intensified experience of being in which the visual domain provides the raw materials by which to affirm the true "más allá." The vocabulary of the final strophes—intense, action-oriented words ("empuje," "se ahinca," "lanza")—suggests that an active outside principle has been replaced with an active inside principle. The poem's content thus becomes an account of the poet's meticulous valuation of an active principle of consciousness that is also a poetic principle. By the poem's conclusion, inner and outer realities have effectively merged. These categories are superseded as three-dimensional reality effectively collapses by virtue of its redefinition in terms of the values of being. The necessary sunlight of empirical representation is superseded by "un rayo de sol más," an inner phenomenon that becomes the true locus of images. The present acquires atemporal characteristics not because of an outside force but by a forceful act of consciousness that has excised ("con empuje henchido") an image of the real world from its temporal mooring. The outside realm acquires "fullness" only when it becomes the pretext for the affirmation of its supplement, the fullness of being. Far from a glorification of the facilitating light of empirical representation, the poem represents a decisive shift in emphasis from a passive theory of image production to a more modern, or modernist, idea about such production. The poet affirms a nontraditional model of picturing in which images acquire fullness by surrendering their three-dimensional perspective to become a plane projection on an activated membrane of consciousness. Through an act of intellectual will that produces a new understanding of the true relationship between the two realities ("un tumulto de acordes"), the image is redefined as it proceeds from a spatial-temporal context in empirical reality to an atemporal locus of representation in the inner consciousness, where spatial distance is not a requirement for the production of images.

Poetic expression responds to an existential need to affirm being by means of a landscape appropriated for that purpose. The resultant image is quite different from that typically associated with nineteenth-century realism-naturalism. The realism of this poetry corresponds not to an objective, observing eye, but to the subjective desire of the poet's eye to seize upon objects that correspond visually to an aesthetic-existential predisposition that needs precisely such an image. The observed object has status only insofar as it communicates to the poet his own aesthetic-existential agenda. The poetic object's preexisting affinity with the active principle of will-consciousness thus signifies that the distance between subject and object has been greatly diminished from the very outset (MacCurdy 34). The poem, in a sense, becomes the process by which the distinction between inner and outer dimensions of the image become blurred. The object thus wills itself as it itself is willed to become part of a more intense and profound landscape that is invariably supplemented by the willful principle of consciousness ("un rayo de sol más"), which also supplies what the object cannot, an affirmation of its own presence in the representation. In formal terms, the effect is a radical oscillation between spatial and plane dimensions, that is, three- and two-dimensional realities. Nearly every poem witnesses the collapse of empirical reality in favor of a better image, in which words and images fuse in ecstatic harmony.

The words that appear on the pages of *Cántico* are, in effect, graphic equivalents of the images from nature that have helped to initiate the creative process that brings the poem into being. The protagonist, however, is not the natural landscape, but rather being itself, through the landscape. Words do not merely imitate or mirror a preexisting image but become the basis for a better image that exists as words and that acquires imagistic status in a plane reality, of being (see also Macrí 32–33). The most explicit expression of these values is found in "Naturaleza viva" ("Still Life

Alive"), where Guillén ascribes to a plane tabletop the quality of maintaining "Resuelto en una Idea / Su plano: puro, sabio, / Mental para los ojos / Mentales . . ." ("Settled in an Idea / Its plane: pure, wise, / Mental for the eyes / Of the mind . . .") (34). The tabletop has no consciousness of its planeness, as do the poet's "ojos mentales." The plane tabletop that was part of a larger spatial reality, a "bosque / De nogal" ("forest / Of walnut") (35), has now achieved a higher perfection. Its rings, signs of the presence of time, still refer it to the other reality but the act of its planing has transformed its essence. It has won a victory over time and by its separation from its original spatial-temporal milieu has become exalted in a new and more intense fullness:

> . . . ¡El nogal
> Confiado a sus nudos
> Y vetas, a su mucho
> Tiempo de potestad
>
> Reconcentrada en este
> Vigor inmóvil, hecho
> Materia de tablero
> Siempre, siempre silvestre!
>
> . . . The walnut tree
> Trusting in its knots
> And grains, in its great
> Time of power
>
> Concentrated in this
> Still vigor, made
> Matter of a tabletop
> Always, always natural!   (35)

The unsubtle play on words of the title is very suggestive of Guillén's low valuation of nature and things natural. As the title suggests, the walnut tree acquires greater life by losing its natural form and acquiring an artificed plane form. This is, indeed, Guillén's fundamental aesthetic value. The planing of the tree trunk removes it from nature but also from the power of time. It acquires, or is at least ascribed, power and autonomy that it could not possess as part of a spatial realm, in the medium of time. Planing thus connotes atemporalization, a transcending of the power and flux of time. These qualities are also those associated with the production of poetic images. The plane does not connote a limitation of imagistic possibilities but rather an intensification. It is not a mere cross section but rather a dynamic receptacle (see Alvar 88). The tabletop's artificed form is a correlative for an alternative epistemology whose goal is an improvement on the natural image.

Spatial perception, which typically characterizes the experience of everyday reality, is also temporal perception since images in space are communicated to the perceiver over a distance. Consciousness, therefore, becomes aware of time through space. The passive consciousness of the empirical model receives images in the tacit awareness that they inscribe themselves temporally. The active will-consciousness, however, imposes itself on these images, collapsing the distinction between itself and the landscape as it banishes the presence of time. In the passive mode of being, nature and time exert power over being, which is unable to establish its full presence in the spatial realm. In the poetry, as an epistemological phenomenon, the spatiality of nature is disrupted in a manner that exactly parallels the act of planing glorified in "Naturaleza viva." By excising the spatial element of the images of reality, the active consciousness negates their temporality. The production of images shifts from an empirical space to an inner plane, a two-dimensional surface whose highest value is being, the principal content of the poetry. The poems of *Cántico* that typically celebrate the presence of being and the vanquishing of time represent such experiences by means of an intensified two-dimensional image. The images of empirical reality have no place in poem-making until they are reassembled as a composite image superimposed in planes. The creative will understands the images of raw reality as fragments, building blocks for a better image that contains every partial, perceived image and that has fashioned the parts into a graphically represented whole.

The poem functions as a two-dimensional image that closely corresponds to the role of words in "Los nombres" ("Names"). Choosing as the subject of this poem a rose, Guillén is inevitably

reminded, despite the rose's beauty and perfection, of the presence of time and its destructive presentiment:

> *¡A largo amor nos alce*
> *Esa pujanza agraz*
> *Del Instante, tan ágil*
>
> *Que en llegando a su meta*
> *Corre a imponer Después!*
> *¡Alerta, alerta, alerta,*
> *Yo seré, yo seré!*
>
> *¿Y las rosas? . . . Pestañas*
> *Cerradas: horizonte*
> *Final. ¿Acaso nada?*

> To long love may lift us
> That bitter forcefulness
> Of the Instant, so quick
>
> That on arriving at its goal
> It hurries to impose After!
> Watch out, watch out, watch out,
> I will be, I will be!
>
> And the roses? . . . Closed
> Eyelashes: final
> Horizon. Perhaps nothing?   (89)

The passive contemplation of nature, which brings him to a
most negative conclusion, makes Guillén acutely aware of his
mortality. The sole reassurance, "Pero quedan los nombres"
("But the names remain"), is that the verbal sign will survive the
death of any particular rose. The name "rose" is sufficient unto
itself to represent it. Names "Están sobre la pátina / De las cosas"
("Are on the patina / Of things") (88), intimately fused with the
things they name. It is names but not things that survive and
assume an importance that the thing itself cannot. Names are
not responses to things but rather the facilitators of all things.[3]
The reality of words, therefore, is identical, or nearly identical,
to the reality of the better images that the poet most values. The
two-dimensional image that I have outlined functions as an image
that is a word or as a word that is an image. Words and images
are not separate, mutually translatable entities, at least not in

poetry. Images from empirical reality are the building blocks of a better poetic image that contains them, of the same essence as words, and whose purpose is the affirmation of the presence of atemporal being within the plane of artifice. In "El prólogo" ("The Prologue") the poetic process is portrayed as an act of refashioning undesirable, temporally experienced images, characterized as "rodeos" ("detours") (47). Poetry is the moment when temporal experiences are redefined to become the means, or prologue, to the act of artifice that takes one out of the flux of daily experiences measured by the passage of days: ". . . ¡Perezcan / Los días en prólogo! / Buen prólogo: todo, / Todo hacia el Poema" (". . . May the days in prologue / Perish! / Good prologue: everything, / Everything toward the Poem") (47).

"Cima de la delicia" ("Height of Delight") describes an opposite experience, a moment so intense that Guillén can reclaim even useless temporal experiences, "¡Bodas / Tardías con la historia / Que desamé a diario!" ("Late wedding / With the history / That I detested daily!") (87), because the landscape, now "Henchido de presencia" ("Filled with presence"), has acquired the passivity necessary to transform its spatiality to planeness: "El mundo tiene cándida / Profundidad de espejo" ("The world possesses the innocent / Depth of a mirror") (87). The world has become a mirror for the presence of being, which in the empirical realm is rendered invisible by the very history that brings about the poet's disaffection. The moment becomes so full—"La plenitud se escape. / ¡Ya sólo sé cantar!" ("The plenitude escapes. / I only know how to sing!") (87)—that song becomes the only spontaneous possibility. The will to make visible and present the plenitude of being portrayed in the poem leads, nevertheless, to a less than affirmative conclusion. Guillén's "cantar" is evidence of a superabundance of plenitude.[4] The "singing" state of being moves him beyond the word-image that constitutes the activity of consciousness. Direct utterances are rare, but when they do occur, as in "Perfección del círculo" ("Perfection of the Circle"), they suggest that direct speech is a negative representational value that marks the limit of this type of poem-making. This poem, a testimony to the two-dimensional perfection of the circle, concludes by admiring the circle's geometrical form, which possesses the ability to make itself fully present in the act of its representation. Such a power contrasts with the difficulty in affirming the same status for being, which requires the forceful excision of an imperfect spatial-temporal reality. The perfection of the circle also exemplifies the mystery and dilemma of the poet's aesthetic-existential ideal, which he underscores with the questions that close the poem: "—¿Quién? ¿Dios? ¿El poema? / —Misteriosamente . . ." ("—Who? God? The poem? /—Mysteriously . . .") (89). The poetic process that traces the perfection of the circle returns to its origin, expressed negatively as direct speech.

While Guillén may admire the circle's form, he is incapable of faithfully retracing its trajectory with words. The perfection of the two-dimensional ideal is disrupted by the reality of its closure, which also becomes the closure of the means available to understand such perfection on its own terms. This relegates the poet to an outside position from which he can only babble in ignorance about what he has just experienced (see Frutos, "Circle"; Poulet; Silver). The attainment of the circle's perfection is possible only in approximate terms for to do so would require the abandonment of consciousness, the antithesis of a desire that exalts the circle, like a god, as the embodiment of the highest value. More than mysteries, both the abstraction of a plane ideal and the imperfection of a spatial-temporal realm embodied in the direct utterance represent limits beyond which the poet's epistemological premises fail him.

Guillén replaces the natural and abstract enigma with the category "understandable." The things that truly exist are things that he can understand, on his terms. Such an activity reverses the traditional definition of understanding, which becomes instead an occasion for affirming the principles of understanding themselves but not the specific object appropriated for contemplation. "Jardín que fue de don Pedro" ("Garden That Belonged to Don Pedro") portrays the poet in the activity of understanding a garden, which provides the opportunity, as the title suggests, for a transfer of ownership, from Don Pedro's artificed landscape to Guillén's consciousness. The contemplation of the more perfect nature of the garden is paralleled by the juxtaposition of this image with an even greater perfection, the processes of understanding that "Funden lo vivo y lo puro: / Las salas de este jardín" ("Fuse the living and the pure: / The rooms of this garden") (190). The resultant image, in the membrane of consciousness, exists in an intermediate yet understandable realm. It is not, like the perfection of the circle, pure abstraction. Nor is it alive since, as part of the understanding, it has been dispossessed of its autonomy. These ideas are more explicitly addressed in Guillén's statement in the Gerardo Diego anthology that poetry should be " 'poesía bastante pura' *ma non troppo*" (" 'fairly pure poetry' *ma non troppo*") (344), an equation that also affirms the basic conditions of knowledge and existence. Poetry must not be understood in absolute terms, for to do so would render it incomprehensible. Absolutely pure or absolutely alive means a poetry that is also absolutely unintelligible. Guillén is not so much concerned with affirming the aliveness of nature as he is the aliveness of being, as compared to the unintelligible purity of being that does not need to understand itself. The not infrequent declarations of his debt to nature—as in "Siempre aguarda mi sangre" ("My Blood Always Waits"), where he declares that "No soy nada sin ti, mundo" ("I am nothing without you, world") (217)—which seem to indicate an affirmative attitude, actually measure Guillén's alienation from the fullness of being. Without recourse to the unwanted otherness of external reality, from which he has actively distanced himself, he is literally nothing, impotent to affirm the primordial value, being, from which he is also distanced. Experiential reality has value because it confirms the presence of being, not because of an intrinsic worth. It is nothing in exactly the same sense that the poet is nothing without the world. Literally nothing has value unless it is affirming and confirming being.[5] Nature, things, and human beings have value only insofar as they provide the opportunities for being to embody itself. Guillén needs the world only insofar as he needs raw images with which to fashion a landscape that corresponds to his desire to know the shape and substance of being. Being demands a landscape, an empty landscape neither pure nor alive.

Of the 125 poems in the second edition of *Cántico,* many represent experiences that take place in nature or rural settings.

This does not mean that Guillén has assigned these landscapes a special value. The natural landscape, for example, the rural countryside in "Relieves" ["Reliefs"], whose solitary edifices—a castle at the top of a hill and a hermitage—and horizontal landscape provide a striking three-dimensional relief, is primarily a focusing device for the production of a better image, which is being. Thus the experience of a relief is superseded by a more significant relief, a product of the poet's understanding that, paradoxically, destroys the natural relief. The destruction is characterized by Guillén as activities of appropriation ("rendición") and of possession ("Posesión"), which epitomize his aggressive epistemology. The plural title is suggestive of the implicit theme of all the poetry, the making of reliefs to supplement being and a thesis about the structure of all landscapes that improves on their reality.

At specific moments nature acquires anthropomorphized feminine form to become what Guillén portrays as an embodiment of fragility and subservience. "El manantial" ("The Source") describes the retracing of the course of a river to its source, a better image of the river's unwieldy chaos rendered imagistically, in the final strophe, as a young girl:

> Y emerge—compacta
> Del río que pudo
> Ser, esbelto y curvo,
> Toda la muchacha.

> And there emerges—compact
> From the slim and curved river
> That could have been,
> The whole girl.   (53)

Affirmed here is an image, taken from nature, of nature's renunciation of its natural role. Form triumphs over the river's chaos. The girl becomes instead the embodiment of an aesthetic principle, a source of images produced at nature's expense. The physical emergence of the girl from the water marks the final step in a trajectory away from a chaotic nature to a realm of compactness, the better source that affirms itself through this image, the antithesis of the natural principle that has produced the chaos of the river. The river's source has provided the pretext for the production of an image, of compact, white, female nakedness, the creation and creature of a different nature.

The most extensive expression of Guillén's attitude toward nature is "Salvación de la primavera" ("Salvation of Spring"), where the natural landscape again acquires anthropomorphized feminine form.[6] The poem seems to be an ode to the presence of Spring, which, in a sense, "saves" him from solitude and alienation from the world. The most telling evidence to the contrary is that Spring appears in the first strophe, already in an altered, prefashioned condition, in the sculptured purity of the female form:

> *Ajustada a la sola*
> *Desnudez de tu cuerpo,*
> *Entre el aire y la luz*
> *Eres puro elemento.*

> Well fitted to the unique
> Nakedness of your body,
> Between the air and light
> You are pure element.   (90)

At the outset, Spring is already something else, characterized as "ajustada" ("well fitted") for a certain role or "adjusted" to ("made to fit") a role by someone else. Both connotations apply here and lead to the conclusion that the Spring in this poem has little to do with sensual reality but with an image-idea of Spring that in turn embodies the aesthetic-existential ideal:

> *¡Eres! Y tan desnuda,*
> *Tan continua, tan simple*
> *Que el mundo vuelve a ser*
> *Fábula irresistible.*

> You are! And so naked,
> So continual, so simple
> That the world becomes again
> An irresistible fable.   (90)

Spring is from the outset a source for the production of a better image that, like the girl in "El manantial," has nothing to do with nature. Empirical reality is simply evidence or confirmation of something already known:

> *A través de un cristal*
> *La evidencia difunde*
>
> *Con todo el esplendor*
> *Seguro en astro cierto.*

> Through a glass
> The evidence spreads
>
> With all the certain
> Splendor in a sure star.   (91)

The "cristal" is the poet's windowpane, through which he notices the physical landscape for the first time:

> *Mi atención, ampliada,*
> *Columbra. Por tu carne*
> *La atmósfera reúne*
> *Términos. Hay paisaje.*

> My attention, expanded,
> Catches a glimpse. Through your flesh
> The atmosphere gathers up
> Limits. There is landscape.   (92)

As Guillén's attention grows, the landscape acquires greater definition until it reaches a "cerrado equilibrio / Dorado" ("closed / Golden equilibrium") (93), the still moment when Spring gives itself over not to the poet's ego but to another "poder" ("power"):

> *Presa en tu exactitud,*
> *Inmóvil regalándote,*
> *A un poder te sometes,*
> *Férvido, que me invade.*

> *¡Amor! ¡Ni tú ni yo,*
> *Nosotros, y por él*
> *Todas las maravillas*
> *En que el ser llega a ser!*

> Captive in your exactness,
> Giving yourself in stillness,
> You submit, ardently,
> To a power that invades me.

Love! Neither you nor I,
We, and through it
All the wonders
In which being becomes!   (94)

Love is the affirmation of being, a metaphor for a special type of
image production.[7] By the fourth section, Spring is even more
explicitly identified with being. As Guillén states: "Somos nuestra
expresión" ("We are our expression") (96). Spring is an image
through which he has been able to understand being, the otherness within himself, and thus the means by which he saves
himself:

La plenitud en punto
De la tan ofrecida
Naturaleza salva
Su comba de armonía.

¡Amar, amar, amar,
Ser más, ser más aún!
¡Amar en el amor,
Refulgir en la luz!

Plenitude at the point
Of such promised
Nature saves
Its curve of harmony.

Loving, loving, loving,
Being more, being even more!
Loving in love,
Shining in the light!   (99)

The image of Spring has afforded him the opportunity to achieve
a personal transcendence, to see himself at, and as, the center of
the experience of the landscape:

Inexpugnable así
Dentro de la esperanza,
Sintiéndote alentar
En mi voz si me canta,

Me centro y me realizo
Tanto a fuerza de dicha
Que ella y yo por fin somos
Una misma energía.

Unshakable thus
Within the hope,
Feeling you rise up
In my voice if you sing to me,

I center myself and materialize
So much by force of happiness
That she and I at last are
One single energy.   (108)

At the "suprema altitud, / Allí donde no hay muerte" ("supreme height, / There where there is no death") (109), a better image, a direct presence, not a represented simulacrum in nature, becomes the fulfillment of desire, its loving, living mirror.

"Profundo espejo" ("Deep Mirror") further exemplifies this phenomenon. The poem begins with the description of the dawn, which with the light of day also opens the landscape as a mirror. The poem, however, departs from a long Western tradition that has considered poetry the most profound mirror of nature. The landscape in this instance becomes the mirror of the creative process through the production of an image that redefines the landscape in terms of the value of being. "Profundo espejo" is interesting because of the self-conscious, almost critical perspective from which it recounts the reversal of the normal functions of the mirror. The first mirror is a vast landscape that cedes to the discovery of a much smaller area within it: "Un material muy límpido y muy leve / Se aislaba exacto y mucho más hermoso. / La exactitud rendía otro relieve" ("A very limpid and very light material / Was isolated, exact and much more beautiful. / The exactness yielded another relief") (227). This "otro relieve" represents the familiar presence of the activated consciousness, which in the act of noticing a more specific landscape within the larger mirror of nature uses the smaller, special mirror to affirm and reflect itself. As Guillén declares in the final verse, this new relief affirms its presence not as a reflection but as the truth, yet at the expense of everything else that has preceded it: "La verdad inventaba a sus expensas" ("The truth, which was invented at its expense") (227), that is, at the expense of the natural mirror in order to affirm the more profound mirror of understanding that produces, but does not reflect, its presence in other images. Nature exists to mirror the poet's will-consciousness, not to fulfill a function for itself. Nature, therefore, is never really nature because it is never recognized as something of intrinsic value. There is never a need to mirror nature in this poetry because beyond the elemental function of providing the raw material for a better image, nature does not effectively exist. In no sense does nature decisively influence the outcome of a creative process in which it is only minimally involved. Its value is its passivity, availability, and malleability, the ease with which it may be made to assume the forms valued by the understanding.

Any landscape that serves as consistent medium for Guillén's representational agenda becomes necessary at the moment it satisfies the requirements of the understanding. This attitude is affirmed in the significant number of poems that take place indoors and feature an object, ordinary or artistic, through which the poet affirms similar existential states. Perhaps the most well known is the armchair invoked in "Beato sillón" ("Blessed Armchair"), in which the invocation of the massive object within the finite space of the house leads to an unexpected generalization about the world: "El mundo está bien / Hecho" ("The world is well / Made") (195). The poem's brevity does not make clear, however, that Guillén's affirmation is due only minimally to the objective physical presence of the armchair in the room. Although "La casa / corrobora su presencia" ("The house / Corroborates its presence") (195), the chair's massive presence in the limited space of the house provides an even more precise correlative for the presence of being, in the same massive and serene proportions. As with nature, it is not the specific object that is valued but rather the better image that emerges from the activity of contemplation. Significantly, Guillén's eyes do not "see," since "No pasa / Nada. Los ojos no ven, / Saben" ("Nothing / happens. The eyes do not see, / They know") (236). The more passive act of observation has long preceded this moment. Not the spontaneous experience of an object but the ecstatic fashioning of an image of being, the true object of exaltation, has refashioned the world once again. This well-made world is the poet's better-made image, which affirms itself through objects, as in nature, with no inherent value except as referents for being (see also Macrí 75).

If such affirmative moments almost invariably herald the presence of being, the negative moments, such as they are, respond to forces that threaten it. "Muerte a lo lejos" ("Death in the Distance") recognizes that death will eventually place a limit on consciousness, which occasions a rather stoic reply to the certainty of definitive disappearance: ". . . diré sin lágrimas: embiste, / Justa fatalidad. El muro cano / Va a imponerme su ley, no su accidente" (". . . I will say without tears: attack, / Just fatality. The white wall / Is going to impose upon me its law, not its accident") (249). This is also an attempt to recast death in more understandable terms.[8] Paralleling the activity of consciousness (often associated in Guillén with a wall), death is understood as a law that will have dominion over life. Guillén's concept of life is that it is also a law operating under the same principle since, like death, life imposes itself actively on space. Guillén has the double satisfaction of knowing that as long as he can define the space of reality, death will remain distant until, in rational fashion as if fulfilling a decree that death itself is incapable of voicing, it succeeds the poet by appropriating his space. Like the other, more affirmative poems, "Muerte a lo lejos" also attempts to redefine the terms of existence in the poet's favor. Similar sentiments are voiced in "El hondo sueño" ("The Deep Dream"), where Guillén cries out to reality not to abandon him as he descends to the depths of unconsciousness, a reference to sleep and dreams, possibly to the dream of death, so that he may "soñar mejor el hondo sueño" ("dream better the deep dream") (253). The more profound reality affirmed throughout the poetry, of course, is the productive principle whose unceasing enterprise is the redefinition of all realms of experience, including dreams and death, on more favorable terms.

Although the specific references to time are not overabundant, Guillén's awareness of it, and its limitations, is constant. Time is rendered as speed in "Profunda velocidad" ("Profound Velocity"), where the "velocísimo Ahora" ("extremely swift Now") causes the landscape to appear as a "presencia escurridiza" ("slippery presence") (187), that is, no presence at all. Only consciousness can restrain the devastation of the temporally imbued landscape by its power to contain the successive images of reality and to transform them into something unchanging and understandable. Speed is indeed a key to the experience of being since the speed associated with the raw landscape can be stabilized only by an even more powerful braking mechanism. The presence of being is accompanied by the falling away of time. A moment of plenitude in "La Florida" ("Florida") becomes "Tiempo en presente mío" ("My present time") (231), time's redefinition in the image of being. The excision of the temporal dimension, therefore, involves simultaneously acknowledging a more profound mechanism than the speed of time. Guillén affirms this idea in "El viaje" ("The Trip"), where he portrays himself in a motorcar, the "speed machine" that so captivates the futurist imagination (Kern 109–30). Despite its "ruedas crujientes" ("creaking wheels"), the imperfect vehicle facilitates covering a much greater expanse of countryside, and thus Guillén is able to see "avanzar los inmortales / Himnos de amor" ("advance the immortal / Hymns of love") (163) of the natural landscape. Guillén evinces none of the futurist fascination with instruments of speed. Indeed, he seems vexed at the most imperfect means he must endure to experience these "love songs" that communicate love in direct proportion to his ability to overcome the speed of their presence in time. In a parody of a modernist ideal, Guillén demonstrates that the instrument of speed runs a poor second to the nullifying activity of being. Being is a better machine that can still an image in motion and make it available for contemplation in an atemporal context. The unintelligibility of the activity of time is overcome by the activity of being in a timeless present of perfect stillness. More than the artifice of a well-made world, the artificing machine of consciousness affirms its greater perfection in nature, but like time, at the expense of nature, in the creation of an even better still presence that is the poetic image.

The poems that portray cityscapes are invariably unflattering and are usually set in cloudy or foggy weather. As in the few negative experiences in nature such as "El desterrado" ("The Exile"), negativity is invariably expressed as incomprehension.

The fog of "El desterrado" effectively erases the landscape and provokes Guillén into a rare direct utterance to proclaim his dumbfoundedness in the confusion of the moment: "—¿Qué es esto? / ¿Tal vez el Caos?" ("—What is this? / Perhaps Chaos?") (159). In this instance, the confusion is feigned as he affirms that "la boba niebla" ("the silly fog") (159) is to blame for his disorientation. In the rare encounters with his fellow humans, Guillén's confusion is decidedly real and uncomplimentary. In "Perdido entre tanta gente" ("Lost among So Many People"), the cityscape leaves him self-absorbed in "Mi abstracción indiferente" ("My indifferent abstraction") (196), the very state that banishes being, expressed here as existential fatigue at having to endure such a context and its inevitably inferior product.

This disdain for society is further emphasized in "Dinero de Dios" ("Money from God"), which summarizes Guillén's attitude toward contemporary society's values. The mocking image of an "Hacedor / Supremo" ("Supreme / Maker") (181), a parody of the liberal idea of a supreme being, manifests its power through the mass production of a false image, "el signo / De la Posibilidad" ("the sign / Of Possibility") (181), printed on money. These false images have acquired an absolute value "Hasta convertirse en . . . el Más Allá" ("Until becoming . . . the Afterlife") (181). Guillén is thus implicitly contrasting his "better image" produced in a "más allá de veras . . . realísimo" with the mass-produced means of image production in capitalist society also governed by the concept of a "más allá." His low opinion of bourgeois society's rather corrupt values becomes particularly evident in the sarcastic conclusion, "—¡Dioses: gastad!" ("—Gods: spend!") (181), a reference to the fact that under capitalism any mortal can become a god by virtue of the acquisition of sufficient quantities of the false images printed on money. The gods define themselves as such through their worship of the supreme maker's graven images, an idolatry that expresses itself in the perverse activity of spending. Such a false economy threatens the privileged status of the well-made images of a different economy.

The disdain of capitalism and its inferior means of image production is an ideological point of departure that leads to Guillén's literal departure from the cityscape to settings where he can produce godlike images of his own. This is the attitude expressed in "Las doce en el reloj" ("Twelve O'Clock"), in which the active contemplation of the natural landscape produces another special moment in which the poet himself becomes "Centro en aquel instante" ("Center of that moment") (279) and thus its nominal divinity. This landscape is valuable and divine because it becomes the medium in which to ground being, a better image through which he also becomes a better god: "Era yo / . . . Quién lo veía todo / Completo para un dios" ("It was I / . . . Who saw it all / Perfect for a god") (279). This experience, however, is a memory. Guillén calls attention to his distance from the actual experience by reference to clock time, the regulatory medium of the city, which serves as the literal frame of the poem since the title is repeated in the final verse. The temporal reference—the hands of the clock overlap each other to point in one direction—signals the intrusion of the cityscape into a moment whose value is its atemporality. The recourse to a temporal metaphor becomes a tacit acknowledgment of the limits of Guillén's power as an image-maker. This image has been reproduced, not produced. The image, like currency, has been devalued because Guillén is forced to remember it, to evoke it in the alien context of the cityscape where, as a citizen of a society organized around a radically different value principle, he is forced to acknowledge that principle. "Las doce en el reloj" represents the dissolution of a full moment as it becomes a memory within the framework of capitalist clock time.[9] "Las doce en el reloj" is an exemplary instance of imagistic inflation. Fully rendered images are not representations. They are being. The represented image of a full moment in memory creates a rather different, less intense image. As a god who recalls an image, the poet ultimately associates himself with the other gods in the cityscape whose presence he is compelled to acknowledge.

"Capital de invierno" ("Capital in Winter"), whose title could refer to capitalism in general as much as to the winter cityscape, expands on these ideas. The poet is acutely aware of the "prisa" ("haste") of city life, seeing in the wind that swirls in the city a symbol of the whirlwind that prevails under the present economic system. Speaking to a passerby swept by the wind, he warns:

> ¡Oh transeúnte, prisa creadora,
> De más viento en el viento:
> Muy claro anuncias el advenimiento
> De los dioses de ahora!

> O passer-by, creative hurry,
> Of more wind in the wind:
> Very clearly you announce the coming
> Of the gods of today!   (151)

This anticapitalism corresponds to a desire for simplicity that can be found only outside the city. Almost as an answer to a prayer, the winter weather neutralizes the speed and complexity of the cityscape: "El dios más inminente necesita / Simple otra vez el mundo. / Lo elemental afronta a lo profundo. / El invierno los cita" ("The most imminent god needs / The world simple again. / The elemental confronts the profound. / The winter summons them") (151). The longing for simplicity expressed here, however, is simply another manifestation of the ongoing desire to render landscapes still. The wind and snow accomplish what the alienated city dweller cannot. In nature is where Guillén encounters cities to his liking, and in his likeness. He discovers, in "Ciudad de los estíos" ("City of Summers"), "La ciudad esencial" ("The essential city") crafted from the "muy elemental" ("very elemental") (120) natural landscape.

The only landscapes of unquestioned value are spaces where the bourgeois cityscape does not intrude and which, in turn, are rendered full, still, and plane as their space is appropriated by the productive principle. The collapsing of space is most evident in poems that contemplate works of art. Whether directed toward sculpture or painting, the activity of contemplation also affords the artificing consciousness occasion to express its own values of production. Sculpture holds an attraction not for its massiveness but because it epitomizes movement immobilized (Matthews 20). In "Estatua ecuestre" ("Equestrian Statue"), the contemplation of an equestrian statue leads to the understanding that "Tengo en bronce toda el alma" ("I have my whole soul in bronze") and that "Permanece el trote aquí, / Entre su arranque y mi mano" ("The trot remains here, / Between its starting point and my hand") (177). The statue is reconstituted as an image held by the hand, a metaphor for the active component of consciousness that has understood a correspondence between the existential ideal and the atemporal, immobile ecstasy of the frozen moment represented in the statue "Inmóvil con todo brío" ("Immobile with full determination") (177). Equally intense sentiments are expressed regarding a group of living horses in "Unos caballos" ("Some Horses") whose "acción" ("activity") is a "destino [que] acaba en alma" ("destiny [that] concludes in soul") (237), a grace that expresses itself as an essential form that makes these horses "ya sobrehumanos" ("already superhuman") (237). As living correlatives of an aesthetic-existential ideal, they transcend their own unconscious "acción" to become "alma," embodiments of a higher principle, a movement toward being.

"Amiga pintura" ("Friend Painting") emphasizes again that Guillén does not recognize an essential difference between a pure art object and a contemplated landscape. Here the activity of perception, the metaphor for which is a "pintor, / Regente de esta hermosura" ("painter, / Regent of this beauty") (193), paints the landscape on the canvas of consciousness, a slow process when compared to the instantaneous reproductive power of photography. The metaphor of painting, however, characterizes only the beginning of a process, not a final product. At the poem's conclusion, Guillén exhorts his painter: "Pinta bien: se me apresura / Todo Mayo hacia un amor" ("Paint well: all May / Hurries me toward a love") (193). The activity of consciousness that renders the landscape as a well-made world, comparable to a work of art, is only the first step in a process of artifice that he understands is leading "hacia un amor," the moment in which he will be able to affirm the better image that is being. As described in "Las alamedas" ("The Poplar Groves"), the poet's task is always that of "profundizando paisajes" ("making landscapes more profound") (197), transforming them into something of greater value, an artificing activity in which the values of being and art exactly coincide. As expressed in "Lo inmenso del mar" ("The Immensity of the Sea"), the sea embodies the ideal of artifice "Monótona, lenta, plana" ("Unchanging, atemporal, plane") (198), but also "Dúctil, manejable, mía . . . en vía / De forma por fin humana" ("Flexible, manageable, mine . . . in the process of acquiring / A form that is finally human") (198). The immensity of the sea is a parallel expression of the immensity of consciousness as it performs its activity on the landscape. As the sea becomes "por fin humana" it becomes as well the vehicle through which the poet expresses his own power as one who can make a given landscape more profound. Another immense landscape, the sky in "El cielo que es azul" ("The Sky That Is Blue"), embodies the same phenomenon. In the fullness of a moment of love in which the poet is able to ". . . Ser más, ser lo más y ahora" (". . . Be more, to be the most and now") (295), he also understands the sky, specifically its qualities of compactness, muteness, and passivity, as a perfect correlative for an ideal aesthetic experience.

What Guillén frequently terms love is actually the moment in which his relationship with being becomes manifest through a better image in being's likeness. In this rather narrow sense, a great many of the poems are love poems. Love is the process by which the poet produces an image of being at the expense of the beloved object, an exchange of realities that devalues the empirical object and more highly values the hybrid love image. In "Los amantes" ("The Lovers") there are no lovers in the traditional sense, only the poet and his love ("Sólo, Amor, tú mismo" ["Only, Love, you yourself"] [49]), expressed as his awareness of the image before him:

> *¡Gozos, masas, gozos,*
> *Masas, plenitud,*
> *Atónita luz*
> *Y rojos absortos!*
>
> *¿Y el día?: lo plano*
> *Del cristal. La estancia*
> *Se ahonda, callada.*
> *Balcones en blanco.*

> Pleasures, masses, pleasures,
> Masses, plenitude,
> Amazed light
> And entranced reds!

And the day?: the planeness
Of the windowpane. The room
Becomes deeper, quiet.
Blank balconies. (49)

The act of love creates the beloved as the empirical landscape is refashioned in the "estancia," the privileged dwelling ground of being. To the poet's amazement, the beloved emerges from the final image of the "Balcones en blanco" at the poem's conclusion: "Nadie, nadie, / Pero . . . —¿Tú conmigo?" ("Nobody, nobody, / But . . . —You with me?") (49). Guillén has been the passive partner in the creation of an unexpected surprise, a plenitude that has transcended mere contemplation in order to produce the person-ified presence of the otherness that is the fullness of being.

A similar amazement is expressed in "Pasmo de amante" ("Lov-er's Amazement"), which describes the contemplation of an object of beauty, again conceived in feminine terms. This be-loved is "necesaria" (178), necessary to see, but not touch ("Con-tacto. ¡Horror! / Esta plenitud ignora, / Anónima, a la belleza" ["Contact. Horror! / This plenitude does not know, / Nameless, beauty"] [178]). Whoever "she" may be (woman, natural land-scape, picture, object, or something else) is unimportant. "She" is necessary because the poet cannot invent exterior reality, only transform it into something better. "Pasmo de amante" represents an early moment in the love experience. Not physical beauty but the abstract whiteness of the beloved object attracts the poet: "Blancura, / Si real, más imaginaria, / Que ante los ojos perdura" ("Whiteness, / If real, more imaginary, / That persists before the eyes") (178). As also expressed in "La blancura" ("Whiteness"), whiteness is an integral aspect of all aesthetic experience, a metaphor for the plane of consciousness on which images are inscribed and made profound:

> *Recta blancura refrigeradora:*
> *¡Qué feliz quien su imagen extendiese,*
> *Enardecida por los colorines,*
> *Sobre tu siempre, siempre justa lámina*
> *Del frío inmóvil bajo el firmamento!*

Straight refrigerating whiteness:
How happy the one who extends your image,

Fired by vivid colors,
Over your always, always just sheet
Of immobile coldness under the firmament!   (216)

"El querer" ("Loving") portrays the concluding moment of this rather slow process of making something profound. The whiteness has by now become a special lighting source described as

Noches de día en secreto,
Encastillados estíos
Con otro sol recoleto,
Lumbre dócil: albedríos

Nights of day in secret,
Fortified summers
With another retreated sun,
Docile light: wills   (204)

—the plane of consciousness whose "otro sol" provides the conditions for the fashioning of the amorous experience of being. Thus in poems like "Desnudo" ("Nude"), where Guillén speaks of the "Plenitud, sin ambiente, / Del cuerpo feminino" ("Plenitude, without milieu, / Of the feminine body") that brings him to the experience of an "absoluto Presente" ("absolute Present") (251), the truth is that such experiences have little to do with the female form (such as a real woman, a nude in a painting, or a naked landscape). The fullness associated with the nude exemplifies the "Monotonía justa" ("Just monotony") (251) of all the poetry. There is essentially one subject, the poet, one object, a landscape in its variant forms, and one value, which is also an economy, of image production: the high valuation of being at reality's expense.

CHAPTER 2

Pedro Salinas

The quest for an alternative mode of understanding and poetic production dominates the poetry of Pedro Salinas.[1] In a well-known declaration in the Gerardo Diego anthology, Salinas defines poetry as process, "una aventura hacia lo absoluto" ("an adventure toward the absolute"); "cuando una poesía está escrita se termina, pero no acaba; empieza, busca otra en sí misma, en el autor, en el lector, en el silencio" ("when a poetry is written it comes to an end, but it does not finish; it begins, searches for another in itself, in the author, in the reader, in silence") (318). In the absence of the poetic end, the absolute, the poetic means, the poems, become the cumulative record of its emerging presence (see Guillén). The initial chapter of *La realidad y el poeta* (*Reality and the Poet*), entitled "El poeta y las fases de la realidad" ("The Poet and the Stages of Reality"), alludes indirectly to the nature of the absolute as Salinas outlines various aspects of reality. He mentions nature (external reality), psychological reality (internal reality), manufactured reality (mechanical civilization and invented products), and cultural reality (artistic production). Cultural reality includes poetry, and its variants, among which

hay una poesía sobre la poesía, sobre el arte mismo. A los antiguos motivos de inspiración, como un paisaje, un arroyo o una mujer, se adicionan hoy otros, como un cuadro, una estatua o una teoría. Así se comprende perfectamente la existencia de una poesía intelectualista; en ella el poeta parece que no se acerca a la realidad ni a través de su reacción espontánea primera, de su propio mundo subjetivo,

ni tampoco a través de las formas externas naturales o artificiales.
Su aproximación se realiza por medio de esa segunda vida refleja
del sentimiento intelectualizado o del puro pensamiento abstracto.

there is a poetry about poetry, about art itself. To the old causes of
inspiration, such as a landscape, a stream, or a woman, are added today
others, such as a painting, a statue, or a theory. Thus one can understand
perfectly the existence of an intellectualist poetry; in this the poet
seems not to be approaching reality by means of his first spontaneous
reaction, from his own subjective world, nor from the natural or
artificial external forms. His approach is realized by means of that
second reflected life of intellectualized feeling or of pure abstract
thought.   (31)

At the essay's conclusion he strongly suggests that this is the
type of poem-making he values most:

Se entra en el verdadero y real mundo poético a través de la fase
psicológica, de la natural, de la social, de cualquiera de las fases de la
realidad que hemos examinado. Pero no nos equivoquemos nunca; el
mundo poético verdadero está más allá de todas ellas, no es el mundo
externo que vemos al abrir los ojos, no es la pura alma individual
del hombre que vemos al cerrar los ojos. Y para mí el deber primero
del poeta hoy, ante los ataques que nos llegan de todas partes, es
afirmar la esencialidad, la incomparabilidad, la "unicidad" del
mundo poético, que trasciende todas las posibles fases de la realidad.

One enters the real and true poetic world by means of the psychological stage, the natural, the social, or whichever of the stages of reality
that we have examined. But let us never deceive ourselves; the true
poetic world is beyond all of them, it is not the external world that we
see on opening our eyes, it is not the pure individual soul of man that
we see upon closing them. And for me the first duty of the contemporary poet, in the face of the attacks that come from all parts, is to affirm
the essentiality, the incomparability, the "oneness" of the poetic world,
which transcends all the possible stages of reality.   (33–34)

In suggesting that the truest reality is an intellectual, almost
abstract "mundo poético," Salinas is affirming the centrality of
the intellectual will in the creation of a private world that responds to laws and values he ascribes to it. What in Guillén is a
repeated, spontaneous-seeming spectacle becomes in Salinas an
indefinite process "toward the absolute" by which the premises
and parameters of the "mundo poético" are initially intuited,
then systematically examined as part of a prolonged intellectual

activity whose goal is the understanding and elaboration of the more highly valued alternative reality. Even in the early poetry, Salinas is dissatisfied with traditional representational models and begins to look for a better image of reality, in contradistinction to ordinary experiences in either external, empirical reality or inner, psychological reality. He subsequently invents a realm that expresses these aspirations and its alternative values. Poetry becomes the vehicle through which to create an alternative world, a better image, of being.

From the outset Salinas clearly expresses dissatisfaction with aspects of traditional reality and its representational requirements and restrictions. In *Presagios* (*Portents*) (1924), Salinas offers a portrait of a dissatisfied artist progressively disappointed in both sensual and psychological reality yet unable to affirm an alternative (Stixrude 41). The external world represents an inadequate image for contemplation, especially the poet's reflected image, as in Poem 2, where the reflecting medium, described as "Agua en la noche, serpiente indecisa" ("Water at night, indecisive serpent") (54), offers none of the answers he seeks about himself and his place in reality. The personified response to his questions offers only a partial satisfaction ("beso te doy pero no claridades" ["I give you a kiss but not light"] [54]) and the negative affirmation that he must not content himself with such solutions because, as the voice declares, "yo he sido hecha / para la sed de los labios que nunca preguntan" ("I have been made / for the thirst of lips that never question") (54). The poetry begins in medias res as an active questioning of the received images of reality, and especially his own.[2] As Salinas emphasizes in the initial poem, his sense of limitation is tempered only by his intellect and the possibilities associated with "la idea pura y en la idea / el mañana, la llave / —mañana—de lo eterno" ("the pure idea and in the idea / tomorrow, the key / —tomorrow—of the eternal") (53). Like Guillén, Salinas comes to reality with a strong sense of its incompleteness and thus the need to supplement it with a form and content of his own (see also González Muela). Empirical images and traditional perception constitute a false consciousness. In Poem 3 the hand, a metaphor for Salinas's intellectual will, is understood to be a better medium for the experiences he is seeking because, unlike the eyes, this hand is

> *Siempre abierta. Es que no sabe*
> *cerrarse, es que tiene*
> *ambiciones más profundas*
> *que las de los ojos, tiene*
> *ambiciones de esa bola*
> *imperfecta de este mundo,*
> *buen fruto para una mano*
> *de ciego, ambición de luz,*
> *eterna ambición de asir*
> *lo inasidero.*

> Always open. The fact is that it does not
> know how to close, it has deeper
> ambitions than do the eyes, it has
> ambitions for the imperfect ball
> that is this world,
> good fruit for a hand
> of a blindman, ambition for light,
> eternal ambition to seize
> the unseizable.   (55)

From a very early moment, Salinas is largely decided on the general means he must employ to affirm a better image of reality. The passive receivers of images in empirical understanding, the eyes, must be replaced with a forceful guide: "Mano de ciego no es ciega: / una voluntad la manda, / no los ojos de su dueño" ("A blindman's hand is not blind: / a will guides it, / not the eyes of its master") (55).

The will that guides the poet in his blindness is his own emerging thesis about the possibility of an alternative realm. Salinas's intuitions require that he rethink his attitudes to traditional images and image-making, as in Poem 8, where he confronts his own "imagen / exacta e inaccesible" ("exact and inaccessible / image") (60) in the mirror, only to conclude that "siento un vacío que sólo / me lo llenará ese alma / que no me das" ("I feel an emptiness that only / the soul that you don't give me / will fill") (60). The sense of absence and distance evoked by his represented image is typical of his attitude to all images from ordinary reality. This attitude becomes openly critical in Poem 38, where he effectively re-creates the empirical mind model in the relationships formed by the external landscape, the window of a house that, like the human eye, frames a portion of the landscape, and a mirror inside the house that reflects the external image that Salinas in turn sees:

> *Aquí a mi lado,*
> *firme pupila la ventana abre:*
> *lo que ella ve de afuera*
> *lo repite en el fondo de la estancia*
> *un viejo espejo familiar, ingenua madre*
> *que la luz y la vida nos trasmite*
> *pura y sin mancha.*

> Here by my side,
> the window opens, a firm pupil:
> what it sees outside
> is repeated in the back of the room by
> an old family mirror, unaffected mother
> that transmits light and life to us
> pure and stainless.   (92)

Although the mirror image is absolutely faithful to the exterior reality, it is insufficient to satisfy Salinas's desire to see in the more intense manner that he has begun to intuit:

> *Miro al espejo y sólo a mí me veo*
> *—ya se borró el crepúsculo indeciso—*
> *en la estampa de mí que me da el rostro.*
> *De lo demás, allí en los ojos algo . . .*
> *A mi rincón me vuelvo. Que la vida*
> *se muera lentamente en el espejo.*

> I look at the window and see only myself
> —the indecisive sunset has already been erased—
> in the imprint of myself that my face renders.
> About the rest, there in the eyes something . . .
> To my corner I return. Let life
> die slowly in the mirror.   (92)

The images of exterior reality offer a composite image of death and the reminder that empirical law is ultimately temporal law grounded in the definitive absence and gradual destruction of such images (see Palley 9–20, 25). The desire is for a new mode of understanding to liberate the poet from "el ansia esta / de ver todo el mundo entero, / sin cuatro partes iguales" ("this longing / to see the world whole, / without four equal parts") (102). Ordinary images of reality "sin bajeza ni altura, / montón de muertas flechas rebotadas / al pie nuestro" ("neither low nor high, / a pile of dead arrows returned / to our feet") must be replaced with a "gran dolor eterno" ("great eternal pain") that "nosotros nos hemos de clavar en el pecho / por voluntad y por mandato interno" ("we ourselves have to stab in our breast / out of will and internal command") (101). The impasse also lies in the understanding whose only medium is words.

Words form the basis of ordinary reality. Like the window that frames the image of the landscape in the mirror in Poem 38, so too language frames, in a limiting sense, our understanding of the images of reality. Language is synonymous with consciousness, understanding, and the framing of raw reality but also with limitation, impotence, and powerlessness. Salinas introduces this idea in Poem 4 with his description of the words that a child uses to describe the objects of his or her experience, in this case "Tatá, dadá" (56) to describe both father and mother. The child's world is confused but unified. Exactly the opposite condition obtains for Salinas, for whom the nonsense words elicit a sense of his limitation with language. The poet can visualize and circumscribe intellectually the child's idea of the world ("una bola confusa; / el mundo 'Tatá, dadá' " ["a confused ball; / the world 'Tatá, dadá' "] [56]) but cannot achieve the preconscious child's unified vision. Salinas's intuition of an alternative reality is thwarted by language that affords the adult a clear understanding of objects but at the expense of a unified vision of them. The child, in effect, names his or her world during that moment before language limits the understanding, paradoxically, by rendering a clear picture of the "clear pictures" that the world makes available to it. Poem 5 explores the dissatisfying consequences of this insight. Speaking to an unidentified object, any among the universe of named objects that must be understood by means of language, he comes to the conclusion that the "Posesión de[l]

... nombre" ("Possession of [the] ... name") of an object is a tainted possession since its "presencia y ... ausencia / sombra son una de otra" ("presence and ... absence / are shadows of each other") (57). Words are incomplete presences that faithfully reflect the emptiness and absence of images from ordinary reality.

The response to language's insufficiency to convey the presence of an object is a willful intensification of the understanding, as underscored in Poem 26, which also portrays Salinas with a child. In this poem, however, the child is only an accidental participant. A walk in the countryside leads him, tracing the child's steps past a lemon tree, to the unexpected discovery of an "amarillo limón escondido" ("hidden yellow lemon"). The poem concludes indoors with the child asleep but with Salinas in intellectual possession of an intensified meaning of the experience which the child is incapable of formulating, rendered as a physical possession:

> *Ahora es de noche y, como fruto cumplido del día,*
> *te tengo en las manos,*
> *limpio limón escondido,*
> *limpio limón discubierto.*
> *(El niño está ya dormido.)*

> Now it's night and, like the full fruit of the day,
> I have you in my hands,
> pure hidden lemon,
> pure revealed lemon.
> (The child is already sleeping.)   (80)

What distinguishes adult from child here is an intellectual willfulness, the need to remain in a state of intellectual vigilance in the face of the phenomena of external reality, to affirm a sense of orderliness and structure to a private experience that in this case refers Salinas to a more intense context. Indeed, he has no interest in communicating the meaning of the lemon to a reader who, like the child, remains distant from a privileged and private experience.

The limitations of language inspire an incipient resolve to reorder his epistemological premises, most clearly expressed in a series of three poems beginning with Poem 23. Salinas chides himself for being fascinated with the artifice of the natural landscape at sunset: "Deja ya de mirar la arquitectura / que va trazando el fuego de artificio / en los cielos de agosto" ("Stop looking at the architecture / sketched by the fireworks / in the skies of August"). He realizes that this is indulging the "vicio de no durar" ("vice of nonendurance") (77). "Hay que ir a buscar lo más durable" ("It is necessary to go and search for the most lasting thing") (77), which, in Poem 24, lies in his relationship to language and the more durable intellectual structure of literary works. This poem examines the reading process, which begins in the book but which reaches its greatest fullness in the human consciousness, which endows the words with a "vida superior" ("superior life") (78). The book's "oro que guardaba tu venero / hoy está libre en mí, no en ti cautivo" ("gold that your mine preserved / today is free in me, not captive in you") (78), which affirms a higher destiny for words and for language. Words acquire new life as means to another end, the private experience that is Salinas's special understanding of the text. The act of reading becomes an occasion to supplement the apparent finality of words and to assign them another purpose, another referent, the poet's understanding "aquí en mi corazón [donde] lo siento vivo" ("here in my heart [where] I feel it alive") (78). Poem 25 represents the logical intellectual culmination of this series, the impetus to poetic creation itself, described metaphorically, but quite accurately, as "El lírico hipogrifo" ("The lyrical hippogriff") that grazes on dreams "en la pradera / más íntima del ser" ("in the most intimate / meadow of being") (79). In a completely inner landscape "libre al fin de la atadura extraña" ("finally free of its strange binding") is where the impetus to produce poetry "dentro de sí sus horizontes crea" ("creates within itself its own horizons") (79).

Even at this early point, Salinas is largely convinced that poetry is an intellectual response to the restricting givens of empirical words and images and their underlying intellectual structure. Such a response, therefore, is also a form of action. The designation of the intellect as a privileged site of poetic production makes his artistic goals indistinguishable from existential con-

cerns. Empirical epistemology impedes the poet's will to experience a better image of reality in which words and images obey
a different set of rules. Language is a conventional construct of
an empirical order that only seems natural. What passes for
reality is a particular epistemological structure premised on the
idea that words and images are translatable, interchangeable
parts. This incomplete hypothesis is the source of Salinas's malaise, the rejection of which provides the point of departure from
which to describe an alternative structure of reality in which
the empirical order becomes its reverse or inverted image, a
mirror opposite.

The mimetic tradition that fundamentally characterizes Western art is also an ideology that subjugates the poet to laws not
of his choosing, temporal laws of graduated change that regulate
both life in organized society and the domain of the creative
artist. In Poem 45, Salinas declares himself in favor of a new
ideal:

> *Agua que nunca huye,*
> *soles que no se ponen,*
> *libros que no traicionan:*
> *quietud, tiniebla, inmóvil, tú, silencio.*
> *Y lo de fuera, sí, sé generoso, afuera.*
> *Mas lo de dentro—dulce secreto eterno—adentro.*

> Water that never flees,
> suns that never set,
> books that do not betray:
> stillness, darkness, immobile, you, silence.
> And the things outside, yes, be generous, outside.
> But the things inside—sweet eternal
>   secret—inside.   (99)

Empirically elaborated words and images betray because they
posit the primacy of a visible, temporal, sound-filled realm to
the exclusion of other possible worlds. Salinas's intuition is
that such a system is not primary but rather secondary to
another that succeeds it—indeed, that also precedes it and
that renders its totalizing premises invalid, the mirror opposite
of empirical representational values: atemporal, dark, silent,
motionless. This realm is also populated by a totally different

creature, the antithesis of the poet's absent form restricted by temporality and societal hierarchies: an ideal female form whom Salinas senses he will call upon later to play a more significant role in the poetry:

> *Te llamaré mañana,*
> *cuando al no verte ya,*
> *me imagine que sigues*
> *aquí cerca, a mi lado.*

> I'll call you tomorrow,
> when, on no longer seeing you,
> I may imagine that you continue
> nearby, at my side.   (103)

Salinas's attitude in the early poetry suggests that he considers that there is not enough room for the competing realities to coexist. He considers himself severely constrained by the given existential order wed to an unsatisfactory mode of artistic production also reflective of cultural and political values. His rather systematic approach to the problem of his existence and its relation to conventional modes of representation is also a complaint against the structure of a society of which he wants little part. He prefers an alternative understanding: the still, dark, silent center of being from which empirical ideology's words and images have estranged him. The poetry becomes a search for an alternative existence that requires a redefinition of reality according to Salinas's intellectual will.

The title of the second volume, *Seguro azar* (*Sure Fate*) (1924–28), introduces the notion that fate is indeed something that can be known, by means of will, an active, willfully sustained intellectual operation. The earlier intuitions about the limitations inherent in the empirical epistemological order elicit more aggressive responses. "El mal invitado" ("The Bad Guest") portrays the poet on a journey lodged in a house from which he contemplates the surrounding countryside. His eyes take active possession of the contemplated scene "para llevárselo, / verlo despacio" ("to remove it, / to see it slowly"), in short

> *Verlo tanto*
> *que esto que me queda ahora*

clavado e inolvidable
como el más alto cantar,
esto, que nunca se olvidará
en mí porque fue del tiempo,
de tan mío, de tan visto,
de tan descifrado, fuera,
eternidad, lo olvidado.

To see it so
that this that now remains
rooted and unforgettable
like the highest song,
this, which will never be forgotten
in me because it was part of time,
so mine, so well seen,
so well deciphered, would that it were,
eternity, the thing forgotten.   (115)

Salinas desires the intellectual possession of the landscape to become independent of perception and cognition. The poem critiques bourgeois epistemology, premised on temporal perceptions and memory, in order to propose an alternative premised on timelessness and forgetfulness, independent of an image or simulacrum of the experience. In "Dominio" ("Domain") he laments the division of reality into conscious and unconscious realms, external and internal landscapes. In such a system one is subject to the confinement inherent in the all-powerful word *adiós* since, if one must be either conscious or unconscious at all times, it is necessary to give up one realm (to say good-bye to it) in order to participate in the other. Speaking to someone who could be himself, Salinas takes note that with the last conscious word, a *good-bye* that signals entry into unconsciousness, "encadenaste / la noche a tu silencio" ("you chained / the night to your silence") (122) and with the first word on awakening, also *good-bye*, to the realm left behind, the new day is created. The poem conveys a growing sense of impasse in the consciousness/unconsciousness cycle and underscores the need for alternative models of understanding.

Modern mechanical inventions allow Salinas to assess how contemporary society seeks these alternative models of under-

standing. In "Nivel preferido" ("Preferred Level") Salinas, trans-
ported to a mountainside by an automobile, gazes at a panoramic
vista that seems like

> ... *unas páginas*
> *enormes, verdes, azules,*
> *servicial, lisa, esquemática,*
> *atlas*
> *para mirarla.*

> ... some pages
> enormous, green, blue,
> obliging, smooth, schematic,
> atlas
> to look at it.   (146)

The power and silent intensity of the moment contrast with the
chaotic movement of man and machine in the city and the
cacophony of "pregón, klaxón, bocina, / sin cesar" ("cry, horn,
megaphone, / without end") (147). In this and other poems
like "Nevacerrada, abril" ("Nevacerrada in April"), which bring
together the poet and a mechanical instrument ("Alma mía en
la tuya / mecánica; mi fuerza, / bien medida, la tuya, / justa: doce
caballos" ["My soul in your / mechanical one; my force, / well
measured, yours, / proper: twelve horsepower"][116]), the automobile's power and rapid movement suggest the intensity of
intellectual activity necessary to transcend the passive modes
of picturing inherent in empirical epistemology. This becomes
explicit in "Far West," where the intense movement of the wind
on the motion-picture screen is understood not as wind but as
the absence of wind: "No es ya viento, es el retrato / de un viento
que se murió / sin que yo le conociera" ("It is no longer wind,
it is the portrait / of a wind that died / without my having made
its acquaintance") (121). "Cinematógrafo" ("Cinema") offers an
even more explicit rejection of film and the empirical values it
embodies (see Feal Deibe 26–27). Regarding the subject of the
film he saw: "La tela rectangular / le oprimió en normas severas"
("The rectangular cloth / oppressed it with strict rules") (133).
The second part affirms a more active mode of image production
via a "tela maravillosa" ("marvelous cloth") (135), a projection

screen that resides in the human intellect. Unlike the cinematic screen, which only receives images, the "tela maravillosa" is independent of light. Its plane can generate its own invented images, not temporally and spatially projected simulacra but immediate presences that originate in the "mundo puro, / la tela blanca" ("pure world, / the white screen") of the intellect. The speed of automobiles and the projection capacities of cinematic art, which possess the ability to accelerate the experience of empirically produced images, are ultimately, however, metaphors for Salinas's desire to affirm a better image that is also a better machine. Like the silent screen, it is a silent presence whose image is not dependent on the imitation of a likeness of something but on the poet's intellectual will. Mechanical reality merely affirms the need for a truly powerful expressive mechanism.

Throughout *Seguro azar* there is a progressively greater association between what Salinas perceives to be his destiny and the fashioning of an alternative realm that is being effected through a subtle yet unmistakable intellectual destruction of the ordinary, inefficient, and outmoded means of understanding.[3] In "Figuraciones" ("Figures") he pictures his fate floating in an undefined space:

> ¡Qué desarraigado, ingrávido,
> entre voces, entre imanes,
> entre orillas, fuera, arriba,
> suelto! Parece el azar.

> How rootless, weightless,
> among voices, magnets,
> shorelines, outside, up,
> loose! It looks like fate.   (108)

This is quietly followed by "Vocación" ("Vocation"), in which he pictures himself rejecting "la luz clara del día / perfecto" ("the clear light of perfect / day") (110) in order to close his eyes

> ... Y ver
> incompleto, tembloroso,
> de será o no será,
> —masas torpes, planos sordos—

Jorge Guillén (left) and Pedro Salinas (right) at the home of Juan
Ramón Jiménez (center) in the 1920s

sin luz, sin gracia, sin orden
un mundo sin acabar,
necesitado, llamándome
a mi o a ti, o a cualquiera
que ponga lo que le falta,
que le dé la perfección.

... And see
incomplete, trembling,
of "it will be" or "it will not be,"
—sluggish masses, deaf planes—
without light, without grace, without order
an unfinished world,
needing, calling to me
or to you, or to whomever
will provide what it lacks,
will give it perfection.   (110)

The otherness addressed here suggests that a major aspect of this perfectible world consists in populating it with a perfect citizen, unlike the female of "Otra tú" ("Another You"), whose fullness Salinas is unable to experience:

No te veo la mirada
si te miro aquí a mi lado.
Si miro al agua la veo.

Si te escucho,
no te oigo bien el silencio.

I do not see your gaze
if I look at you here by my side.
If I look at the water I see it.

If I listen to you,
I do not hear well your silence.   (109)

The dissatisfaction lies in his possessing either her image or her presence, her voice or her silence, but not both simultaneously. He is demanding an image that is also a presence and a voice that is also silence. This is possible only in an alternative realm where empirical rules do not apply, a realm that he embellishes or supplements ("que ponga lo que le falta, / que le dé la perfección"). The perfect citizen of this realm, therefore, is not another full being but the fullness of being, the better image that supplements his lack. Salinas's destiny is "seguro," sure and safe, because he has willed it into being: "escogí: / el otro. / Cerré los ojos" ("I chose: / the other. / I closed my eyes") (110).

"Amada exacta" ("Exact Beloved") underscores the limitations of a traditional beloved whose image and presence are two different things. When his beloved, "hecha / para la presencia pura" ("made / for pure presence"), is by his side he forgets her memory, her remembered image. When she is absent his memory remakes her with "ojos falsos" ("false eyes") (142). Such a love depends on empirical laws and, like life in ordinary reality, is ultimately unsatisfying. Salinas is looking for something still absent from his life: "Estás, estoy, a tu lado: / estás dentro de la niebla" ("You are, I am, at your side: / you are inside the fog") (151). A greater commitment to the alternative realm is required. By the end of the volume, in "Fe mía" ("My Faith"), he pledges himself to the "rosa verdadera" ("true rose") and not to the "rosa / de papel, tantas veces que la hice / yo con mis manos" ("rose / of paper, / that so many times I / made with my hands") (158). That is, he pledges himself to an entire process of poetic creation in which the beloved is understood as an alternative principle of artistic, and existential, production:

> De ti que nunca te hice,
> de ti que nunca te hicieron,
> de ti me fío, redondo
> seguro azar.

> In you whom I never made,
> in you whom they never made,
> in you I trust, round
> sure fate.   (158)

The dimly glimpsed otherness will, in effect, become his new eyes, a lens with which to redefine an unfulfilling ordinary reality. As he declares in "Amiga" ("Friend"):

> Para cristal te quiero,
> nítida y clara eres.
> Para mirar al mundo,
> a través de ti, puro,

de hollín o de belleza,
como lo invente el día.
Tu presencia aquí, sí,
delante de mí, siempre,
pero invisible siempre,
sin verte y verdadera.
Cristal. ¡Espejo, nunca!

I want you for a lens,
you are spotless and clear.
To look at the world,
through you, pure,
of soot or beauty,
as the day invents it.
Your presence here, yes,
before me, always,
but invisible always,
without seeing you and truthful.
A lens. A mirror, never!   (159)

Mimesis, the mirror of nature, is reformulated to become a lens, a means to understanding further the unseen alternative. Poetry is the vehicle for bringing into focus a realm that "No se le ve, / pero está detrás, seguro" ("Cannot be seen, / but is behind, secure") (162). The most formidable presence, and the surest value, is being:

Yo lo sé:
lo mío no es mío, es suyo.
Lo eterno, suyo. Vendrá
—¡qué bien le siento!—por ello.
Voy a verle cara a cara:
porque ya se está quitando,
porque está tirando ya,
los cielos, las alegrías,
los disimulos, los tiempos,
las palabras, antifaces
leves que yo le ponía
contra—¡irresistible luz!—
su rostro de sin remedio
eternidad, él, silencio.

I know:
what's mine is not mine, it is his.

The eternal, his. He will come
—how well I feel him!—for it.
I am going to see him face to face:
because he is already shedding,
because he is already throwing away,
the skies, the joys,
the dissimulation, the times,
the words, light masks
that I put on him
against—irresistible light!—
his face of irremediable
eternity, him, silence.   (162)

The activity of his intellectual will thus affords a first glimpse of his destiny.

Fábula y signo (*Story and Sign*) (1931) begins with a more acute sense of the need to go beyond empirical relationships. "Mar distante" ("Distant Sea"), nominally about the seascape, expresses open dissatisfaction with the representational and cognitive means through which the sea can be known, the empirical system that defines the conditions of understanding:

Si no es el mar, sí es su voz
. . . .
Si no es el mar, sí es su nombre
. . . .
Si no es el mar, sí es su idea
de fuego, insondable, impia:
y yo,
ardiendo, ahogándome en ella.

If it's not the sea, it is its voice
. . . .
If it's not the sea, it is its name
. . . .
If it's not the sea, it is its idea
of fire, bottomless, impious:
and I,
burning, drowning in it.   (169)

As suggested by the title, to know an object by empirical means one must understand it at a distance. The more one wishes to know, in fact, the more distant the object becomes. One can never know the sea but rather the image, voice, word, and idea that represents the sea, a stand-in but not its presence. "La estatua" ("The Statute") moves closer to affirming an alternative mode of understanding. Touching a stone statue leads to the conclusion that his silent, sightless contact ("ese tacto tan puro" ["that touch so pure"]) has bridged the distance between the object and his understanding. Both poet and statue affirm a measure of their truer natures, which transcends form and heralds the advent of being in its purest sense:

> *Es ese tacto tan puro,*
> *con que vuelves a tu ser*
> *piedra, con alma de piedra:*
> *a ser lo primero, tierra, lo primero que tú eras,*
> *lo primero*
> *(pero no esa forma falsa)*
> *que fui yo.*

> It is that touch so pure,
> with which you turn to
> stone, with soul of stone:
> to be the first, earth, the first that you were,
> the first
> (but not that false form)
> that was I.   (170)

The statue has value only as part of an act of understanding that makes more clear to Salinas the truer object of desire and its accompanying epistemological premises. The meaning of this experience is to realize "lo primero," an existential condition that transcends empirically constituted words, images, voices, and ideas. Salinas's first value becomes the transcendence of the distancing factors that relegate him to a secondary existence whose paradigm is the mirror image communicated over space and time. The task, therefore, is to create a privileged medium that will facilitate his access to "lo primero."

In "Paris, abril, modelo" ("Paris, April, Model") the sculptured landscape of a Paris garden within the cityscape attracts Salinas to the exquisiteness of the artifice that remakes it into an "estatua de sí misma" ("statue of itself") (173). The landscape has achieved a higher perfection, reflective of an artistic will and purpose: "nunca en Venus / buscaste forma, tú, / inventora de formas, modelo" ("never in Venus / did you search for form, you, / inventor of forms, model") (173). This "primavera modelo" ("spring model") is independent of a mode of artifice that requires the artificer lovingly to copy a preexisting model but not to supply the model.[4] The Spring that manifests its presence in the garden setting is its own model. It is nature that has transcended its nature, that does not need to mirror itself. Likewise, Salinas's artistic ideal transcends the need for models. "Muertes" ("Deaths") parodies the failure of traditional cognitive and philosophical models to know in a profound sense. Indeed, such models bring the opposite of understanding, as Salinas enumerates in relation to his model female, the progressively more frequent subject of address. In a parody of both Christian and Platonic traditions, he suggests what will happen to his beloved if they have to depend exclusively on empirical values:

> *Andarás tú, tu nombre, que eras tú,*
> *ascendido*
> *hasta unos cielos tontos,*
> *en una gloria abstracta de alfabeto.*

> You will wander, your name, which was you,
> ascended
> to some foolish heavens,
> in an abstract glory of alphabet.   (178)

In "Rapto a la primavera" ("Rapture to Spring") Salinas, once again in his car, sees two dried leaves of fall in the spring landscape, which he pictures as rushing at high speeds to save themselves from a premature fate. His solution is to reattach the leaves to "la más descuidada rama / de un árbol distraído" ("the most neglected branch / of an absent-minded tree") (180), to circumvent natural-empirical laws, which in this instance seem as incongruous as the spectacle of autumn leaves in spring. Indeed, the landscapes in *Fábula y signo* become progressively less natural, as in "Font-Romeu, noche de baile," ("Font-Romeu, Night of Dance"), in which Salinas, driving in his car, witnesses the spectacle of billboards along the road. The billboards and their models remind him of the vacuousness of a culture that considers such products significant but, more important, of his own "voluntad vacante aquí en lo blanco" ("vacant will here in the whiteness") (183). These ironic, even flippant poems demonstrate Salinas's deep-seated dissatisfaction and frustration with the direction of modern culture. He is caught between an admiration for the inventiveness of mechanical production and the realization that it is but another reformulation of the values he detests. Industrial society has not changed anything, only made the evidence of cultural failure more glaring and garish, as demonstrated by the billboards, crafted images of society's impotence.

An alternative ideology of the image requires a new model of artistic production, described in "Vida segunda" ("Second Life") as the willful formulation of a better image, a form worthy of becoming loved. The conditions of the form's birth are the total erasure of her form from the poet's consciousness ("tú naciste al borrárseme / tu forma" ["you were born on erasing for me / your form"] [188]) and her escape from his memory ("te escapaste del recuerdo" ["you escaped from memory"] [188]). Her willful escape requires an equal willfulness on the poet's part: "te tuve que inventar" ("I had to invent you") (188). This beloved is not a strict otherness, as Salinas tells her: "Eras ya de mí, incapaz / de vivirte ya sin mi" ("You were already mine, incapable / of living yourself without me") (188). The transcendence of her image in the memory refers her to the will-understanding. It also recasts the traditional definition of love—something that leaves an indelible impression after the act of seeing—as an intellectual response to the false images of ordinary reality that make Salinas feel impotent. The second life of the beloved is a new life for Salinas. She is not a reproduced or remembered image but a crafted presence independent of the empirical world:

> *A mis medidas de dentro*
> *te fui inventando, Afrodita,*
> *perfecta de entre el olvido,*
> *virgen y nueva, surgida*
> *del olvido de tu forma.*

> To my inner measurements
> I was inventing you, Aphrodite,
> perfect out of oblivion,
> virgin and new, arisen
> from your forgotten form.   (189)

He intensifies this idea in "Escorial I," in which the statuesque again embodies the highest artistic ideal. The mass of the Escorial reveals that form itself is the real purpose of the building; ("Piedra / dimensión, forma" ["Stone / dimension, form"] [190]). Words are not necessary to interpret the building; "Sin traducción ya le entiende" ("It is understood without translation") (190). Likewise in "Ruptura sin palabras" ("Rupture without Words") Salinas describes his own rupture with empirical reality in order to experience the "tiempo lentísimo" ("very slowest time") (192) that contrasts with time's will to impose an order that stifles and frustrates him.

In "Tú, mía" ("You, Mine") Salinas associates his will to transcend time with the beloved whom he imagines to have grown tired of living "en los espejos, / en las sombras, en los ojos, / de verte tan parecida / a ti" ("in mirrors, in shadow, in eyes, / of seeing you so similar / to yourself") (194–95), in the lesser representational realm. He also imagines that she has grown tired of being an image and that she will want simply to "ser tú" ("be you"):

> ... *aquí, a la cima*
> *más alta de ti, al momento*
> *tan perfecto, tan sin par,*
> *imposible en lo mejor,*
> *que quise dejarte así,*
> *y me marché de tu lado*
> *diciéndole al tiempo: basta.*
> *Vivir era ir hacia atrás.*
> *Ya se te había acabado*
> *—te tengo así—el más allá.*

> ... here, at the highest
> height of yourself, at a moment
> so perfect, so without equal,
> impossible to make better,

that I tried to leave you thus,
and I left your side
saying to time: enough.
To live was to go backward.
Already the beyond
—I have you thus—had put the finishing
    touches on you.   (195)

"Más allá" ("The beyond"), the alternative reality where the
beloved achieves her fullness, is the realm where Salinas has
redefined the conditions of knowledge. Seeing and hearing are
unimportant in a realm where the beloved's pure presence is
capable of surpassing temporal laws. Words, images, and other
conventional means of representation are grounded in time, the
despoiler of being. The beloved created in a "here" thus also
embodies the poet's form in the alternative reality. She has been
defined as an exact opposite of the life that Salinas must endure
in ordinary reality and thus underscores again that his distance
from a transcendent existence is a consequence of his involvement with the wrong set of values, the wrong set of ideological
assumptions. The beloved embodies the values of an alternative
milieu grounded in silence, blindness, and immobility and as
such becomes the perfect means for an expanded understanding.

Extending these momentary insights becomes the preoccupation of the concluding poems. In "El teléfono" ("The Telephone"), the telephone becomes a symbol for Salinas's inability
to sustain his glimpse of the other reality. The telephone voice
which proclaims " 'Aquí estoy. / Aquí.' " (" 'Here I am. / Here.' ")
(199) is not "here" in a satisfying sense. Nevertheless, the disem-
bodied voice that makes its "cama / de acero tenso, en alambre, /
por el aire" ("bed / of tense steel, in wire, / through the air")
(200) is suggestive of an ideal voice, a fully present voice independent of utterances which makes all others seem absent. The
somewhat flippant tone of this poem and the better-known "Underwood Girls" underscores Salinas's growing dissatisfaction
with ordinary means of communication (see Stixrude 87). In
"Underwood Girls" the real protagonists are not the countless
secretaries that reproduce mechanically the words, and wills, of
their bosses in order to make capitalist society function effi-

ciently but rather the "treinta, eternas ninfas" ("thirty, eternal nymphs") (203), the letters of the Spanish alphabet that "sostienen el mundo" ("sustain the world") (203). By conflating the secretaries and the typewriter letters that secretaries strike to make words, Salinas succinctly comments on the confused nature of modern society and the way it conducts its business as well as the restrictions that conventional models of language have imposed on his own art. The image is one of mutual domesticity, language and the secretaries that reproduce it reduced to the lowest common denominator. Like the secretaries who do the will of others, so too language has become domesticated because its users have forgotten its origins and higher purpose. These false female images contrast sharply with the ideal partner Salinas wishes to know in the alternative reality. In "La sin pruebas" ("The Untested One") he imagines her so pure and virginal that "cuando no vivas más / yo no sé en qué voy a ver / que vivías" ("when you no longer live / I do not know in what I am going to see / that you lived") (209) because "no hay señal: / no dejas huella detrás" ("there is no sign: / you do not leave a trace behind") (208). His "intención, ansia, proyecto" ("purpose, will, project") is "puro / querer, de querer sin más" ("pure / love, loving pure and simple") (213), a desire that describes the beloved, a "salvada, / virgen ímpetu primero / de todo y nunca de nada. / Inútil héroe blanco, con venas sin estrenar" ("saved, / first virgin impetus / of everything and never of anything. / Useless white hero, with untested veins") (213), a new set of epistemological-existential relationships.

La voz a ti debida (*The Voice Owed to You*) (1933) establishes the elaboration of this new understanding as its primary focus. Salinas's strategy is simple, to ascribe agency for these alternative values to the beloved, simultaneously a real flesh-and-blood person and a creature of his intellectual will:

> *A ti debértelo todo*
> *querría yo.*
> *¡Qué hermoso el mundo, qué entero*
> *si todo, besos y luces,*
> *y gozo,*
> *viniese sólo de ti!*

To owe everything to you
is what I would want.
How beautiful the world, how complete
if everything, kisses and lights,
and delight,
were to come only from you!   (262)

Her simply being herself—becoming the embodiment of an alternative mode of understanding—provides the surest means for Salinas to elucidate his understanding of her and the better reality she inhabits: "Ese es tu sino: vivirte. / No hagas nada. / Tu obra eres tú, nada más" ("That is your fate: living yourself. / Do nothing. / Your work is you, nothing more") (261). A flesh-and-blood woman, the beloved is also an orientation device, a medium through which to affirm alternative existential-representational values. Each encounter with her becomes an opportunity to delineate her qualities, indistinguishable from those of her realm and the alternate intellectual conditions necessary for knowing her more profoundly. A real-life extramarital affair (see Havard) thus provides the inspiration, but also the intellectual ground, for a further investigation of an alternative reality.

The beloved offers the means to transcend conventional representational laws; to discover her truly Salinas must seek her "por detrás de las gentes" ("behind people") (223), apart from society and historical time. Indeed, he rejects knowing her through conventional means:

No en tu nombre, si lo dicen,
no en tu imagen, si la pintan.
Detrás, detrás, más allá.
Por detrás de ti te busco.
No en tu espejo, no en tu letra,
ni en tu alma.
Detrás, más allá.

Not in your name, if they say it,
not in your image, if they paint it.
Behind, behind, farther away.
From behind you I search for you.
Not in your mirror, not in your letter,
nor in your soul.
Behind, farther away.   (223)

The main obstacle to knowing the beloved's higher order of existence is the epistemological barrier that has fractured reality into divisive parts. Her name, the fact that she has been named, keeps them apart:

> *Si tú no tuvieras nombre,*
> *todo sería primero,*
> *inicial, todo inventado*
> *por mí,*
> *intacto hasta el beso mío.*
> *Gozo, amor: delicia lenta*
> *do gozar, de amar, sin nombre.*
>
> *Nombre: ¡qué puñal clavado*
> *en medio de un pecho cándido*
> *que sería nuestro siempre*
> *si no fuese por su nombre!*

> If you did not have a name,
> all would be primal,
> initial, all invented
> by me,
> intact up to my kiss.
> Pleasure, love: slow delight
> of enjoying, of loving, without a name.

> Name: what a dagger stuck
> in the heart of an innocent breast
> that would be ours always
> if it were not for your name!   (233)

The name referred to is not the name of a woman but the more fundamental requirement of traditional epistemology that all entities be assigned a name, a place in a representational order. Poetry exists to overturn the epistemological barriers to the experience of the beloved and thus to critique mimetic representational values.[5]

Separation from the beloved also means absence from being since, as a lover, Salinas is also a prisoner of the naming process. When he muses how delightful it could be to "vivir en los pronombres" ("live in pronouns") where the beloved could be "pura, libre, / irreductible: tú" ("pure, free, / irreducible: you") (243), the real intention is a more radical overturning: "enterraré los nombres, / los rótulos, la historia" ("I will bury names, / labels, history") to return to the "anónimo / eterno del desnudo, / de la piedra, del mundo" ("eternal / anonymity of the nude, / of the stone, of the world") where he can tell the beloved " 'Yo te quiero, soy yo.' " (" 'I love you, it's me.' ") (243). Such statements indicate that the experience of a higher self is also a goal of Salinas's extended dialogue. To experience a love that is being he must create a realm for the beloved that meets its requirements, the supersession of empirical form:

> *Y ya siento entre tactos,*
> *entre abrazos, tu piel*
> *que me entrega el retorno*
> *al palpitar primero,*
> *sin luz, antes del mundo,*
> *total, sin forma, caos.*

> And already I feel among touches,
> among embraces, your skin
> that bestows on me the return
> to the first palpitation,
> without light, before the world,
> total, without form, chaos.   (249)

This is a realm in which "El tiempo no tenía / sospechas de ser él" ("Time did not / suspect being itself") (250) in which beloveds can exist "en el puro vivir, / sin sucesión, / salvados de motivos, / de orígenes, de albas" ("in pure being, / without sequence, / saved from motives, / origins, dawns") (251). It is a place where Salinas hopes to discover "lo desnudo y lo perdurable" ("the naked and the lasting") which he visualizes as being the "centro puro, inmóvil" ("pure, immobile center") (258) of the beloved.

This immobile center is a projection where, in relation to the beloved, the poet can "Ser / la materia que te gusta . . . y que ves ya sin mirar / a tu alrededor" ("Be / the matter that is pleasing to you . . . and that you see already without looking / about you") (259), or, more in terms of love, he can experience "el amor del que tú te enamorases" ("the love of which you become enamored") (260). He desires to share what the beloved has "created" as he provides the very conditions for sharing. This is possible only under a new intellectual-poetic hypothesis, a new epistemology, impossible in the "mundo descolorido / en donde yo vivía" ("discolored world / in which I lived"):

> *Para sentirte a ti*
> *no sirven*
> *los sentidos de siempre,*
> *usados con los otros.*
> *Hay que esperar los nuevos.*
>
> To perceive you
> the usual senses,
> used with the others,
> are useless.
> One must wait for the new ones.   (269)

These new senses understand ordinary words and images as by-products of a more intense reality that has preceded them. The values of silence and darkness underpin the alternative epistemology, a sculpturesque ideal dominated by solidity and massiveness. Color and light play no role here. The fullness of being, not the impotent images of memories and dreams that define amorous values in ordinary reality, becomes the supreme value. Salinas often portrays himself "perdido, ciego" ("lost, blind") (274), willfully blinded and free to imagine union with the beloved in a frozen moment beyond words and images "en la absoluta espera inmóvil / del amor, inminencia, gozo, pánico, / sin otras alas que silencios, alas" ("in the absolute, immobile hope / of love, imminence, delight, panic, / without other wings than silences, wings") (274).

The remembrance of the beloved complicates their love. Dreaming of her is "una larga despedida de ti" ("a long good-bye to you") (265) because dreams and memories are aspects of conventional understanding whose products are simulacra and not direct presences. All traditional senses must be redefined, including sight, a refined version of which is reserved for the most intense moment: "yo no quiero ya otra cosa / más que verte a ti querer" ("I want nothing else / but to see you love") (276), at a point beyond "las diferencias, invencibles, arenas, / rocas, años" ("the differences, invincibles, sands, / rocks, years") (277) that constitute conventional reality. At a point when Salinas thinks the beloved incapable of demonstrating "otra cosa de ti más perfecta" ("another aspect of you more perfect") (279), he discovers—"límpida, insospechada— / otra hermosura nueva: / parece la primera" ("limpid, unsuspected— / another new beauty: / it seems the first one") (279)—that the beloved is continually supplementing his definitions of her. Each new aspect becomes a new starting point that undermines the previous one. She is "aumentada en sus dones sin fin" ("endlessly augmented in her gifts") (278), destructive of any hypothesis about her nature. She defies remembrance, the foundation stone of traditional epistemology.[6] Each new experience, which "seems the first one," banishes memory and time: "Mejor no amarse / mirándose en espejos complacidos" ("Better not to love / looking in satisfied mirrors") (281). The only possible ideal is "Amor total, quererse como masas" ("Total love, to love like masses") (281), to love outside of time. None of the conventional senses is adequate to achieve an understanding of the beloved who defies temporality: "lentamente vas / formándote tú misma, / naciéndote, / dentro de tu querer" ("slowly you are / forming yourself, / giving birth to yourself, / within your love") (283). Finally she reveals her statuesque beauty as a "nuevo ser" ("new being"), a "desnuda Venus cierta" ("sure, naked Venus") (284). Salinas's task is to "sacar / de ti tu mejor tú" ("take / from you your best you") (285), to discover the beloved under the best terms, in the context of the fullness of being.

Being, as opposed to temporality, is characterized by its silence, darkness, and immobility, by its repudiation of empirical values, as is the beloved: "La forma de querer tú / es dejarme que te quiera. / El sí con que te me rinde / es el silencio. . . . Jamás palabras" ("The way to love you / to allow myself to love you. / The yes that conquers me / is silence. . . . Never words") (282). To speak words to her trivializes her. Likewise, "Su gran obra de amor / era dejarme solo" ("Your great work of love / was to leave me alone") (295), in a position to understand the distance that remains between them:

Tú no puedes quererme:
estás alta, ¡qué arriba!
Y para consolarme
me envías sombras, copias,
retratos, simulacros,
todos tan parecidos
como si fueses tú.
Entre figuraciones
vivo, de ti, sin ti.

You cannot love me:
you are high, so high up!
And to console me
you send me shadows, copies,
portraits, simulacra,
all so lifelike,
as if each were you.
I live among
images, of you, without you.   (297)

He lashes out at these images as "criaturas falsas, / divinas, inter-
puestas" ("false creatures, / divine, inserted") (298) and, in a
subsequent poem, beseeches the symbol of this mode of understanding, the mirror:

Distánciemela, espejo;
trastorna su tamaño.
A ella, que llena el mundo,
hazla menuda, mínima.
Que quepa en monosílabos,
en unos ojos;
que la puedas tener
a ella, desmesurada,
gacela, ya sujeta,
infantil, en tu marco.

Distance her from me, mirror;
change her size.
The one that fills up the world,
make her small, minimal.
Let her fit in monosyllables,
in some eyes;
may you be able to hold her,

beyond measure,
gazelle, already subdued,
infantile, in your frame.   (302)

The mirror and the mimetic values it epitomizes are incapable of circumscribing her form. A beloved image will not suffice, only her "carne" ("flesh"), her presence, the experience of her body in and as the "body" of being:

> *tu vivir conmigo*
> *es signo puro, seña,*
> *en besos, en presencias,*
> *de lo imposible, de*
> *tu querer vivir*
> *conmigo, mía, siempre.*

> your life with me
> is a pure sign, mark,
> in kisses, in presences,
> of the impossible, of
> your wanting to live
> with me, mine, always.   (309–10)

The beloved is simultaneously an erotic, existential, and artistic ideal, the embodiment of all the values of being and the principles of an intensified understanding. His "amor con ella / y todo lo que fue" ("love with her / and all that it had been") has been an attempt to create something "que nunca ha existido, / que sólo fue un pretexto / mío para vivir" ("that never has existed, / that only was a pretext / of mine in order to live") (319). The exclusive means to this goal has been "Signos y simulacros / trazados en papeles / blancos, verdes, azules" ("Signs and simulacra / scratched on / white, green, blue paper") that "querrían ser tu apoyo / eterno, ser tu suelo, / tu prometida tierra" ("would want to be your eternal / support, to be your ground, / your promised land") (321). They have proven insufficient because "se deshacen, en tiempo, / polvo, dejando sólo / vagos rastros fugaces, / recuerdos" ("they break up, in time, / dust, leaving only / vague, fleeting traces, / memories") (321). Salinas is again complaining of his incomplete understanding which has created only "leves mundos frágiles" ("light, fragile worlds"), the "amor que inventamos / sin tierra ni sin fecha" ("love that we invent / without land and without date") (324) in an "otra luz" ("another light") beyond form, where they can be "libres / de sospecha de materia" ("free / of the suspicion of matter") (328). Ironically, the means to effect such an end is a "retorno / a esta corporeidad mortal y rosa / donde el amor inventa su infinito" ("return / to this mortal and rose corporality / where love invents its infinity") (329).

Razón de amor (*Reason of Love*) (1936) introduces a more active beloved, a force and not the somewhat intellectualized abstraction of *La voz a ti debida,* an embodiment of the means of salvation from a temporal destiny estranged from the fullness of being. Salinas's emphasis on her corporality signals an intensification of his will to know the conditions of salvation, the

> *gran afán de salvación constante*
> *de cuyo no cesar se está viviendo:*
> *el ansia de salvarme, de salvarte,*
> *de salvarnos los dos, ilusionados*
> *de estar salvando al mismo que nos salva.*
>
> great constant zeal for salvation
> because of whose very ceaselessness it is living:
> the zeal to save myself, to save you,
> to save us both, eager
> to be saving the same thing that saves us.   (339)

Love is a total interdependence among lover, beloved, and love itself, a salvation. It does not require the lovers actually to achieve the "paraíso sin lugar, isla sin mapa, / donde viven felices los salvados" ("placeless paradise, mapless island, / where the saved live happily") (340). Rather, Salinas understands that "nos llenará la vida / este puro volar sin hora quieta, / este vivir buscándola: / y es ya la salvación querer salvarnos" ("life will fill us with / this pure flight without a quiet hour, / this life searching for it: / and just wanting to save ourselves is salvation") (340). The will to salvation is the true reason for love. The intellectual understanding of love is coeval with any fortuitous experience that flesh-and-blood lovers might actually have. Salinas defines love in terms favorable to him since loving entails both being

saved and saving the medium in which love is realized. The will
to know love is sufficient in itself without the participation of
factors beyond human control—that is, the specific phenomenon of love as a corporeal experience. Salinas wants to understand, and control, an uncontrollable, inexplicable, spontaneous
phenomenon. To understand the reason for love is to achieve
intellectual understanding and control over the things that leave
him dissatisfied, impotent, and uncomprehending.

The beloved exists to assist Salinas in clarifying the practical
issues of his life, thus making it necessary to bring his idea-
beloved into greater interaction with the world. Thinking back
on his previous experiences with the beloved, he realizes that
"Estabas, pero no se te veía, / aquí en la luz terrestre, en
nuestra luz / de todos" ("You were here, but I did not see
you, / in the terrestrial light, in the light / of everybody")
(346). Yet he realizes that she lies beyond the power of those
that "Te iban buscando / por tardes grises" ("Went searching
for you / on gray afternoons") (346). As opposed to empirical
light, which anyone can see, her special light is only for "mis
ojos ... los únicos / que saben ver con ella" ("my eyes ... the
only ones / that know how to see her") (346). As he sees her
here he can declare that "Ni recuerdos nos unen, ni promesas"
("Neither memories unite us, nor promises") but rather "tú
para ser mirada, yo mirándote" ("you to be contemplated, I
contemplating you") (346–47). This light created by the
beloved, underscores an intensification of her role. She has
become identified as an alternative source of images, which
only the poet can see, not defined or limited by memories or
by "ese oscuro mundo que se llama / no volvernos a ver"
("that dark world which is called / not seeing each other
again") (347). The following poem describes the beloved in
terms of the marks she is capable of making in Salinas's life
in ordinary reality: "la seña de tu ser" ("the sign of your
being") (348), her primordial function, which transcends "las
presencias de siempre" ("the usual presences") (349) to take
him "hacia su pleno más" ("toward their greater fullness")
(349), "el prodigioso / saber ... que no sufre memoria, / como
sufren las fechas / los nombres o las líneas" ("the marvelous /

knowledge ... that does not suffer memory, / as the dates, / names, or lines suffer") (350–51), "ese dónde" ("that place") where, in contradistinction to remembrance that is "la pena de sí mismo" ("its own grief"), he can experience "eternidad: relámpago" ("eternity: a flash of lightning") (351). This leads to the idea of a "Lengua de paraíso" ("Language of paradise") (353) different from the ordinary language, which "no deja huella / en memoria ni en signo" ("leaves no trace / in memory or sign") (353), through which the beloved's real name can be known. Begotten by special means ("de tu propia criatura origen, / del vago simulacro de tu antes / te sacas tu nacer" ["origin of your own creature, / of the vague simulacrum of your before / you bring forth your birth"] [372]), the beloved embodies a new linguistic principle, which creates her physical image:

> ... *tu voz crea su cuerpo. Nacen*
> *en el vacío espacio, innumerables,*
> *las formas delicadas y posibles*
> *del cuerpo de tu voz....*

> ... your voice creates your body. Born
> in the empty space, innumerable,
> are the delicate and possible forms
> of the body of your voice....   (377)

The corporality of the beloved does not depend on the mirror image of a thing. Her form and being, voice and image are identical because the beloved is a presence, not a simulacrum of something else. She is her own origin, a unified presence that has transcended the contradictions of ordinary reality, the origin, idea, image, and body of the constituting values of the alternative realm, the ideal love in which the values of being transcend "los besos, / las miradas, las señales" ("the kisses, the glances, the signs") to affirm a love "tan sepultado en su ser, / tan entregado, tan quieto, / que nuestro querer en vida / se sintiese / seguro de no acabar" ("so buried in your being, / so given over, so quiet, / that our love in life / would feel / sure of never ending") (384–85).

Salinas proposes an idea of love in which "Los vastos fondos del tiempo, / de las distancias, se alisan / y se olvidan de su drama: separar" ("The vast depths of time, / of distances become smooth / and forget their drama: to separate") (387–88). The fragmentation and compartmentalization characteristic of conventional reality have impelled Salinas to create his own intellectual-artistic alternative, compared here to water, an apt metaphor for the type of artistic medium he has been articulating. In the plane surface of the water

> *Todo se junta y se aplana.*
> *El cielo más alto vive*
> *confundido con la yerba,*
> *como en el amor de Dios.*
> *Y el que tiene amor remoto*
> *mira en el agua, a su alcance,*
> *imagen, voz, fabulosas*
> *presencias de lo que ama.*

> All is united and made plane.
> The highest sky lives
> confused with the grass,
> as in the love of God.
> And one who possesses remote love
> sees in the water, within his grasp,
> image, voice, imaginary
> presences of what he loves.   (388)

Not the water but the active plane of the intellectual will allows Salinas to "querer / lo querido" ("love / what is loved") (388). The water epitomizes an artistic-existential ideal that has superseded the fractured and distantiating aesthetic of conventional representation and has fused them into one plane. Space and distance cede to massiveness, the temporal elaboration of reality to immobility, traditional words and images to a condition in which their functions fuse. As he tells the beloved:

> *En nuestros ojos visiones,*
> *visiones y no miradas,*
> *no percibían tamaños,*
> *datos, colores, distancias.*
> *. . . . .*
> *Palabras sueltas, palabras,*

deleite en incoherencias,
no eran ya signo de cosas,
eran voces puras, voces
de su servir olvidadas.

In our eyes visions,
visions and not glances,
did not perceive shapes,
data, colors, distances.
. . . .
Loose words, words,
delight in incoherences,
were no longer a sign of things,
they were pure voices, voices
that had forgotten their function.   (398)

And finally

Las manos, no era tocar
lo que hacían en nosotros,
era descubrir; los tactos
nuestros cuerpos inventaban,
allí en plena luz, tan claros
como en la plena tiniebla.

The hands, it was not to touch
what they were doing in us,
it was to discover; the touches
our bodies invented,
there in full light, so clear
as in full darkness.   (398–99)

The traditional senses cease to be ends and become the means to fulfill an alternative role, compelled by an alternative ideology, love: "todas / tienen letra distinta / cuando cuentan sus breves / amores en la arena" ("all / have a different letter / when they write their brief / loves in the sand") (400). Taken as a whole the "diferencias minúsculas" ("minuscule differences") of human experience provide the basis for "la alegría / inmensa de ser otras" ("the immense happiness / of being others") (400). As a part of a new order they form the amorous links in a chain constantly "buscando / un más detrás de un más" ("searching for / a more beyond a more") that "va / seguro a no acabarse:

toca / techo de eternidad" ("moves / certain of never ending and
touches / the roof of eternity") (401). The goal of alternative
experience is eternity, the opposite of temporal experience; it
is a different intellectual order, which repudiates the "Leyes
antiguas del mundo, / ser de roca, ser de agua" ("Old laws of the
world, / to be made of rock, to be made of water"), which
"indiferentes / se rompen porque las cosas / quieren vivirse
también / en la ley de ser felices" ("indifferently / burst because
things / want also to live / by the law of being happy") (409).
Such an order proclaims the fullness of being as its highest value.

Being becomes central in the concluding poems as Salinas
visualizes with increasing clarity "la dócil materia / eterna, con
que se labre / el gran proyecto del alma" ("the docile, eternal /
matter, with which is shaped / the great project of the soul")
(411). This is expressed in "Salvación por el cuerpo" ("Salvation
by the Body") as "el ansia de ser cuerpo ... cumplirse en la
materia" ("the desire to be a body ... to fulfill oneself in matter")
(419), a desire to give solidity and substance to what has been
an intellectual hypothesis. The poetry has been describing a
rebirth into a new reality, created under Salinas's own terms
"con los ojos cerrados, y los puños / rabiosamente voluntarios"
("with closed eyes, and fists / rabidly willful") (420), a process
that he describes as "tentativas de presencia" ("attempts at presence"), a concerted effort to know the body of being. More than
any singular human body the ultimate "cuerpo" is the body that
contains both lover and beloved, "su cuerpo, el del amor, último
y cierto" ("its body, the body of love, final and certain") (423),
a timeless unity "que inútilmente esperarán las tumbas" ("that
the tombs will await in vain") (423), alternative landscapes "que
en la sangre encontramos, invisibles, / y que el solo camino / es
ese que hay que abrirse / con el alma y las manos" ("that we find
in the blood, invisible, / and the sole road / is one that must be
opened / with the soul and the hands") (437). This is the ultimate
value that lies beyond the ordinary measure of value,

> *sin señas de que nadie exista,*
> *sin la demostración desconsolada*
> *que es tener en las manos*
> *monedas de oro o un retrato.*

without signs that exists,
without the disconsolate demonstration
that is having in one's hands
gold coins or a portrait.   (442)

There is no trace of this love. Their "posesión lenta ... del
paraíso" ("slow possession ... of paradise") has happened because of the will to know that "El paraíso está debajo / de todo
lo supuesto" ("Paradise lies beneath / all that is presupposed")
(443), beyond the representational system whose products are
impotent testimony of its inability to create presences. Salinas's
relationship with the beloved ultimately makes them "suicidas
hacia arriba, / en el final acierto, / de nuestra creación, / que es
nuestra muerte" ("upward suicides, / in the final success, / of our
creation, / which is our death") (443), since their experience of
each other leaves no trace, no product. An experience beyond
value has consumed itself completely and perfectly.

The final poem of *Razón de amor* is a commentary on the
entire phenomenon of the beloved's corporality, the need to
make the idea flesh. The conclusion is that both poet and beloved, in her incorporeal and corporeal aspects, are necessary
supplements of each other: "soy necesario a su gran ansia / de
ser / algo más de la idea de su vida" ("I am necessary to her great
desire / to be / something more than the idea of her life") (447).
And likewise, she needs to be

> *Viva, ser viva, en algo humano quiere,*
> *encarnarse, entregada, pero al fondo*
> *su indomable altivez de diosa pura*
> *en el último don niega la entrega,*
> *si no es por un minuto, fugacísima.*
> *En un minuto solo, pacto,*
> *se la siente total y dicha nuestra.*
> *Rendida en nuestro cuerpo,*
> *ese diamante lúcido y soltero,*
> *que en los ojos le brilla,*
> *rodará rostro abajo, tibio, par,*
> *mientras la boca dice: "Tenme."*
> *Y ella, divino ser, logra su dicha*
> *sólo cuando nosotros la logramos*

en la tierra, prestándola
los labios que no tiene.

Alive, to be alive, in something human she wants,
to become incarnate, given over, but at the bottom
    of it all
her indomitable arrogance of a pure goddess
in a last gift denies her surrender,
if only for a minute, most fleetingly.
In a sole moment, pact,
one feels her totally along with our happiness.
Surrendered in our body,
that lucid and solitary diamond,
which shines in our eyes,
will tumble down, tepid, even,
while her mouth says: "Have me."
And she, divine being, attains her happiness
only when we attain it
on earth, lending her
the lips she does not have.   (447–48)

Ultimately, the beloved has never had lips, but she has provided the ground, the reason for love, the means to the carnal experience of a fuller reality. In the end, the embodiment of her better idea of being expresses itself through and in the flesh, where love ultimately makes sense as the expressive body of a private human will.

CHAPTER 3

Vicente Aleixandre

Vicente Aleixandre's poetry, like Salinas's and Guillén's, may also be read as a progressively more intense investigation of an alternative reality.[1] Aleixandre, however, explores an existential order over which the intellectual will is incapable of exerting immediate and definitive control. If Guillén willfully reconstitutes ordinary reality into a better image and if Salinas willfully summons his beloved in order to make objective a better intellectual order, Aleixandre's desire to know a better reality requires an extended struggle to impose his will on a force that defies attempts to circumscribe it (see Volek 83–87). What seems almost spontaneous for Guillén and what is for Salinas a carefully controlled exercise becomes for Aleixandre a protracted engagement to understand and to dominate a medium that communicates by radically different means.[2] Aleixandre is not so much interested in self-understanding as in the self-aggrandizement that accompanies the presence of being. The poetry rejects a psychoanalytic purpose (see Schwartz) in order to create a private world whose primary meaning is for "un único pecho" ("a unique heart") (478), a privileged experience to which the poetry is testimony.

The preparatory moment to a new value orientation is *Ambito* (*Boundary*) (1924–27), which chronicles Aleixandre's dissatisfaction with the limitations of the given reality as it subtly undermines and devalues traditional representational and epistemological assumptions (see also Carnero 95). The volume's most persistent image, the reflected light of the moon, epitomizes the limited possibilities of ordinary consciousness as well as the young poet's awareness, as an adult, of his distance from being. "Adolescencia" ("Adolescence") conveys this most acutely as the young poet remembers his adolescent self and consciousness then, as now, "mirando / aguas abajo la corriente, / y en el espejo tu pasaje / fluir, desvanecerse" ("watching / the waters beneath the current, / and in the mirror your passage / flow, disappear") (105). The dissatisfaction is intensified by the realization that there is no essential difference between past and present. Both have been dominated by the passive contemplation of represented images of the self, representations of being but not its presence. "Juventud" ("Youth") underscores the impotence of this passivity as Aleixandre looks back on youth as innocent and hopeful but also blind: "cerrados / los ojos. Derribados / paredones. Al raso, / luceros clausurados" ("eyes / burned out. Fallen / walls. Skyward, / closed stars") (117). A confining consciousness becomes the consequence of his misspent youth. More than one poem, for example "Retrato" ("Portrait"), alludes to masturbation as a means of combating the tedium of life, experiences that invariably summon an even greater sense of limitation that "cierra ya el sentido" ("seals the senses") (96). Self-contemplation and self-gratification are also acts of self-containment, a failure of the will: "El gesto blando que / mi mano opone al viento" ("The bland gesture that / my hand uses against the wind") (97).

Images of weakness and impotence abound in *Ambito*. One of the few poems that expresses a more forceful attitude treats symbolic antagonists, an imagined fight in "Riña" ("Fight") between the moon and the shadow that would extinguish the moon's weak light if victorious (Olivio Jiménez 20–21). Such a battle underscores at a symbolic level the weakness of Aleixandre's ordinary consciousness. That he favors the triumph of the shadow suggests a growing dissatisfaction with traditional consciousness, embodied in the moon's weak light. Aleixandre begins to understand that the shaping forces in his life are invariably associated with the idea of mimetic reproduction and their doubled product: mirror reflections, simulacra, and words that translate into images. He begins to dissociate himself from these agents of existential dilution as he declares to an imaginary lover: "Lo que yo no quiero / es darte palabras de ensueño, / ni propagar imagen con mis labios" ("What I do not want / is to give you daydream words, / nor to propagate an image with my lips") (108). He is looking for an alternative means of representing love, his better self. What he is suggesting is a new expressive mode, a new "Filosofía. Nueva / mirada hacia el cielo / viejo" ("Philosophy. New / gaze toward the aged sky") and hope for a new "Definición que aguardo / de todo lo disperso" ("Definition that I await / of everything scattered") (137). An integral aspect of the alienation from empirical values is the devaluation of memory. Just as in empirical epistemology words and images become doubles for each other, so too memories, as simulacra of past events, distance the poet from being by reduplicating, inflating, and thus devaluing his presence. Thus, in "Cabeza, en el recuerdo" ("Head, in Remembrance"), as he speaks to his adolescent countenance, memory must be transfigured into "su escultura" ("your sculpture"), something more substantial than an image or simulacrum, to acquire positive value. In "Memoria" ("Memory"), however, memory is pictured as a "Valle de ausencias" ("Valley of absences") that leaves him "sediento" ("thirsty") (168) to experience the presence of things that memory cannot supply. He is left at the volume's conclusion with a sense of expectation as "Toda mi boca se llena / de amor, de fuegos presentes" ("My whole mouth fills / with love, with present fires") (172).

Pasión de la tierra (*Passion of the Earth*) (1928–29) chronicles Aleixandre's initial experience with the alternative mode of understanding and the expanded existential possibilities it heralds.[3] In this volume he is concerned more with characterizing and describing the new landscape than with making conclusions, since the new intuitions about an intensified existence are overwhelming in every sense. Nevertheless, like Salinas, Aleixandre populates this realm with a female creature as the poetry abandons its conventional form and becomes prose. There is a direct correlation between the prose-poem form and the female creature who is the frequent subject of address ("ella quedaba desnuda, irisada de acentos, hecha pura prosodia" ["she remained

naked, iridescent with accents, made into pure prosody"] [181]),
which suggests that the poetry is responding to a more powerful
will and theory of production that has overturned the earlier
artistic-existential premises. A new representational framework
emerges as Aleixandre declares conventional understanding inoperative: "Me descrismo y derribo, abro los ojos contra el cielo
mojado" ("I explode and destroy, I open my eyes against the
liquid sky") (180). Aware from the outset that his relationship
with the unconscious center of being is a learning process, he
tells his female companion: "Tu compañia es un abecedario"
("Your company is a spelling book") (179). The old understanding is so many "dibujos ya muy gastados" ("already used-up
drawings") (179). The principal communicative medium of the
alternative realm is a new form of language, "la tos muy ronca
[que] escupirá las flores oscuras" ("the very hoarse cough [that]
will spit out dark flowers") (180), which requires new means of
understanding, "esa puerta" ("that door") that will allow "todos
[a besarnos] en la boca" ("everybody [to kiss each other] on the
mouth") (182), as a special but peculiar form of "love" begins
to affirm itself ("qué oscura misión mía de amarte" ["what a
dark mission mine, loving you"] [182]). Aleixandre, however, is
frightened by the power of the alternative existence, attracted
to and repelled by a realm where "Los amantes se besaban sobre
las palabras" ("The lovers kissed each other above words") (182)
and where he is able to "sentir en el oído la mirada de las cimas
de tierra que llegan en volandas" ("hear in my ear the view
from the peaks of land that come through the air") (187). His
liberation is also a new epistemological burden (see Molho 143).

To become the worthy lover of the feminine realm Aleixandre
must overcome its power to overwhelm vision. "Ser de esperanza
y lluvia" ("Being of Hope and Rain") acknowledges his willingness to become a prisoner in "ese dulce pozo escondido ... en
busca de los dos brazos entreabiertos" ("that sweet hidden well
... in search of the two half-open arms") (187) but also his
willful determination to begin to exert an influence over the
rush of sounds, images, and language he cannot understand:
"Horizontalmente metido estoy vestido de hojalata para impedir
el arroyo clandestino que va a surtir de mi silencio" ("Horizon-

tally situated, I am clothed with tinplate to impede the clandes-
tine stream that is going to spurt from my silence") (188).
This silence, suggestive of Salinas's preferred medium, remains
unknown, uncircumscribable, and thus powerful. The desire
becomes to "extender mi brazo hasta tocar la delicia" ("extend
my arm until I touch delight"): "Si yo quiero la vida no es para
repartirla. Ni para malgastarla. Es solo para tener en orden los
labios. Para no mirarme las manos de cera, aunque irrumpa su
caudal descifrable" ("If I want life it is not to share it. Nor to
waste it. It is only to put my lips in order. In order not to look
at my hands of wax, even though their decipherable volume may
erupt") (191). As he begins to decipher the strange messages of
this medium, he declares that "estoy aquí ya formándome.
Cuento uno a uno los centímetros de mi lucha. Por eso me nace
una risa del talón que no es humo. Por ti, que no explicas la
geografía más profunda" ("I am here forming myself. I count one
by one the centimeters of my struggle. This is why there emerges
a smile of a smokeless heel. Through you, who do not explain
the deepest geography") (192). Understanding the physical terrain of this new geography is a means of acquiring its power,
which in turn endows the poet with more substantial form, a
new understanding that is a means to the values of full being.
Called "pretérita" ("past") (194), the beloved is acknowledged
as previous to the poet, a privileged point of origin, a better
image by which to orient himself to a primal reality. Becoming
her lover, Aleixandre also becomes her philosopher and transla-
tor. Loving means learning to speak the beloved's new language.

Naming and representing the beloved is also a means of self-
aggrandizement. A force understood as both a "perla de amor
inmensa caída de nosotros" ("immense pearl of love fallen from
us") and an aspect of the "infinito universal que está en una
garganta palpitando" ("universal infinite that is in a palpitating
throat") (195), she is a medium of being but also uncontrollable
and destructive, a "rojo callado que [crece] monstruoso hasta
venir a un primer plano" ("silent red color that [grows] mon-
strous until it comes to the fore") (196). Aleixandre must master
the epistemological premises underlying his love before he can
participate in her liberating energy. The beloved brings a new

thesis regarding the possibilities of understanding, which impels the poet to "olvidarse de los límites y buscar a destiempo la forma de las núbiles, el nacimiento de la luz cuando anochece" ("forget limits and seek at an inopportune moment the form of the nubile ones, the birth of the light when night falls") (199). She is a productive principle that contradicts traditional models unable to account for a "luz cuando anochece." She brings her own light, independent of traditional representational formulas, and thus heralds herself as a primary apparition, a presence and not a simulacrum or copy of something else. Although Aleixandre is still lamenting his impotence and weakness ("nunca he conseguido ver la forma de vuestros labios" ["I have never got to see the form of your lips"] [199]), he is also very much aware of his will to penetrate and to capture this medium's power: "Mi brazo es una expedición en silencio" ("My arm is an expedition in silence") (200).

In "Del color de la nada" ("Of the Color of Nothingness") Aleixandre takes another step toward understanding the new reality as he describes in physical terms what has been happening epistemologically. He sees "los ojos, salidos, de su esfera ... [que] acabarían brillando como puntos de dolor, con peligro de atravesarse en las gargantas" ("eyes, wandered from their sphere ... [that] would wind up shining like points of pain, with fear of piercing each other in the throats") (204). A form of vision independent of the mimetic paradigm is making him tired of "tristes acordeones secundarios" ("sad secondary accordions") (205). Like Guillén and Salinas, Aleixandre is becoming convinced that it is possible to render the presence of a thing, to erase the distance between the word or image that stands for an object. Aleixandre intuits this new type of language in "El crimen o imposible" ("The Crime or the Impossible"): "Yo espío la palabra que circula, la que yo sé un día tomará la forma de corazón. La que precisamente todo ignora que florecerá en mi pecho" ("I watch the word that circulates, the one that I know one day will take the form of a heart. The one that is precisely unaware that it will flower in my chest") (208–09). He is also aware of the failure of traditional words and images to summon the alternative reality: "el misterio no puede encerrarse en una cáscara de huevo, no puede saberse por más que lo besemos diciendo las palabras expresivas, aquellas que me han nacido en la frente cuando el sueño" ("the mystery cannot be enclosed in an eggshell, it cannot know itself however much we kiss it while saying expressive words, those that have been born in my forehead during dreams") (209). The concept "word" is acquiring an entirely different meaning as Aleixandre becomes progressively aware of empirical limitations, as in "El mar no es una hoja de papel" ("The Sea Is Not a Sheet of Paper"): "Sí, esperad que me quite estos grabados antiguos" ("Yes, wait so I can get rid of these old engravings") (210), a rather pointed reference to the mimetic requirements of empiricist representation and the necessity to confront "grabados"—the printing process—but also to the "imprinting" metaphor that characterizes cognition in empiricist terminology—the presence of absences.

In "El solitario" ("The Solitary One"), as Aleixandre searches for "palabras que certificarían mi altura, los frutos que están al alcance de la mano" ("words that would certify my height, the fruits within reach of my hand") (219), he becomes more aware of the nature of his struggle and his power as a lover.[4] He declares that it is he, and not this "señorita," who is actually in control of the course of his life, metaphorized into a game of solitaire: "yo manejo y pongo en fila [esta señorita] para completar" ("I direct and align [this girl] in order to perfect") (220). The true locus of the other reality is an inner silence from which emanate new words and images. This brings a new understanding about their production during "ese minuto tránsito que consiste en firmar con agua sobre una cuartilla blanca, aprovechando el instante en que el corazón retrocede" ("that transitory minute that consists in signing one's name with water on a white sheet, taking advantage of the instant in which the heart retreats") (221). But he will not be satisfied with a poetry that "oculta el armazón de [los] huesos" ("hides the framework of [the] bones"); he wants to limit the power of his "muchacha" ("girl"), to transform her "en una bahía limitada, en una respiración con fronteras a la que no le ha de sorprender la luna nueva" ("into a slow-witted bay, into a breath with boundaries that the new moon will not surprise") (222). He wants a source of strength to call upon in order to discover "donde los ojos podrán al cabo presenciar un paisaje caliente, una suave transición que consiste en musitar un nombre en el oído mientras se olvida que el cielo es siempre el mismo" ("where the eyes will be able finally to witness a hot landscape, a soft transition that consists of muttering a name in my ear while it is forgotten that the sky is always the same") (222). His love is a means to a better end, a "paisaje caliente," the true source from which this new language and its startling images proceed.

The continued experience of the new medium without some greater finality, however, is akin to the dubious product of masturbation, "esa dolorosa saliva que resbala y que me está quemando mis manos con su historia, con su brillo de cara reinventada para morir en al arroyo que ignoro entre las ingles" ("that painful saliva that slides and that is burning my hands with its history, with its gleam of reinvented face in order to die in the stream of which I am unaware in my groin") (222). The solution is to invent a goal to which lover and beloved can aspire together. As he proposes, "Si cantas te prometo la castidad final, una imagen del monte último donde se quema la cruz de la memoria contra el cielo" ("If you sing I promise you the final chastity, an image of the last mountain where the cross of memory is burned against the sky") (224). Aleixandre is proposing the elimination of the final barrier to unmediated being, the surpassing of memory and temporality, in order to achieve the "destino que ilumina las letras sin descarga, de las que no se pueden apartar los ojos" ("destiny that illuminates the unfired letters, the ones from which the eyes cannot move") (224). Word, image, poetry, and plenitude are all contained in the same experience, which exists beyond the final empirical barrier. Aleixandre's surrealistic songbird "busca aguas, no espejos" ("searches for waters, not mirrors") (224), presences, not mimesis. In "Del engaño y la renuncia" ("Of Deception and Renunciation") he emphasizes the inner strength available to him, symbolized in his "brazo muy largo" ("very long arm"), which is "presto a cazar pájaros incogibles" ("ready to hunt uncatchable birds") and, especially, his "pierna muy larga ... destruyéndome todas las memorias" ("very long leg ... destroying all my memories") (226).

This assault on the premises of empirical epistemology continues in "Ansiedad para el día" ("Anxiety for the Day"), where
Aleixandre again makes a value comparison between his empirical eyes, "dos lienzos vacilantes que me ocultaban mi destino"
("two vacillating canvases that were hiding my destiny"), and
"aquella dulce arena, aquella sola pepita de oro que me cayó de
mi silencio una tarde de roca" ("that sweet sand, that lone gold
nugget that fell to me from my silence one afternoon of rock")
(228), his new intuition of an alternative existence. By now
there is no question of his high valuation of the alternative realm,
even though he takes pains to protect "mi nivel sobre el agua"
("my level above the water") (229). He still fears "el monstruo
sin oído que lleva en lugar de su palabra una tijera breve, la justa
para cortar la explicación abierta" ("the unhearing monster that
carries instead of its word short scissors, the right size to cut off
an open explanation") (229). Such is also the vision in "El mundo
está bien hecho" ("The World Is Well Made"), an allusion to
Guillén's well-known verse, in which he contrasts both the positive aspect of the hidden center of being, "la mujer del sombrero
enorme" ("the woman with a huge hat") (233), and the more
ominous aspect of the same force that appears as a "gran serpiente larga" ("a great, long serpent") (234). Both utter what
appear to be contradictory appeals: " 'Amame para que te
enseñe' " (" 'Love me so I can teach you' "), and the other,
" 'Muere, muere' " (" 'Die, die' ") (234). The contradiction is not
to be resolved by choosing, or seeking to avoid, one possibility
over the other. Aleixandre must achieve the same understanding
as the "ojo divino" ("divine eye") (234), the unique perspective
from which this alternative world truly reveals itself as "bien
hecho" ("well made") and thus capable of synthesis. At the
volume's conclusion, he calls for "un vaso de nata o una afiladí-
sima espada con que yo parta en dos la ceguera de bruma, esta
niebla que estoy acariciando como frente" ("a glass of cream or
an extremely well-sharpened sword with which I may split in
two the blindness of the mist, this fog that I am caressing like a
forehead") (237), that is, the raw will and virility necessary to
overcome his confusion. There is an indication that he has begun
to understand that the knowledge he seeks can be conveyed

only by radically different means: "toser para conocer la existencia, para amar la forma perpendicular de uno mismo" ("to cough in order to know existence, in order to love the perpendicular form of oneself") (239). He must understand the involuntary manifestations of "existencia" that happen as irrationally as a cough. To "amar la forma perpendicular" of himself he must also learn to love the involuntary coughing that holds the key to the mystery of who he is and can be. It is to that "misterio, la cámara vacía donde la madre no vivió aunque gime, aunque el mar con mandíbulas la nombra" ("mystery, the empty room where the mother did not live even though she moans, even though the sea with jaws names her") (240) that he now directs his energies.

Espadas como labios (*Swords Like Lips*) (1930–31) begins with the awareness that "[es posible] ya ... el horizonte, / ese decir palabras sin sentido / que ruedan como oídos ... entre la luz pisada" ("the horizon ... [is] already [possible], / that saying of words without meaning / that roll around like ears ... in the trampled light") (247; see Novo Villaverde 104–06). He acknowledges two types of words and images, each responding to a different mode of production. The words "sin sentido" are possible only after the light, the source of empirically produced images, has been trampled, which leaves him at the mercy of an alternative mode of production he cannot understand. This is the posture in "La palabra" ("The Word"), where he portrays himself, or rather, his consciousness, as "un caracol pequeñísimo" ("an extremely small snail") but, nevertheless, "capaz de pronunciar el nombre, / de dar sangre" ("capable of pronouncing the name, / of giving forth blood") (248–49), of retaining his existential integrity in the face of a force that threatens to overwhelm it. As he declares,

> *que mi voz no es la tuya*
> *y que cuando solloces tu garganta*
> *sepa distinguir todavía*
> *mi beso de tu esfuerzo*
> *por pronunciar los nombres con mi lengua.*

> my voice is not yours
> and whenever you sob, may your throat
> still know how to distinguish

my kiss from your force
by pronouncing the names with my tongue.   (249)

Aleixandre is laying claim to a more willful role in the poetic process, however insignificant in comparison to the power of the alternative realm. He must confront the unconscious "silencio que es carbón" ("silence that is coal") (251), which brings unintelligible words and, in "Muerte" ("Death"), the vision of a "morir sin horizonte por palabras, / oyendo que nos llaman con los pelos" ("horizonless death through words, / hearing that they call to us fully") (251). "Circuito" ("Circuit") postulates the existence of "sirenas vírgenes / que ensartan en sus dedos las gargantas" ("virgin sirens / that string together throats on their fingers") (252), willful counterforces that will control the involuntary production of the throats, followed by the declaration that "Yo no quiero la sangre ni su espejo. . . . Por mis venas no nombres, no agonía, / sino cabellos núbiles circulan" ("I do not want the blood nor its mirror. . . . Through my veins not names, not agony, / but rather nubile hairs circulate") (252). Finding the correct circuit means rejecting empirical epistemology: not "nombres" or "espejos," words or images that impotently mirror each other, but a new circuit connected to a different set of intellectual-existential premises. This brings forth the "ojo profundo que vigila" ("deep eye that watches") (253), a counterforce "para evitar los labios cuando queman" ("in order to avoid the lips when they burn") (253), a new willfulness that allows him to proclaim: "Soy esa tierra alegre que no regatea su reflejo" ("I am that happy earth that does not bargain away its reflection") (257). He is the ultimate ground of the alternative reality: "he dominado el horizonte" ("I have dominated the horizon") (257). Rejuvenated, he becomes "alto como una juventud que no cesa" ("tall as ceaseless youth") (257). The question now becomes "¿Hacia qué cielos o qué suelos van esos ojos no pisados / que tienen como yemas una fecundidad invisible?" ("Toward what skies or what floors go those untrammeled eyes / that have an invisible fecundity like that of yolks?") (257): to see with transforming eyes the invisible force that surges within

him, "ese crecimiento que acabará como una muerte recienna-
cida" ("that growth that will finish as a newborn death") (258).

It is with eyes of experience that Aleixandre continues his
exploration, as he declares in "El vals" ("The Waltz"): "Todo lo
que está suficientemente visto / no puede sorprender a nadie"
("Everything that is sufficiently seen / cannot surprise anybody")
(261). Learning to see in this new way offers a means to resist
the involuntary eruptions from "este hondo silencio" ("this deep
silence") of the "garganta que se derrumba sobre los ojos"
("throat that hurls itself on the eyes") (264). It heralds the
advent of the fullness of being, "la eternidad" ("eternity"), when
"El tiempo [es] solo una tremenda mano sobre el cabello largo
detenida" ("Time [is] a terrible slow hand laid on long locks")
(264). "Toro" ("Bull"), which recounts what may be a masturbatory episode or even a wet dream, parodies the presence of
being and the "vastedad de esta hora" ("vastness of this hour")
(266) with "sus fuerzas casi cósmicas como leche de estrellas"
("its almost cosmic forces like star milk") (266). "El más bello
amor" ("The Most Beautiful Love") critiques such episodes:

> *Falsa la forma de la vaca que sueña*
> *con ser una linda doncellita incipiente.*
> *Falso lo del falso profesor que ha esperado*
> *al cabo comprender su desnudo.*

> False the form of the cow that dreams
> of being a cute incipient little maiden.
> False that of the false professor who has hoped
> finally to understand his nude.   (269)

Both accusations are leveled at himself since this cow is but
another aspect of his own sexual frustration that assumes masculine form in "Toro." Aleixandre has also been a "falso profesor"
since his inadequate means achieve only partial understanding.
To experience "esa forma imperiosa que sabe a resbaladizo infinito" ("that imperious form that tastes of slippery infinity") (270),
he turns to "un tiburón en forma de cariño" ("a shark in the form
of affection") (269). Force must match force:

> *Te penetro callando mientras grito o desgarro,*
> *mientras mis alaridos hacen música o sueño,*

porque beso murallas, las que nunca tendrán ojos,
y beso esa yema fácil sensible como la pluma.

I penetrate you, keeping silent while I shout or
       cough up,
while my shrieks make music or I dream,
because I kiss walls, the ones that will never have eyes,
and I kiss that easy yolk sensitive like
       the feather.   (270)

Only his will confirms his presence and importance in this order:

La verdad, la verdad, la verdad es esta que digo,
esa inmensa pistola que yace sobre el camino,
ese silencio—el mismo—que finalmente queda
cuando con una escoba primera aparto los senderos.

The truth, the truth, the truth is this that I say,
that immense pistol which lies in the road,
that silence—the same one—that finally remains
when with the first broom I separate the paths.   (270)

This is also the theme in "Poema de amor" ("Love Poem"), where
amid the "concéntricas ondas, sí, detenidas" ("concentric waves,
yes, arrested"), the timeless alternative realm, he is able to declare that "me busco, oh centro, oh centro, / camino ... del
futuro existente / más allá de los mares, en mis pulsos que laten"
("I search for myself, O center, O center, / road ... of the existing
future, / beyond the seas, in my pulses that beat") (272). He
defines his centrality as a willful proximity to the beloved center,
his hope for a new understanding: "La esperanza ... es un inmenso párpado donde yo sé que existo" ("Hope ... is an immense
eyelid where I know that I exist") (272).
    The new understanding, however, also brings risk since images
produced in this realm can also be false and misleading, such as
the empty dolls in "Muñecas" ("Dolls") "respirando ese beso
ambiguo o verde" ("breathing that ambiguous or green kiss")
(274). The poetry is more and more becoming the record of a
contest of wills, the triumph of the poet's will or that of the
involuntary producer of unintelligible images. Aleixandre finds
himself in an adversarial relationship with the otherness that is
being, a victim of a love whose finality seems inevitably to be

the affirmation of one of the parties of this relationship at the other's expense. Aleixandre reacts to this impasse in "Acaba" ("Finish"), which recalls his deficient understanding ("he visto golondrinas de plomo triste anidadas en ojos / y una mejilla rota por una letra" ["I have seen swallows of sad lead nested in eyes / and a cheek broken by a letter"] [275]) and which in turn reminds him that he remains distant from "la única desnudez que yo amo" ("the only nakedness that I love"), that is, "mi tos caída como una pieza" ("my cough fallen like a coin") (275). The means of capturing such an evasive prize is an imposition of will that arises from within "como un ojo herido / se va a clavar en el azul indefenso" ("as a wounded eye / is going to fix its gaze on the defenseless blue") to "convertirlo todo en un lienzo sin sonido" ("convert it all into a soundless canvas") (276), to remake his consciousness into "ese rostro que no piensa" ("that face which does not think") (276). This "will-to-willfulness" is epitomized in the word-command "ACABA" ("FINISH"), which entitles and concludes the poem, providing substantive evidence of the poet's desire to assert his will and to place a framework of understanding on the force responsible for producing the images and the understanding associated with a higher form of truth.

In "Por último" ("Finally") Aleixandre declares himself among "todo lo que se nombra o sonríe" ("all that names itself or smiles") (277), an entity capable of giving order and names to a realm he earlier thought to be "palabras sin sentido" ("meaning-less words") (247). To achieve an understanding that transcends the specific word or image involuntarily "coughed up" requires that he take matters into his own hands: "No aquí. Aquí está tendido lo más fácil; / voy a inventar un cuento o una espuma; / aquí están las miradas o las aguas" ("Not here. Here is extended the easiest thing; / I am going to invent a story or a foam; / here are the glances or the waters") (278). And later, "Yo aspiro a lo blanco o la pared, ¿quién sabe? Aspiro a mí o a ti o a lo llorado" ("I aspire to the whiteness or to the wall, who knows? I aspire to me or to you or to what was already cried") (278); he aspires to a new means of understanding and representation, a new plane ("lo blanco o la pared") on which to inscribe the full and present image of himself. His experience is "este aprender la dicha" ("this learning of happiness") (283), a search for "lo ardiente o el desierto" ("the ardent or the desert"), the absolute limits of existential possibility undertaken "allí entre la mentira sí esperada" ("there among the hoped-for lie") (283). He has learned that these involuntary images must be understood as means and not ends, that their reality is a lie that, nevertheless, can lead to higher truths and thus a better image of reality.

"Madre, madre" ("Mother, Mother") acknowledges the growing awareness that words and images must be viewed as means. The mother is the transformed image of the beloved that has assumed various shapes throughout the poetry ("Madre, madre, esta herida, esta mano tocada, / madre, en un pozo abierto en el pecho o extravío" ["Mother, mother, this wound, this touched hand, / mother, in an open well in the heart or deviation"][258]). Here, however, the female figure becomes a self-conscious evocation of Aleixandre's intuitions about the realm she populates. He sees this mother as "espejo mío silente" ("my silent mirror") (285), which has begun to respond to his will. The images emanating from her are now understood not as traditional reflections but as embodiments of the poet himself. Likewise, in "Palabras" ("Words") words become the agents by which the image of a "muchacha casi desnuda" ("almost naked girl") (287), a familiar symbol of the alternate realm, becomes "manchad[a] de espuma delicada" ("stained with delicate foam") (287). Compared to the masturbatory act and the ejaculation of semen, the understanding traditionally offered by words ("Nave, papel, o luto, borde o vientre, / palabra que se pierde como arena" ["Ship, paper, or mourning, border or stomach, / a word that gets lost like sand"] [287]) simply does not compare to "Este pasar despacio sin sonido, / esperando el gemido de lo oscuro" ("This slow and soundless passage, / hoping for the cry of the darkness") or to the "mármol de carne soberana" ("marble of sovereign flesh") (288), the intuited presence of the fullness of being, which begins to loom as a greater possibility.

In "Ida" ("Departure") the sense of distance from this goal is diminished. The sleeping girl who "en silencio se marcha hacia lo oscuro" ("in silence goes off toward the dark") (289) heralds the route to the silent darkness that Aleixandre must penetrate if he is to learn more. He knows that the desired landscape is comparable to "El pueblo en lontananza / del tamaño de un ojo entornado / [que] yace sin respirar aún" ("The town in the distance, / the size of a half-closed eye, / [which] rests without yet breathing") (291). He also declares in "Instante" ("Instant"), an allusion to a momentary insight concerning this process, that his own power of vision-will is growing: "Mira mis ojos. Vencen el sonido" ("Look at my eyes. They defeat the sound") (292). "El frío" ("The Cold") takes him a step closer as he makes contact with "esta muralla [donde] están las letras" ("this wall [where] the letters are") and also where the light, the medium of empirical representation, "escapa sin notarse" ("escapes without being noticed") (294). Indeed, in "Río" ("River") he proclaims the death of his empirical consciousness, a necessary death that heralds his entrance, somewhat in Dantean fashion, to the unknown underworld of being: "Así la muerte es flotar sobre un recuerdo no vida" ("Thus death is to float over a memory not life") (295). His self-destructive problem all along, as recounted in "Suicidio" ("Suicide"), has been "saliendo del fondo de sus ojos" ("leaving the bottom of your eyes") (301), his separation from direct and present images in order to partake of reality at a distance. As with Guillén, where the idea of an interior plane of image production is prominent, Aleixandre is affirming a representational model for which empirical theories cannot account. The desire is not to reproduce the image at a distance but rather to encounter the image at its origin, to make an image that is the thing itself.

Although Aleixandre is seeking a new way of seeing this involuntary language, he nevertheless makes use of the empirical idea that words and images are translatable hieroglyphs. The significant difference is that with these peculiar words and images there are no conventions or referents, only the poet's will that these chaotic sounds and signs acquire meaning. Indeed, there are only two effective possibilities: Aleixandre can impose a meaning by intellectual force or he can continue to be tormented. Evidently, he chooses the former option, which requires the repudiation of empirical epistemology. The correct route does not lie in "leaving his eyes," in separating words and images into equivalent spheres, but rather in discovering the principle by which such unintelligible images, which have meaning for the poet only at the "bottom of his eyes," are produced. The special words and images that Aleixandre encounters are unsatisfying because he has yet to grasp that understanding their means of production is also the means to a full existence. Being, not representation, is the ultimate goal, to "responder con mi propio reflejo a las ya luces extinguidas" ("respond with my own reflection to the already extinguished lights") (304). The old representational system is characterized in "Con todo respeto" ("With All Respect") as "esta limitación sobre la que apoyar la cabeza / para oír la mejor música, la de los planetas distantes" ("this limitation on which to rest my head / to listen to the best music, that of the distant planets") (306). Only through the intellectual will can Aleixandre penetrate the alternative reality: "Con mis puños de cristal lúcido quiero ignorar las luces, / quiero ignorar tu nombre, oh belleza diminuta" ("With my fists of lucid crystal I want to be ignorant of the lights, / I want to be unaware of your name, O diminutive beauty") (309). He wants to transcend the empirical premises that make light the exclusive medium for images and the words that translate them. The new intuition of a "belleza diminuta" is a realm in which words are not signs but presences, "lingotes de carne que no pueden envolverse con nada" ("ingots of flesh that cannot become involved with anything") (310). Likewise, in this realm "no sirve cerrar los ojos" ("it is useless to close your eyes") (310) since the reality of images is also a carnal, existential one that also responds to the throat, the involuntary center of production. The volume concludes hopefully that "esa piel desprendida que no puede ya besarse más que en pluma" ("that plucked skin that cannot now be kissed any more than when it was feathered") (316) will manifest itself as a direct presence.

La destrucción o el amor (*Destruction or Love*) (1932–33) intensifies the struggle to achieve direct knowledge of the alternative reality and thus of the fullness of being (Puccini 69–73). In "La selva y el mar" ("The Jungle and the Sea") Aleixandre expresses, in much more willful terms, his growing desire to

"Mirar esos ojos que solo de noche fulgen" ("See those eyes that only shine at night") (323), to understand the productive principle of the alternate reality. His own understanding, characterized here as "el pequeño escorpión ... con sus pinzas" ("the small scorpion ... with its pincers"), wants to "oprimir un instante la vida" ("oppress life for a moment"), defined as "la menguada presencia de un cuerpo de hombre que jamás podrá ser confundido con una selva" ("the diminished presence of the body of a man that can never be confused with a jungle") (324). Desire is equated with exercising the will to summon the full and unconfused presence of his "cuerpo de hombre," or full being. Aware of his continued distance from "ese mundo reducido o sangre mínima: ("that reduced world or minimal blood") (326), he is equally aware of his will, which "busca la forma de poner el corazón en la lengua" ("seeks a means of putting the heart in the tongue") (329), which seeks to unify his understanding through the new discourse. Such a presentiment of unity is expressed in "Unidad en ella" ("Unity in Her"), which again features a female figure, a "rostro amado donde contemplo el mundo" ("beloved face where I contemplate the world"), being, "la región donde nada se olvida" ("the region where nothing is forgotten") (331). Such an experience, called love, is also destruction, as the volume's title underscores, in the same sense that it is the antithesis of ordinary experience (see especially Bousoño 72–76). The declaration that nothing "podrá destruir la unidad de este mundo" ("will be able to destroy the unity of this world") (332) is an affirmation that such a world is not a separate and distinct reality, that his alienation from being has an epistemological origin.

In "Sin luz" ("Without Light") Aleixandre penetrates further into this realm via an "inmóvil pez espada cuyo ojo no gira" ("immobile swordfish whose eye does not rotate") (335). He uses the strength of his raw will to encounter the region beyond light, where empirical principles have been rendered inoperative, "Ese profundo oscuro donde no existe el llanto" ("That deep darkness where lament does not exist") and "donde aplacado el limo no imita un sueño agotado" ("where, appeased, the slime does not imitate an exhausted dream") (336). Penetration to this point brings him to the end of mimetic possibility, a point beyond psychoanalytic discourse where a more powerful and profound unconscious seems consciously to reject dream interpretation and other such empirically based enterprises as means of self-knowledge. The presence of an eye that "does not rotate" suggests a more radical position that has by now rejected the strictly personal aspect of an unconscious in order to affirm a much more elemental experience, being. The desired union is one in which the medium of darkness ("Ese profundo oscuro") will avail itself of the eye that does not rotate, the will to produce form in the darkness, a better image, the product of the encounter between the pure presence of the alternative reality and the pure human will to master its discourse. Such is the sentiment expressed in "Mina" ("Mine"), which alludes to the darkness to which Aleixandre has penetrated, where he is "comprendiendo que el hierro" ("understanding that the iron"), this mine's existential product, "es la salud de vivir, / que el hierro es el resplandor que de sí mismo nace" ("is the health of living, / that the iron is the brilliance that is born from itself") (337). He is affirming a principle of understanding described metaphorically as a production, a brilliance originating from itself, from within, not from an external source.

Affirming the fullness of being means understanding the premises under which being is possible. Such intuitions become intensified in subsequent sections, as in "Mañana no viviré" ("Tomorrow I Will Not Live"), where Aleixandre affirms to his beloved, whom he now summons to him, that "besándote tu humedad no es pensamiento" ("kissing your dampness is not thought") (346). He understands it as a different type of intellectual experience and says that the beloved is "amorosa insistencia en este aire que es mío" ("amorous insistence in this air that is mine") (346). Their association is a contest of wills within a landscape of being that he understands is all his. In "Ven, ven tú" ("Come, Come") he also senses a domain "donde las palabras se murmuran como a un oído" ("where words whisper as to an ear"), a unifying principle under which "Ni los peces innumerables que pueblan otros cielos / son más que lentísimas aguas de una pupila remota" ("Not even the innumerable fish that populate other skies / are more than the slowest waters of a remote pupil") (347). Eye and ear, as newly defined, begin to work in concert as Aleixandre senses that "Esta oreja próxima escucha mis palabras" ("This nearby ear listens to my words") (348) and as "el mundo rechazado" ("the rejected world"), the empirical system, "se retira como un mar que muge sin destino" ("retreats like a sea that moos without a destiny") (348). A better destiny looms as a consequence of "esa dureza juvenil" ("that youthful hardness"), the intensified will that is now able even to "iluminar en redondo el paisaje vencido" ("illuminate all around the defeated landscape") (349), the site of a new mode of image production described as "ese ojo profundo sin párpado que en el fondo / demuestra con su fijeza que nunca ha de acabarse" ("that deep lidless eye that at the bottom / demonstrates with its fixity that never has to end") (350).

As the poems progress, Aleixandre becomes more explicit in his characterization of the alternative realm, as in "Paisaje" ("Landscape"), a reference to the existential inscape acquiring more definition. As he draws closer, he is also able to speak to, and for, the otherness that defines being: "no existes y existes, / Te llamas vivo ser" ("you do not exist and you exist, / You are called living being") (351). In more familiar antiempirical terms, the domain of being becomes "Pájaro, nube o dedo que escribe sin memoria" ("Bird, cloud, or finger that writes without memory") and "mirada que en tierra finge un río" ("a gaze that on earth simulates a river") (352). At a later point in "A ti, viva" ("To You, Living One"), Aleixandre again expresses his desire to know his beloved ("Mirar tu cuerpo sin más luz que la tuya" ["To look at your body with no more light than your own"] [355]) but, more important, his growing conviction that she is also the source of a new mode of understanding that values words and images only as presences and not as mere representations (see also Olivio Jiménez 49–50). This becomes consciously articulated in "Quiero saber" ("I Want to Know"), whose title emphasizes that the process of epistemological adjustment facilitating these new insights is inseparable from the goal itself. Thus when he tells his beloved that he wants to know "el secreto de tu existencia" ("the secret of your existence") (358) he is referring to his own. There is no separation between the experience of being and the epistemological premises of the alternative realm. Or more explicitly, "el mundo todo es uno, la ribera y el párpado" ("the world is all one, the shore and the eyelid") (358). The section entitled "Elegías y poemas elegíacos" ("Elegies and Elegiac Poems") heralds, among other things, the death of conventional epistemology. "A la muerte" ("To Death") looks back on "esa mirada humilde de una carne / que casi toda es párpado vencido" ("that humble gaze of a flesh / that is almost all defeated eyelid") (364), his old understanding that has died. "La luz" ("The Light"), on the other hand, eulogizes the principal empirical medium, light, separated from its origin ("¿De dónde vienes, celeste túnica . . . ?" ["From where do you come, celestial tunic . . . ?"] [365]): "tan pronto pareces el recuerdo de un fuego ardiente tal el hierro que señala" ("so soon you seem the memory of an ardent fire like the iron that brands") (365). The facilitating light of conventional understanding, however, does not compare to the more intense medium that produces better images "como la pronunciación de un nombre / que solo pueden decir unos labios que brillan" ("like the pronunciation of a name / that only some lips that shine can say") (365). External light is the subject of an elegy because Aleixandre has by now come to understand it as an embodiment of dead things. The true light is the "celeste luz temblorosa o deseo. . .de un pecho que se lamenta como dos brazos largos" ("celestial trembling light or desire . . . of a breast that mourns like two long arms") (366), the light that is a presence, not the diffuse absence through which things are ordinarily experienced. In "Canción a una muchacha muerta" ("Song to a Dead Girl") the poet calls for experiences that require a new and different light, the only suitable medium for "esos ojos por donde solo boga el silencio" ("those eyes through which silence sails alone") (370).

The desire is for the fullness of being, as expressed in "Plenitud" ("Plenitude"), a type of palinode in which Aleixandre realizes the extent of the falsity of his past assumptions, defined as "todo lo que es un paño ante los ojos" ("everything that is a cloth before the eyes") (372). The truth does not lie in the words or images he may happen to perceive but in the higher principle

responsible for their origin, "una música indefinible, / nacida en
el rincón donde las palabras no se tocan, / donde el sonido no
puede acariciarse" ("an undefinable music, / born in the corner
where the words are not touched, / where sound cannot be
caressed") (372). He has realized that there is no longer a radical
separation among words, images, and their "unintelligible" origin: "Todo es sangre o amor o latido o existencia, / todo soy yo
que siento cómo el mundo se calla / y cómo así me duelen el
sollozo o la tierra" ("Everything is blood or love or heartbeat or
existence, / everything am I who feels how the world grows
quiet / and how thus the sob or the earth gives me pain") (373).
The goal becomes to summon this "amorosa presencia de un día
que sé existe" ("loving presence of a day that I know exists")
(384), to make present what is presently absent. With each
poem, the hope grows that such a goal can be realized: "Yo sé
quien ama y vive, quien muere y gira y vuela. / Sé que lunas se
extinguen, renacen, viven, lloran. / Sé que dos cuerpos aman,
dos almas se confunden" ("I know who loves and lives, who dies
and turns and flies. / I know that moons extinguish themselves,
are reborn, live, cry. / I know that two bodies love, two souls are
mingled") (386). And further, in "Sobre la misma tierra" ("On
the Same Earth"), "que la noche y el día no son lo negro o lo
blanco, / sino la boca misma que duerme entre las rocas" ("that
night and day are not the blackness or the whiteness, / but rather
the same mouth that sleeps among the rocks") (389): the two
realities are inextricably intertwined. Those who live exclusively
"sobre la misma tierra," however, cannot know the better aspect
of reality. The desire for existential presence is to know an
"inmensa mano que oprime un mundo alterno" ("immense hand
that oppresses an alternative world") (390), which brings the
necessity to "Matar la limpia superficie sobre la cual golpeamos, /
... superficie que copia un cielo estremecido" ("Kill the clean
surface on which we pound, / ... a surface that copies a trembling
sky") (391), the epistemological assumptions that keep this
realm distant. The experience of this other world finally brings
Aleixandre to "notar ya blanco el corazón inmóvil" ("notice
already white the immobile heart") (391), to transcend the
bounds of the empiricist equation. As he proclaims in "Soy el

destino" ("I Am Destiny"): "renuncio a ese espejo que donde-
quiera las montañas ofrecen, / pelada roca donde se refleja mi
frente / cruzada por unos pájaros cuyo sentido ignoro" ("I re-
nounce that mirror which the mountains offer anywhere, /
sheared rock where my face is reflected / traversed by some
birds whose meaning I do not know") (395). The values of
mimesis cede to the experience of himself in the fullness of
being:

> *Soy el destino que convoca a todos los que aman,*
> *mar único al que vendrán todos los radios amantes*
> *que buscan a su centro, rizados por el círculo*
> *que gira como la rosa rumorosa y total.*

> I am the destiny that convokes all who love,
> only sea to which come all the lovers, like spokes,
> that search for their center, rippling around the circle
> that turns like the murmuring and total rose.   (396)

The antimimetic alternative reality, "el oscuro chorro [que]
pasa indescifrable / como un río que desprecia el paisaje" ("the
dark stream [that] passes undecipherable / like a river that de-
spises the landscape") (399), prefers "una lengua no de hombre"
("a tongue not of man") (400), a language of presence beyond
representation. "La luna es una ausencia" ("The Moon Is an
Absence") looks back to the familiar symbol of the moon, the
embodiment of the inadequacies of ordinary consciousness, and
to the "otro lado donde el vacío es luna" ("to the other side
where the emptiness is moon") (402), where presences become
represented absences. In "Quiero pisar" ("I Want to Step") Aleixandre reaffirms his will to know a different medium, "esa garganta
o guijo fría al pie desnudo" ("that throat or gravel cold to the
naked foot") (403) and to confront the "pupila lentísima que
casi no se mueve" ("slowest of pupils that almost does not
move"), that "yo casi no veo, pero que sí que escucho; / aquel
punto invisible adonde una tos o un pecho que aún respira, /
llega como la sombra de los brazos ausentes" ("I almost do not
see, but certainly hear; / that invisible point where a cough or a
breast that still breathes, / arrives like the shadow of the absent
arms") (405). The desire to confront "un amor que destruye"

("a love that destroys") (406) is to know a loving presence capable of destroying absent images that distance Aleixandre from full being. The proximity to such a destructive encounter signals in "Cobra" the transformation of Aleixandre's willful self or consciousness, now a phallic cobra that is "todo ojos" ("all eyes") (407) and to whom he beseeches, "ama todo despacio. . . . Ama el fondo con sangre donde brilla / el carbunclo logrado" ("love everything slowly. . . . Love the bottom with blood where there shines / the attained carbuncle") (408). "Que así invade" ("That Invades Thus") continues this slow act of love in which Aleixandre "regresa a su seno recobrando su forma" ("returns to his breast recovering his form") (409), and in which he also discovers that his beloved "no destruye mis manos / ni mis ojos cuando apoyo los párpados" ("does not destroy my hands / or my eyes when I rest my eyelids") (410). This leads to yet another image of the will-consciousness in "El escarabajo" ("The Beetle"), the image of the plodding, durable, and virtually indestructible scarab, an apt metaphor for Aleixandre's strength in the face of the alternative reality's destructive power. The insect's arrival also signals that it "por fin llega al verbo también" ("finally also arrives at the verb") (411); it achieves the long-sought understanding, able now to descend "a unos brazos que un diminuto mundo oscuro crean" ("to some arms that create a diminutive dark world") (412) and thus the triumphal declaration in "Cuerpo de piedra" ("Body of Stone") that "Ya no quema el fuego que en las ingles / aquel remoto mar dejó al marcharse" ("No longer burns the fire which that remote sea left behind in my groin / when it retreated") (414). Indeed, Aleixandre has now made contact with a vaster source of power (see also Colinas 72).

In the final section, Aleixandre examines even more closely his relationship to the beloved at the center of being, who is now understood to possess "ojos que no giran" ("eyes that do not turn") and a "corazón constante como una nuez vencida" ("heart constant like a defeated walnut") (417). He beseeches her to become the full presence that he has desired her to be: "Vive, vive, despierta, ama, corazón, ser, despierta como tierra a la lluvia naciente, / como lo verde nuevo que crece entre la

carne" ("Live, live, awaken, love, heart, being, awaken like land
to an incipient rain, / like the new green that grows in the flesh")
(418). In "Hija de la mar" ("Daughter of the Sea") he once again
invokes a "muchacha" ("girl") who is also "corazón o sonrisa, /
caliente nudo de presencia en el día" ("heart or smile, / hot knot
of presence in the day") (419) whom he hopes will be the final
partial image before he finally experiences "el son de tu madre
imperiosa" ("the sound of your imperious mother") (419), the
principle of existential presence that he most highly values. In
"Las águilas" ("The Eagles") he draws another step closer when
he envisions "el celeste ojo victorioso / [que] vea solo a la tierra
como sangre que gira" ("the victorious celestial eye / [that] sees
the earth only as blood going round") (421), the full presence
of being. "La noche" ("The Night") describes "el viaje de un ser
quien se siente arrastrado / a la final desembocadura en que a
nadie se conoce" ("the journey of a being who feels dragged /
to the final river's mouth in which no one is recognized") (422).
Such a climactic moment, which resists precise description, is
recounted in "Se querían" ("They Were Loving") where the
male-female, conscious-unconscious, willful-involuntary aspects
of Aleixandre's struggle achieve a brief unity: "mar o tierra, navío,
lecho, pluma, cristal, / metal, música, labio, silencio, vegetal, /
mundo, quietud, su forma. Se querían, sabedlo" ("sea or earth,
ship, bed, pen, windowpane, / metal, music, lip, silence, vegeta-
ble, / world, stillness, its form. They were loving, know it") (425).
The quest has been one of knowing, the affirmation of being: "la
luz ... como el corazón ... / que pide no ser ya él ni su reflejo,
sino el río feliz, / lo que transcurre sin la memoria azul, / camino
de los mares que entre todos se funden / y son lo amado y lo
que ama, y lo que goza y sufre" ("the light ... / like the heart ... /
that asks to be neither it nor its reflection, but rather the happy
river, / that which moves along without the blue memory, /
avenue of the seas that are all fused together / and that are
the beloved and that which loves, and that which delights and
suffers") (426).

Aleixandre has portrayed an existential quest in amorous
terms. Lover and beloved are aspects of the same phenomenon,
a willful self-understanding via

El amor como lo que rueda,
como el universo sereno,
como la mente excelsa,
el corazón conjugado, la sangre que circula,
el luminoso destello que en la noche crepita
y pasa por la lengua oscura, que ahora entiende.

Love like that which rolls along,
like the serene universe,
like the exalted mind,
the conjugated heart, the blood that circulates,
the luminous gleam that in the night crackles
and passes through the dark tongue, which
      now understands.   (427)

The act of love is, as in Salinas, an act of self-affirmation that requires the destruction of the intellectual premises that have prevented Aleixandre from achieving this special understanding. The bourgeois self is destroyed to bring into being "lo que no vive, / lo que es el beso indestructible . . . mientras la luz dorada está dentro de los párpados" ("that which does not live, / that which is the indestructible kiss . . . while the golden light is inside the eyelids") (428). That such a light of existential presence is not summonable at will does not negate its absolute value. In the volume's concluding poem, "La Muerte" ("Death"), being brings an invocation of "death":

Mátame como si un puñal, un sol dorado o lúcido,
una mirada buida de un inviolable ojo,
un brazo prepotente en que la desnudez fuese el frío,
un relámpago que buscase mi pecho o su destino.

Kill me as if a dagger, a gilded or lucid sun,
a pointed glance of an inviolable eye,
a strong arm in which nakedness were the cold,
a lightning flash that searched for my breast or
      its destiny.   (433)

The death of the bourgeois self heralds the birth of a new mode of seeing and existence, the principal theme of the final pre–Civil War volume, *Mundo a solas* (*World Alone*) (1934–36).

When Aleixandre declares in "No existe el hombre" ("Man

Does Not Exist") that "el hombre no existe. / Nunca ha existido, nunca" ("man does not exist. / He has never existed, never") (442), he is referring again to bourgeois definitions of manhood and being incapable of expressing the better truth he has experienced. The true embodiment of the nature of existence is found in the "árbol [que] jamás duerme" ("tree [that] never sleeps"), which is "verde siempre como los duros ojos" ("always green like the hard eyes"), and about which it can never be said that it "quiera ser otra cosa" ("may want to be another thing") (443). The tree symbolizes the existential state to which Aleixandre's intuitions have led him: "un árbol es sabio, y plantado domina" ("a tree is wise, and planted it dominates") (443). The poetry has been, in a sense, the history of the planting of the tree of the fullness of being that "vive y puede pero no clama nunca, / ni a los hombres mortales arroja nunca su sombra" ("lives and is able but that never clamors, / nor to mortal men does it ever extend its shade") (444). The mortals are those necessarily lesser beings trapped in ordinary reality who must continue to experience and to think via "esos ojos que te duelen, / en esa frente pura encerrada en sus muros" ("those eyes that throb, / in that pure face enclosed in its walls") (445). This lies in contrast, in "Bajo la tierra" ("Below the Earth"), to the underground realm where being resides: "Debajo de la tierra hay, más honda, la roca, / la desnuda, la purísima roca donde solo podrían vivir seres humanos" ("Below the earth there is, deeper, the rock, / the naked, the purest rock where only human beings can live") (450). The center of being is solid, massive, silent, immobile: a frozen, statuesque, pristine realm from which a new definition of his humanity has emerged. In "Humano ardor" ("Human Ardor") he affirms to his beloved that "Besarte es pronunciarte" ("To kiss you is to pronounce you") (451). He has seen her "pasar arrebatando la realidad constante" ("pass taking away the constant reality") (451) and now understands that her "labios" ("lips"), her presence, "eran, no una palabra, / sino su sueño mismo, / su imperioso mandato que castiga con beso" ("were, not a word, / but your dream itself, / your imperious command that punishes with a kiss") (451–52). This love that is also death has redefined his humanity: "Morir, morir es tener en los brazos un cuerpo /

del que nunca salir se podrá como hombre" ("To die, to die is to have in your arms a body / from which one will never be able to escape as a man") (452). At the center of being, traditional definitions of manhood are superseded by one that uses words not to define or describe but to be "su sueño mismo."

The eventual separation from this state of existential fullness does not change Aleixandre's opinion of its value, only of his ability to invoke the "otra tierra invisible" ("other invisible land") (460). He persists in affirming that "yo te sentí, yo te vi, yo te adiviné" ("I felt you, I saw you, I foretold you") (460). Even as the beloved recedes, he remembers this transforming existential experience as the most sublime form of love: "Sí. Tú extendida no imitas un río detenido, / no imitas un lago en cuyo fondo al cabo el cielo descansa" ("Yes. You extended do not imitate an arrested river, / you do not imitate a lake at whose bottom the sky finally rests") (463). The beloved, the creature of the realm of being, is, finally, "mínima" ("minimal") (465), the only fitting word to describe an experience that has transpired in immobility and silence. Aleixandre has penetrated to the "Profundidad sin noche donde la vida es vida" ("Depth without night where life is life") (470) in order to aggrandize his understanding as "un ojo inyectado en la furia / de presenciar los límites de la tierra pequeña" ("an eye injected into the fury / of witnessing the limits of the small earth") (473). The volume's final poem, "Los cielos" ("The Heavens"), offers what may be read as a last will, in the aftermath of his death in and after love: "buscad la vida acaso como brillo inestable, / oscuridad profunda para un único pecho" ("look for life perhaps like an unstable brilliance, / a profound darkness for a unique breast") (478). These concluding sentiments express in large part the principal theme of all the early poetry, which most of Aleixandre's critics consider concludes here, a search for a "brillo inestable" capable of being understood only by "un único pecho" whose guiding values have been "los fuegos inhumanos" ("the inhuman fires") (479), the slow but methodical transcendence of ordinary human consciousness.

Through an intellectual will to master the epistemological-ideological premises that govern the alternative reality, in which being is definitively experienced as a presence and no longer through an empirical filter, Aleixandre affirms a better image of reality and thus aligns his poetry with that of others dedicated to affirming private landscapes of will. Notwithstanding obvious expressive differences with Guillén and Salinas, Aleixandre ultimately shares more ideologically with these poets (see especially Bousoño 43) than with Cernuda, García Lorca, and Alberti. Despite a multitude of obstacles and difficulties only alluded to in Salinas and consciously suppressed in Guillén, Aleixandre's fundamental position regarding being is that, ultimately, it is knowable and representable on his terms.

CHAPTER 4

Luis Cernuda

The early poetry of Luis Cernuda provides the most explicit avowal of an alternative reality.[1] Unlike the previously discussed poets, who affirm the fullness of being in "well-made" worlds, Cernuda can only affirm his distance from being, the consequence of his experience of a better reality, which defeats his attempt to comprehend and possess it. If Cernuda's rejection of ordinary reality is more intense than that of his contemporaries, his inability to possess his alternative vision does not necessarily mean that he is forced to accept less. For Cernuda, less in relation to ordinary standards clearly means more. This is why, despite the insistence of Cernuda's most prominent critics that the principal theme of the early poetry is his "fall" from an edenic state (Silver) or his "loss of innocence" (Harris, *Study*), the early poetry is better understood as affirming a more positive content: the process by which Cernuda becomes a maker of better images, a poet.

A good deal of Cernuda's mature critical writing is dedicated to dispelling false images, a growing body of critical opinion that considered him less than an original and distinctive poetic talent. These critics cited, among other things, his alleged discipleship to Guillén and, to a lesser extent, his early mentor Salinas (see Harris, *Perfil* 45–78; Delgado 67–75). Guillén and Salinas, along with Dámaso Alonso and Aleixandre, became the increasing focus of Cernuda's critical polemics after the Civil War, when Cernuda desired to counter what he considered wrong opinions about himself and other contemporaries (Harris, *Poetry* 10–14).

Aleixandre became, in Cernuda's "Supervivencias tribales en el medio literario" ("Tribal Survivals in the Literary Milieu"), in *Desolación de la Quimera* (*Desolation of the Chimera*), the insensitive "Poeta en Residencia" ("Poet in Residence"), a reference to his remaining in Spain after the Civil War, and, in *Los encuentros* (*Encounters*), the subject of a strong denunciation regarding Aleixandre's remembrance of Manuel Altolaguirre as a boyish "Manolito." According to Cernuda, always invoking the youth but never recognizing the mature poet was a means of trivializing Altolaguirre's talent: "Quisieron consignar al olvido su raro don poético, / Cuidando de ver en él tan sólo y nada más que a 'Manolito' / Y callando al poeta admirable que en él hubo" ("They tried to consign to oblivion his special poetic gift, / Taking care to see in him only and nothing more than 'Manolito' / And silencing the admirable poet that was present in him.")

He most bitterly denounces Alonso's evocation of Lorca in "Una generación poética" ("A Poetic Generation"), where Alonso calls Lorca his "prince." This elicits from Cernuda in "Otra vez, con sentimiento" ("One More Time, with Feeling"), also from *Desolación,* the following commentary, addressed to the dead poet: "¿Príncipe tú de un sapo? / ¿No les basta a tus compatriotas haberte asesinado? / Ahora la estupidez sucede el crimen" ("You the prince of a frog? / Isn't it enough for your countrymen to have murdered you? / Now stupidity follows the crime"). These well-connected figures possess virtually unlimited influence in establishing definitive images of this period of Spanish literary history. In Cernuda's case, the principal culprit is Salinas, who, in reference to Cernuda's difficult personality, labels him a "Licenciado Vidriera" ("Licentiate of Glass"), which occasions Cernuda's "Malentendu" (also from *Desolación*) and the opinion that Salinas has made him "un fantoche a su medida: / Raro, turbio, inútilmente complicado" ("a puppet to your dimensions: / Strange, disturbed, uselessly complicated").

The most severe judgment that the unconventional Cernuda can level against Salinas and Guillén—Cernuda discusses them together in *Estudios sobre la poesía española contemporánea* (*Studies on Spanish Contemporary Poetry*)—is to call them "bourgeois poets" (an opinion with which my own reading disagrees). Guillén's poetry "aún más que la de Salinas, [expresa] un concepto burgués de la vida y que en ella la imagen del poeta no trasciende al hombre sino a una forma histórica y transitoria del hombre, que es el burgués" ("even more than that of Salinas, [expresses] a bourgeois concept of life and in it the image of the poet does not transcend man but rather a historical and transitory form of man, which is the bourgeois") (*Prosa* 432; all prose quotations are from this volume). The phrase "imagen del poeta" is quite suggestive. Cernuda concurs with Salinas that poetry's principal theme is poetry and the poet. Such a protagonist, however, should be not a persona-less flesh-and-blood poet, the representative of the narrow interests of a particular class. If art aspires to the production of better images, transcendent images of art and artist, the clear implication is that Cernuda's "imagen del poeta" is superior to that of Guillén and Salinas (see Gil de Biedma).

If these are the scholarly judgments of a person approaching his sixtieth year, it is safe to assume that the young Cernuda (who, regarding the subject of bourgeois reality, declares, in the Gerardo Diego anthology, "La detesto como detesto todo lo que a ella pertenece" ["I detest it as I detest everything that belongs to it"] [516]) had formed quite similar conclusions before the appearance in 1936 of the first edition of *La realidad y el deseo* (*Reality and Desire*), which recounts the emergence not of a disciple but of a very singular "imagen del poeta." His introduction to the volume, "Palabras ante una lectura" ("Words before a Reading") hopes only for "esa simpatía honda y recatada de unos cuantos" ("that deep and discreet sympathy of a few") (876). Cernuda was apprehensive, worrying that his poetry would not appeal to a middle-class audience incapable of understanding the "experiencias fragmentarias" ("fragmentary experiences"), the individual poems, "que nos [permiten] suponer el pensamiento completo del poeta" ("that [allow] us to surmise the complete thinking of the poet") (871). "Palabras ante una lectura" echoes the poetry, which proclaims both its impotence and arrogance in championing an "imagen del poeta" understood as a superior way of life (see also Paz).

Cernuda ascribes responsibility for his becoming the special poet he is to a larger-than-life force against which he must struggle, a "daimonic power," which parallels at an invisible level his struggle against bourgeois society:

La sociedad moderna, a diferencia de aquellas que la precedieron, ha decidido prescindir del elemento misterioso inseparable de la vida. . . . Pero el poeta no puede proceder así, y debe contar en la vida con esa zona de sombra y de niebla que flota en torno de los cuerpos humanos. Ella constituye el refugio de un poder indefinido y vasto que maneja nuestros destinos . . . un poder demoníaco, o mejor dicho, daimónico, que actúa sobre los hombres. . . . Ese poder . . . está estrechamente unido a mis creencias poéticas.

Modern society, unlike those that preceded it, has decided to do without the inseparable mysterious element of life. . . . But the poet cannot proceed in this manner, and in his life he must count on that area of shadow and fog that floats around human bodies. It constitutes the refuge of a vast and indefinite power that controls our destinies . . . a demonic power, or rather, daimonic, that works on men. . . . That power . . . is closely wed to my poetic beliefs. (874)

Daimonic power describes the phenomenon and process through which Cernuda becomes a different poet, a principle of poetic production that inspires him with images of the world's beauty as it also demonstrates to him their transitoriness.[2] The poet is doomed to lament "la pérdida y la destrucción de la hermosura" ("the loss and the destruction of beauty") (875), to understand the circumstantial nature of all images of reality while at the same time being irresistibly attracted to them "tal el fuego en la zarza ardiente que vio Moisés" ("like the fire in the burning bush that Moses saw") (876). As "esa oscura fuerza daimónica que rige el mundo" ("that dark daimonic force that rules the world") (875), daimonic power exists in a dark realm beyond images but communicates to mortals by imagistic means, compared to the biblical burning bush, the brightest of divine images. This is not a contradiction but an affirmation of the working premise of *La realidad y el deseo:* some images are better than others, and no image is an end in itself. The bourgeois understands life as a matter of affirming and accepting the images of ordinary reality as the exclusive ground of existence. Cernuda confronts poetry and the task of image-making as both a distrustful iconoclast and one invariably enamored of better images he knows to be indices of a better reality.

This is certainly true of *Primeras poesías* (*First Poems*), a much reworked version, possibly as late as 1935, primarily of the rather poorly received *Perfil del aire* (*Profile of the Air*) (1927) but also of other uncollected poems of the same period. This retrospective anthology does not faithfully capture the essence of the early poetry, which was written long before the intuition of daimonic power.[3] *Primeras poesías* reinterprets the past in terms of the later existential equation "la realidad y el deseo" ("reality and desire"), which understands ordinary reality as a realm of false images and desire as the inadequate human means of understanding a divine-demonic force that provides a better image. Cernuda's "pensamiento poético" ("poetic thinking") begins with the adolescent's victimization by traditional models of understanding and image-making. The initial poems recount representative moments in the development of the adolescent as he becomes aware of desire as a force in his life and of his calling as a poet. The initial poem is dominated by the landscape contemplated from the open window of the adolescent's room, which functions almost as a photographic lens that also re-creates the conditions of empirical cognition. The daylight images from the window seem to confirm a passive consciousness absent and distant from the world indolently contemplated:

> *Tan sólo un árbol turba*
> *la distancia que duerme:*
> *así el fervor alerta*
> *la indolencia presente.*

> Only a tree disturbs
> the distance that sleeps:
> thus the ardor makes alert
> the present indolence.   (73)

With the advent of the night, however, the window plays a different role:

> *En su paz la ventana*
> *restituye a diario*

las estrellas, el aire
y el que estaba soñando.

In its peace the window
restores daily
the stars, the air,
and the one who was dreaming.   (74)

In the darkness and in the absence of the visual spectacle of
the landscape, the real activity continues under more favorable
conditions. The images of visible reality are understood from
the outset as simply one possible source of understanding.
Thus although he seems to establish his artistic origin, in *La
realidad y el deseo,* in an apparently classical empiricism in
which sensory experiences form the sole and passive basis for
cognition, knowledge, and thus for desire, Cernuda is actually
overturning empiricism, if imperfectly, which is already intuited as a hindrance (see also Aguirre 225–27). The young
dreamer must wait until dark to resume this more useful
activity in the absence of empirical images. Such impotence
lies in contrast to the strength of Guillén in the face of the
landscape that invariably affirms his will to being and the
activity of his consciousness.

The adolescent's unsuitability as a medium for the production
of images is emphasized in the following poems in which his
"afán, entre muros / debatiéndose aislado" ("desire, inside / de-
bating itself, isolated") (76) is becoming dissatisfied with the
monotony of his life:

Desengaño indolente
y una calma vacía,
como flor en la sombra,
el sueño fiel nos brinda.

Indolent disillusionment
and an empty calm,
like a flower in the shadow,
the faithful dream gives us.   (75)

His dreaming is becoming unproductive:

La almohada no abre
los espacios risueños;

dice, sólo, voz triste,
que alientan allá lejos.

The pillow does not open
the smiling spaces;
it says, only, sad voice,
that they inspire from afar.　(76)

By the fourth poem, the monotony becomes a "Morir cotidiano,
undoso / entre sábanas de espuma" ("Daily, wavy death / between
sheets of foam") (76). The adolescent wants to bring his dream
to the world, to affirm its presence in the world and thus to erase
the distance, and difference, between the two domains. Cernuda
describes this experience in poem V as "el acorde total" ("the
total harmony") (78). Although it resembles the experience of
the fullness of being recounted in Guillén's *Cántico,* the "acorde"
experience in *La realidad y el deseo* is confined to this poem
only. There is a prehistory beyond which Cernuda must move
to affirm the "imagen del poeta" that distinguishes him from his
contemporaries. The "acorde" is recounted much later in the
prose poetry of *Ocnos* (see Valender 88–89), where it is described as an "unidad de sentimiento y conciencia; ser, existir,
puramente y sin confusión" ("unity of emotion and consciousness; being, existing, fully and without confusion") (104), a state
in which "la vida se intensifica y, llena de sí misma, toma un
punto más allá del cual no llegaría sin romperse" ("life intensifies
and, filled with itself, goes to the point beyond which it would
break") (103). While the "acorde" is a very positive existential
experience, it has very little to do with *La realidad y el deseo*
despite the importance ascribed to it by Cernuda's critics (see
Silver 30–50, 57–62; Harris, *Poetry* 23, 98). The "acorde" that
"nunca ... se produce de por sí" ("never ... is generated by
itself") (103) lies beyond the poet's power to will or summon
it and thus differs greatly from the willed experience of full being
in Guillén, Salinas, and Aleixandre.

Poem V, however, also underscores the emptiness of the adolescent's life. The sky that he addresses provides the mirror
image of his own existential nullity, "nuestra nada divina" ("our
divine nothingness") (78), as empty as it is vast and divine.
Poem VI describes the corollary moment to the "acorde." The

adolescent is again in his room but is now aware of his solitude, and of time.[4] The fullness of the earlier timeless moment now becomes a

> ... *Tibio vacío,*
> *ingrávida somnolencia [que]*
> *retiene aquí mi presencia,*
> *toda moroso albedrío,*
> *en este salón tan frío,*
> *reino del tiempo tirano.*

> ... Tepid void,
> weightless somnolence [that]
> retains my presence here,
> all sluggish will,
> in this room so cold,
> realm of the tyrant time.   (78)

The bourgeois concept of time brings the adolescent to an understanding of the unsuitability of continued adherence to bourgeois images, time's inseparable companions, and its limiting existential possibilities. Such an awareness spurs Cernuda to a new way of thinking and to the first of a number of manifestos regarding the question of being:

> *Existo bien lo sé,*
> *porque le transparenta*
> *el mundo a mis sentidos*
> *su amorosa presencia.*

> *Mas no quiero estos muros,*
> *aire infiel a sí mismo,*
> *ni esas ramas que cantan*
> *en el aire dormido.*

> *Quiero como horizonte*
> *para mi muda gloria*
> *tus brazos, que ciñendo*
> *mi vida la deshojan.*

> *Vivo un solo deseo,*
> *un afán claro, unánime;*
> *afán de amor y olvido.*

> I exist and well I know,
> because the world

makes transparent to my senses
its amorous presence.

But I don't want these walls,
air unfaithful to itself,
or those branches that sing
in the sleeping air.

I want as a horizon
for my mute glory
your arms, which girding
my life strip away its leaves.

I live a single desire,
a clear, unanimous zeal;
a desire for love and oblivion.   (79)

Love, the goal of existence, is much different from that affirmed by Salinas and Aleixandre since it cannot be willfully summoned. Cernuda makes his existential presence contingent on the presence of another desiring body, the antithesis of the solitary "acorde" experience. From the outset, Cernuda defines himself as an absence unable to validate his existence by means of his will alone. Love becomes the means to forget his ordinary understanding, which is that he is the sum total of the remembered images of visual reality.

The adolescent's rejection of the bourgeois formula of existence is accompanied by a growing distrust of ordinary images as well as the products of impotent dreaming, which brings him to his first intuitions about poetry. Poem VIII recounts the initial attempt to give form to desire through poetry. The attempt fails because the adolescent is still given to a "sueño maravillado que indolente / entre sus propias nieblas va sujeto" ("astonished dream that indolently / moves subdued among its own fogs") (80). Poem IX burdens him with the insight that "No acercarán amistades / la tierna imagen ajena" ("friendships will not bring near / somebody else's tender image") (81), the better image to remedy his "ternura sin servicio" ("unused tenderness") (81). The closest the adolescent comes to this better image is poem X, which recounts in allegorical terms the adolescent's discovery via the appearance of an angel looking for "Un soneto . . . / perdido

entre sus plumas" ("A sonnet ... / lost among his feathers").
As he describes it:

> *La palabra esperada*
> *ilumina los ámbitos;*
> *un nuevo amor resurge*
> *al sentido postrado.*

> The hoped-for word
> illumines the boundaries;
> a new love revives
> the prostrate senses.   (82)

At this point, poetry offers something of an outlet, a substitute
for love's absence and a means by which to avoid indolent
dreaming ("Olvidados los sueños / los aires se los llevan" ["The
dreams forgotten, / the breezes take them away"] [82]). Poetry,
however, brings the corollary awareness that it is also susceptible
to temporal laws, as suggested by poem XI, in which music, here
a symbol for all art, is likened to a bird that flies "por la cámara
en olvido" ("through the room cast into oblivion") (82), through
a hostile medium to an ignominious mortal destiny. At this
moment in his life, the necessary commitment to a medium that
seems to hold little transcendent promise seems hardly worth
the effort.

As a consequence, the adolescent becomes progressively
inner-directed and narcissistic, in poem XIII a "Narciso enamor-
ado" ("enamored Narcissus") (84), with only a fragmentary
image of love. He returns to his room to continue dreaming
as before but with a growing sense of desperation:

> *Levanta entre las hojas,*
> *tú, mi aurora futura;*
> *no dejes que me anegue*
> *el sueño entre sus plumas.*

> Arise from among the leaves,
> you, my future dawn;
> don't let the dream
> overwhelm me in its feathers.   (86)

In poem XIX, the darkened window becomes an oppressive
medium, a mirror for his reflection in the darkness that renders

the impotent image of "un cuerpo que se sueña / en el cristal, fingido irreparable" ("a body that dreams itself / in the glass, irreparably false") (89). The existential unity proclaimed earlier now becomes the realization that "alma y vida son ajenas" ("soul and life are alien") (90), an estrangement from the fullness of being complemented by his equal failure to embrace poetry as a vocation, "Tu juventud nula, en pena / de un blanco papel vacío" ("Your youth nil, grieving / over an empty sheet of white paper") (92). In the final poem, set in a garden, existential emptiness defines the adolescent who understands quite clearly that "En vano / resplandece el destino. / Junto a las aguas quietas / sueño y pienso que vivo" ("In vain / shines destiny. / Next to the quiet waters / I dream and think that I am alive") (92). The setting embodies the adolescent's domestication in a space where he can dream and think but not affirm a better destiny. Since "el tiempo ya tasa / el poder de esta hora" ("time already regulates / the power of this moment") (92), the garden is no different from other settings that have brought him to compromise his earlier intuitions of a better reality.[5]

In "Historial de un libro" ("Record of a Book") (1958), a commentary on the making of *La realidad y el deseo,* Cernuda holds no fond memories for the compositions of the second section and remarks that "mucha parte viva y esencial en mí no hallaba expresión en dichos poemas" ("a large living and essential part of me did not find expression in those poems") (905). *Egloga, elegía, oda (Eclogue, Elegy, Ode)* (1927–28) intensifies the contradictions of the garden thoughts and dreams of poem XXIII (see Valdés). Originally an homage to Fray Luis de León, the initial poem, "Homenaje" ("Homage"), also refers to its adolescent poet narrator. Poetry, "un eco ... tan solo" ("an echo ... so alone") (98), is still an uninviting medium. Even its ability to endure over time intensifies the poet's sense of absence from the scene of his creation. As much an homage to his own poetry and himself as to any other past poet that "ya no siente / quien le infundió tan lúcida hermosura" ("no longer senses / the one who instilled in him such lucid beauty") (98), "Homenaje" is indirectly a critique of the adolescent's inability to affirm his full presence in poetry. The insufficiency of his concept of being becomes explicit in "Egloga" ("Eclogue"), whose protagonist is an idyllic landscape, notable among its beautiful objects being a rose, the embodiment of adolescence that

> ... *asume*
> *una presencia pura*
> *irguiéndose en la rama tan altiva,*
> *o equívoca se sume*
> *entre la fronda oscura,*
> *adolescente, esbelta, fugitiva.*

> ... assumes
> a pure presence
> swelling pridefully on the haughty branch,
> or equivocally it sinks
> among the dark fronds,
> adolescent, svelte, fleeing.   (99)

The adolescent-roses cannot affirm a higher meaning to their purity and presence and thus come under the influence of the narcissistic "agua tan serena, / gozando de sí misma en su hermosura" ("water so serene, / enjoying itself in its beauty") (100), which in turn only vaguely approximates the intensity of the sky:

> *sólo copia del cielo*
> *algún rumbo, algún vuelo*
> *que vibrando no burla tan ingrata*
> *plenitud sin porfía.*

> it only copies from the sky
> some direction or flight
> that vibrating does not deceive such ungrateful
> plenitude without persistence.   (29)

The poem effectively retraces the trajectory of *Primeras poesías,* concluding that this form of presence is actually "Nula felicidad; monotonía" ("Null happiness; monotony") (100), which heralds the presence of the "horror nocturno de las cosas" ("nocturnal horror of things") (103).

The nocturnal horror is embodied in "Elegía" ("Elegy") in the self-contemplative form of the adolescent, naked this time, yet again in his familiar indoor setting, a "pura presencia" ("pure presence") who offers to a mirror "su estéril indolencia / con un claro, cruel escalofrío" ("his sterile indolence / with a clear, cruel shiver") (104). The adolescent, however, is a presence in physical terms only who expresses his self-desire in "Soledad amorosa" ("Amorous solitude") (105) as masturbation: "Melancólica pausa. En triste nieve / el ardor soberano se deshace" ("Melancholy pause. In sad snow / the supreme ardor comes undone") (105). What remains of this nocturnal experience is "una lejana / forma dormida ... ausente y vana / entre la sorda soledad del mundo" ("a far-off / sleeping form ... absent and unreal / among the deaf solitude of the world") (105). This faint image provides the basis for the final poem, "Oda" ("Ode"), and the emergence "vivo, bello y divino [de] / un joven dios" ("alive, beautiful, and divine [of] / a young god") (106) to fulfill this dream's impotent promise. This god, a "contorno tibiamente pleno" ("tepidly full contour") (107) that in every way resembles the adolescent of "Elegía," cedes his presence to an "eco suyo ... / el hombre que ninguna nube cela" ("echo of himself ... / the man that no cloud watches") (107). The man is a self-sufficient being who "sólo fía / en sí mismo ese orgullo tan altivo; / claramente se guía / con potencia admirable, libre y vivo" ("only trusts / in himself that arrogant pride; / he guides himself clearly / with admirable power, free and alive") (108), a self-conscious echo of an echo whose reason for being is to justify a loveless existence:

> *a su vigor tan pleno*
> *la libertad conviene solamente*
> *no el cuidado vehemente*
> *de las terribles y fugaces glorias*
> *que el amor más ardiente*
> *halla en fin tras sus débiles victorias.*

> to such a full vitality
> only freedom is suitable
> not the vehement care
> of the terrible and fleeting glories
> that the hottest love
> finally discovers after its weak victories.   (109)

The man, however, has nothing to do in this empty paradise except to pursue his "extraña imagen" ("strange image") (109), to become a "nuevo dios" ("new god") (110), and thus to dilute further whatever essence he may have originally possessed.

The realization of the untenability of such an existential posture occasions the tortured *Un río, un amor* (*A River, a Love*) (1929), whose title makes explicit reference to the solitary loving of earlier experiences. The form of love that for Guillén, Salinas, and Aleixandre is a means to expanded consciousness and creativity is for Cernuda conclusive proof of his impotence and failure. Adolescence has been an unrequited wait for "somebody else's tender image", which has failed to materialize. *Un río, un amor* represents the first attempt to reestablish desire as a transcendent value by rejecting the self-absorbed impotent innocence into which he has drifted. Such an undertaking requires a renewed artistic and existential commitment to the better image. As Cernuda recalls in "Historial de un libro," his definitive commitment to poetry came after 1927 and the unfavorable critical reception of *Perfil del aire,* as a gradual realization that "el trabajo poético era razón principal, si no única, de mi existencia" ("poetry was the principal, if not the sole, reason for my existence") (903). *Un río, un amor* is perhaps best read as an extended palinode, a chagrined and bitter renunciation of a failed way of life (see also Summerhill; Harris, *Poetry* 33–36).

In the initial poem, "Remordimiento en traje de noche" ("Remorse in Evening Dress"), an "hombre gris ... un cuerpo vacío" ("gray man ... an empty body") (115), a new protagonist but one not essentially different from the presences of the previous section, comes forth, as "remorse" but also as "el tiempo pasado" ("past time") (115), to embody the inadequacy of the earlier existential-amorous commitment, which has engendered false images with destructive power. The site of these images' production, an inner landscape of "ligeros paisajes dormidos en el aire" ("light landscapes asleep in the air") (116) called "the south" in "Quisiera estar solo en el sur" ("I Want to Be Alone in the South"), seems to be an idyllic locale but is in reality the physical image of desolation and absence from full being that has actually caused the present remorse: "El sur es un desierto que llora mientras canta, / . . . hacia el mar encamina sus deseos amargos / abriendo un eco débil que vive lentamente" ("The south is a desert that cries as it sings, / . . . toward the sea it directs its bitter desires / opening a weak echo that lives slowly") (116). This medium has populated the adolescent universe with images of which Cernuda wishes to be rid but which must continue to endure, as in "Sombras blancas" ("White Shadows"). These white apparitions "dormidas en su amor, en su flor de universo, / el ardiente color de la vida ignorando" ("asleep in their love, in their flower of the universe, / ignoring the ardent color of life") (116) embody the adolescent's impotence to affirm a viable form of love. Their kisses that fall into "el mar indomable como perlas inútiles" ("the indomitable sea like useless pearls") (117) recall the "triste nieve" ("sad snow") of the adolescent's masturbatory episode in "Elegía" and thus strongly suggest that, far from being nostalgia for an edenic past, the "sombras blancas" are the haunting image of values ("sin amor ni dolor, en su tumba infinita" ["without love or pain, in their infinite tomb"] [118]) that have occasioned Cernuda's "monótona tristeza, emoción en ruinas" ("sad monotony, emotion in ruins") (118).

The vacuity of adolescence is also underscored in "Nevada," where "el estado de Nevada" ("the state of Nevada") becomes synonymous with adolescent impotence, which has yielded "amor inconstante" ("inconstant love") (120), the "nieve dormida / sobre otra nieve, allá en Nevada" ("snow sleeping / on top of other snow, there in Nevada") (120), again reminiscent of the "sad snow" of "Elegía." As a consequence, Cernuda is left "Gritando locamente" ("Shouting wildly"), obsessed with the tormenting memory that "sin embargo vine como luz" ("I nevertheless came as light") (121). Instead of the presence of being, he has encountered "La presencia del frío" ("The presence of the cold") (121), a new medium beyond light that leads "por un espacio ciego de rígidas espinas" ("through a blind space of rigid thorns") (121) to the painful truth about love: "ningún cuerpo viene ciegamente soñando" ("no body comes forth blindly dreaming") (121). As a consequence, he is forced to confront the truth of himself, that he is an "incesante fantasma con mirada de hastío" ("unceasing phantom with a look of loathing") (121), a "fantasma que desfila prisionero de nadie, / falto de voz, de manos, apariencia sin vida" ("phantom that marches past, the prisoner of no one, / lacking voice, hands, an apparition without life") (122). He has penetrated to an "oscuridad completa" ("complete darkness"), a medium beyond light where he is forced to understand the impotence "De mis sueños copiando los colores de nubes, / de mis sueños copiando nubes sobre la pampa" ("Of my dreams copying the colors of clouds, / of my dreams copying clouds above the prairie") (123). Despite these realizations, Cernuda continues to "verter de mis labios vagamente palabras; / palabras de mis ojos, / palabras de mis sueños perdidos en la nieve" ("vaguely pour words from my lips; / words from my eyes, / words from my dreams lost in the snow") (123), which nevertheless suggests a different attitude toward his dreams and their means of production. If in adolescence existence is a by-product of "copying dreams," it becomes here, in "complete darkness," an act of "spilling" or "pouring" words. Words, not images, flow from the sites of an earlier "copying" (his lips, eyes, and dreams). The poetry ceases to be an attempt to establish correspondences with images in nature and becomes instead an attempt to fathom his uncomprehending commitment to a new medium ("no sé por qué he de cantar" ["I don't know why I must sing"] [123]).

Succeeding poems mark the initial steps toward such an understanding and commitment to words. "Habitación de al lado" ("Room Next Door") is an examination of "la muerte" ("death"), presided over by a goddess that "sin vida está viviendo solo profundamente" ("without life is living profoundly alone") (123). The death referred to is quite similar to Aleixandre's characterization of an alternative medium where empirical laws are rendered invalid and where the false images of an earlier time are exposed for what they are. This culminates in the condemnation of the adolescent experience itself in "Durango." In a parody of the open window of *Primeras poesías,* Cernuda sees "Por la ventana abierta" ("Through the open window") that "muestra el destino su silencio" ("destiny reveals its silence") (126). The adolescent has had no destiny. His only accomplishment is the making of "Durango postrado, / con hambre, miedo, frío, / pues sus bellos guerreros sólo dieron, / raza estéril en flor, tristeza, lágrimas" ("Durango prostrate, / with hunger, fear, cold, / whose beautiful warriors only produced, / a sterile race in blossom, sadness, tears") (126). This conclusion leads to the affirmation that "hoy es impossible / buscar la luz entre barcas nocturnas" ("today it is impossible / to search for the light among nocturnal boats") (126): the dreams of adolescence must end. Cernuda further concludes in "Desdicha" ("Bad Luck") that attempts to will love's presence are futile but that words remain the only vehicle, however unsatisfying, to bring him "hacia el amor" ("toward love"):

> ... *él con sus labios,*
> *con sus labios no sabe sino decir palabras;*
> *palabras hacia el techo,*
> *palabras hacia el suelo.*
> *Y sus brazos son nubes que transforman la vida*
> *en aire navegable.*

> ... he with his lips,
> with his lips he knows only how to say words;
> words toward the ceiling,
> words toward the floor.
> And his arms are clouds that transform life
> into navigable air.   (128)[6]

The poems that follow "Desdicha" bring increased understanding of the adolescent's failure as they establish words as the only available means of understanding. "No intentemos el amor nunca" ("Let's Never Try Love") is a misleading title since it suggests a despairing attitude. It actually refers to the temptation of the sea (symbolic of the poet's vitality) to return to the earlier unviable adolescent love. The sea returns to cities whose names (Cielo Sereno, Colorado, Glaciar del Infierno) are "todas puras de nieve o de astros caídos" ("all pure snow or fallen stars") (128) and which, by virtue of their inaccessibility ("el mar se cansaba de esperar las ciudades" ["the sea got tired of waiting for the cities"] [129]), might as well not have existed. The same attitude is expressed in "Linterna roja" ("Red Lantern") where Cernuda looks back on the earlier time embodied in "mendigos" ("beggars") who were "los reyes sin corona" ("the uncrowned kings") of unfulfilled adolescence "que buscaron la dicha más allá de la vida" ("that searched for happiness beyond life") (129). Their images "palidecen como olas" ("grow pale like waves") and reveal their true "essence": "las sombras no son mendigos o coronas, / son los años de hastío esta noche con vida" ("the shadows are not beggars or crowns, / they are the years of disgust alive tonight") (130). "Razón de las lágrimas" ("Reason for the Tears") confronts the fundamental problem of the adolescent more directly via the image of the night, who, like a cheap prostitute, "retuerce sus caderas, / aguardando, quien sabe, / como yo, como todos" ("shakes her hips, / waiting, who knows, / like me, like everyone") (131). The adolescent has settled for a false form of love. He has waited too long, and alone. As expressed in "Todo esto por amor" ("All This for Love"), it is "este amor cerrado por ver sólo su forma" ("this love shut off by seeing only its form") (132) that must now discover a means to "imponer la vida" ("impose life") so that "mis ojos, estos ojos, / se despiert[e]n en otros" ("my eyes, these eyes, / awaken in others") (132).

The first of such attempts follows in "No sé qué nombre darle en mis sueños" ("I Don't Know What Name to Give You in My Dreams"), where Cernuda calls out to the image-idea of a beloved who does not exist in reality, only

> detrás de la cabeza,
> detrás del mundo esclavizado,
> en ese país perdido
> que un día abandonamos sin saberlo.

> behind the head,
> behind the enslaved world,
> in that lost country
> that we abandon one day without knowing it.   (133)

The idea of love has now brought him to the threshold of a new affirmation, a future beyond adolescence, which he must pursue in the world:

> sólo sabemos esculpir biografías
> en músicas hostiles;
> sólo sabemos contar afirmaciones
> o negaciones, cabellera de noche;

sólo sabemos invocar como niños al frío
por miedo de irnos solos a la sombra del tiempo.

We only know how to sculpt biographies
in hostile music;
we only know how to count affirmations
or negations, comet tail of the night;
we only know how to invoke the cold like children
out of fear of going alone into the shadow
        of time.   (58)

The message of the concluding poems, beginning with "La canción del oeste" ("The Song of the West"), is the need to move
beyond this disappointment, to relegate the false images that
live in "the west," if not to oblivion, at least to their proper place.
"¿Son todos felices?" ("Is Everybody Happy?") declares, among
other things, that Cernuda must no longer "esperar ese pájaro
con brazos de mujer, / con voz de hombre oscurecida deliciosa-
mente" ("wait for that bird with the arms of a woman, / with the
deliciously obscured voice of a man") (139). He must turn away
from the images engendered during this long process of self-
examination and thus avoid repeating the error of the adolescent
that "como cualquier monarca / aguarda que las torres maduren
hasta frutos podridos" ("like any monarch / waits for the towers
to ripen into rotten fruits") (139). The poem concludes with a
protest against the reality of the adolescent: "gritemos a un ala
enteramente, / para hundir tantos cielos, / tocando entonces
soledades con mano disecada" ("let's scream entirely at one
wing, / to collapse so many skies, / then touching solitudes with
a stuffed hand") (139).

    This is a necessary step, however, in reaffirming the lost prom-
ise of adolescence and to renew the potential of "los deseos
cortados a raíz / antes de dar su flor, / su flor grande como un
niño" ("the desires cut at the root / before yielding their flower, /
their flower as big as a child") (140). Indeed, for the first time,
poetry and desire evince a conscious common purpose: "Los
labios quieren esa flor / cuyo puño, besado por la noche, / abre
las puertas del olvido labio a labio" ("My lips want that flower /
whose fist, kissed by the night, / opens the doors of oblivion lip
to lip") (140). The concluding poem returns to the adolescent's

window, the symbol of ordinary understanding of the early poetry, now a "Ventana huérfana con cabellos habituales" ("Or-
phaned window with habitual hair") (140), to look inwardly
upon an

> *atroz paisaje entre cristal de roca*
> . . . .
> *penetrando en los huesos hasta hallar la carne,*
> *sin saber que en el fondo no hay fondo,*
> *no hay nada, sino un grito,*
> *un grito, otro deseo*
> *sobre una trampa de adormideras crueles.*
>
> atrocious landscape among rock crystal
> . . . .
> penetrating into the bones until it finds the flesh
> without knowing that at the bottom there is no bottom,
> there is nothing, only a scream,
> a scream, another desire
> above a trap door of cruel poppies.   (140)

An insubstantial medium of words has demonstrated the insub-
stantiality of the false images engendered during adolescence.
Desire is also little more than words, an acknowledgment of
Cernuda's present emptiness and distance from a better vision.

By 1931, the date of *Los placeres prohibidos* (*The Prohibited
Pleasures*), Cernuda has become aware of the "poder daimónico"
("daimonic power"). At this earlier date, however, it is understood in more positive terms as a force that "va rigiendo nuestras
vidas" ("is governing our lives") (1095) and that "tiene siempre
un sutil afinidad más o menos exacta, con nuestro espíritu"
("always has a subtle and more or less exact affinity, with our
spirit") (1236). The darker, irresistible aspect of this force,
which dominates "Palabras ante una lectura," has yet to manifest
itself. This is because daimonic power, Cernuda's belief in the
agency of an outside presence that will confirm his unfulfilled
adolescent dreams, manifests itself initially as the invoked intuition of a better image of reality. The narrator-teacher, presumably Cernuda himself, of the prose piece "La escuela de los
adolescentes" ("School for Adolescents") relates to his listener-
pupil that it has been necessary for him to "creer en una presen-

cia, presencia que nosotros mismos evocamos de la nada con el poder taumatúrgico del amor, y que surge, al fin, radiante y amenazadora, ante nuestros ojos cegados" ("to believe in a presence, a presence that we ourselves call up from nothingness with the wondrous power of love, and that emerges, finally, radiant and threatening, before our blinded eyes") (1237). If in *Un río, un amor* all Cernuda can do is write "words" in "complete darkness" about the adolescent's hesitation to affirm love, *Los placeres prohibidos* becomes a rewriting, a justification after the fact of his having waited so long to affirm the "pleasures" that he himself has prohibited.

The introductory poem, "Diré como nacisteis" ("I Will Tell How You Were Born"), often interpreted as a diatribe against society (Capote Benot, *Surrealismo* 147–48; Harris, *Poetry* 46–47), is also a critique of the "régimen caído" ("fallen regime") (145) of Cernuda's own failed adolescence and mode of image-making. Although it is justifiable to interpret the poem's polemical references to the regime and values of Alfonso XIII and his conservative followers, the poem also certainly alludes to the "reyes sin corona" and the "monarca" of *Un río, un amor,* the adolescent "king" who has indeed fallen. When Cernuda shouts "Abajo, estatuas anónimas, / sombras de sombras, miseria, preceptos de niebla" ("Down with you, anonymous statues, / shadows of shadows, squalor, precepts of fog") (147), he is lashing out at his own vacuous past as well. The "placeres prohibidos" promise a new "fulgor [que] puede destruir vuestro mundo" ("radiance [that] can destroy your world") (147), the false worlds and mediums, inner and outer, self-inflicted and society-inflicted, that have thwarted the poet's freedom. This new freedom is a new existential ideology that repudiates the solitary self of adolescence, expressing itself instead as "alguien, cruel como un día de sol en primavera, / [que con] su sola presencia ha dividido en dos un cuerpo" ("someone, cruel as a sunny day in spring, / [that with] his sole presence has divided a body in two") (147). In "Adónde fueron despeñadas" ("Where They Were Thrown") Cernuda returns as a "peregrino" ("pilgrim") to the site of his earlier existence, where he confronts the image of that self, called Corsario, a self-absorbed pleasure seeker "que

se goza en tibios arrecifes" ("who enjoys himself in tepid reefs")
(148). The demand is that Corsario become his lover:

> Vierte, viértete sobre mis deseos,
> ahórcame en mis brazos tan jóvenes,
> que con la vista ahogada,
> con la voz última que aún broten mis labios,
> diré amargamente cómo te amo.

> Pour, pour yourself over my desires,
> hang me in my arms so young,
> so that with my drowned vision,
> with the last voice that my lips still spout forth,
> I will bitterly say how I love you.   (148)

The poet desires that the misguided love and energy of adolescence become directed to the present goal of invoking love,
even if by the inadequate means of "mis labios" ("my lips"). This
is ultimately a new profession of faith in desire that, even though
it remains a "pregunta cuya respuesta nadie sabe" ("question
whose answer nobody knows") (150), will encounter a reply:
"Otro cuerpo que sueñe; / mitad y mitad, sueño y sueño, carne
y carne, / iguales en figura, iguales en amor, iguales en deseo"
("Another body that dreams; / half and half, dream and dream,
flesh and flesh, / equal in figure, equal in love, equal in desire")
(150).

Faith in the unseen beloved intensifies in "Si el hombre pudiera
decir" ("If Man Could Say") as the beloved becomes the reposi-
tory of all value and the means by which to forget "esta existencia
mezquina" ("this miserable existence") (151): "Tú justificas mi
existencia. / Si no te conozco, no he vivido; / si muero sin
conocerte, no muero, porque no he vivido" ("You justify my
existence. / If I do not know you, I haven't lived; / if I die without
knowing you, I do not die, because I haven't lived") (151). "Unos
cuerpos son como flores" ("Some Bodies Are Like Flowers")
affirms what the adolescent was unable to accomplish, a total
commitment to love, the desire to become love's medium, "camino / que cruzan al pasar los pies desnudos" ("a road / that
naked feet cross in passing") (152). The highest value of love,
especially for one who has yet to experience it, is "un amor que
se entrega" ("a love that gives itself over") (152). The amorous

preparation ushers in the first brief glimpse of its better image, the sailors of "Los marineros son las alas del amor" ("Sailors Are the Wings of Love"). Although they emanate a dazzling "luz cegadora erguida sobre el mar" ("blinding light over the sea"), they are ultimately "los espejos del amor" ("the mirrors of love") (152), invoked presences, and thus absences, hypothetical evocations of what love must be like. The succeeding poems support such an interpretation. "Quisiera saber por qué esta muerte" ("I'd Like to Know Why This Death") addresses the fading image of his adolescent self, described as a "mar dormido bajo los astros negros" ("sea asleep under black stars") (153) but also "rubio igual que la lluvia" ("blond like the rain") (153), almost identical to the sailors' features. The poem reiterates a lesson the adolescent may have known but never practiced, that "el amor es lucha / donde se muerden dos cuerpos iguales" ("love is a struggle / in which two equal bodies bite each other") (153).

Disenchanted with his inability to encounter a satisfying image of love, Cernuda returns to a familiar posture in "Déjame esta voz" ("Leave Me This Voice") and the realization that his voice, his will to invoke the better reality, remains his only knowledge of it. This inspires another return, to an even more remote landscape, in "De qué país" ("From What Country"), where Cernuda addresses his earlier self, this time as an infant before the presence of "el deseo que se corrompe" ("desire that is corrupted") (155). This poem fulfills a double function. The first is the necessary killing off of the adolescent self, which has prevented Cernuda from being able to "besar con inocencia, / ni vivir aquellas realidades que te gritan con lengua inagotable" ("kiss with innocence, / or live those realities that shout at you with an inexhaustible tongue") (156). Cernuda tells the infant its destiny, which has already been decreed by the adolescent: "escuchar lo que digan / las sombras inclinadas sobre tu cuna" ("to listen to what the shadows say / bent over your cradle") (155). In telling this innocent infant "muérete bien a tiempo" ("die in good time") (156), Cernuda is voluntarily rejecting an entire phase of existence dominated by "sombras," the false images of ordinary reality in which the adolescent subsequently became diverted and which have debilitated the contemporary efforts to affirm "realidades que te gritan con lengua inagotable."

The second function of the poem refers to the "sombras," certainly an allusion to bourgeois society. Their lingering effects are also attributable to the adolescent consciousness that has believed in them. Cernuda has realized that it is not enough simply to condemn the "sombras" if he wishes to redeem the lost promise of what still remains of his innocence. "De qué país" is significant in that the double deaths of the adolescent and his infant predecessor mean that the country or territory ultimately affirmed is poetry. Abandoning the inner landscapes, Cernuda sees his form in a truer light as "Tu pequeña figura, sola en algún camino, [que] / cae lentamente desde la luz" ("Your small figure, alone in some road, [which] / falls slowly from the light") (156). What may seem to be the acknowledgment of a fall from an earlier state of happiness is actually a conscious choice fraught with danger: "abandonas la hierba tan cariñosa / para pedir que el amor no te olvide" ("you leave the grass so tender / in order to ask that love not forget you") (156), since the only force he can call upon is his own "Palabras de demente o palabras de muerto" ("Words of a madman or words of a deadman") (156).

The distance established between himself and the child-adolescent is a positive development that allows Cernuda in "El mirlo, la gaviota" ("The Blackbird, the Seagull") to reformulate his relationship to adolescence. Cernuda transcends the image of his own adolescence, and as a consequence the poem becomes the occasion for a much stronger amorous profession:

> *Creo en el mundo,*
> *creo en ti que no conozco aún,*
> *creo en mí mismo;*
> *porque algún día yo seré todas las cosas que amo:*
> *el aire, el agua, las plantas, el adolescente.*
>
> I believe in the world,
> I believe in you whom I still do not know,
> I believe in myself;
> because one day I will be all the things I love:
> the air, the water, the plants, the adolescent.   (159)

The succeeding poems supplement this new faith as Cernuda now is able, in "Como leve sonido" ("As a Light Sound"), to equate "todo aquello que de cerca o de lejos / me roza, me besa, me hiere" ("all that from near or far / rubs me, kisses me, wounds me") (160) with the image of love:

> *tu presencia está conmigo fuera y dentro,*
> *es mi vida misma y no es mi vida,*
> *así como una hoja y otra hoja*
> *son la apariencia del viento que las lleva.*

> your presence is with me outside and in,
> it is my life and it is not my life,
> just as one leaf and another leaf
> are the outward sign of the wind that
>   carries them.   (160)

This leads in turn to Cernuda's even greater commitment to poetry, which in "Te quiero" ("I Love You") is equated with the various means, all inadequate, that he has employed to say the words *I love you.* The ultimate conclusion is that even the "terribles palabras" ("terrible words"), the surrealistic discourse of *Un río, un amor* and the present volume, have proven insufficient to express such sentiments:

> *así no me basta;*
> *más allá de la vida,*
> *quiero decírtelo con la muerte;*
> *más allá del amor,*
> *quiero decírtelo con el olvido.*

> that way is not enough;
> beyond life,
> I want to say it to you with death;
> beyond love,
> I want to say it to you with oblivion.   (161)

However inadequate his professions and intuitions, they are the only means to keep strong such a faith. At the volume's conclusion, Cernuda finds himself once again with himself, alone and waiting for the time a beloved's "propia presencia / haga inútil este triste trabajo / de ser yo solo el amor y su imagen" ("own presence / will make useless this sad work / of being by myself alone love and its image") (162).

Donde habite el olvido (*Where Oblivion Dwells*) (1932–33) recounts the painful memory of precisely the experience for which Cernuda has been preparing himself and actively invoking. If *Los placeres prohibidos* is a blind invocation of an intuition of love as yet unknown, which only love's better image can redeem, *Donde habite el olvido* represents a blinded account of an all-consuming love whose image has surpassed the poet's ability to understand its positive meaning. Such a meaning emerges only after love's presence becomes an absent, haunting image. "Olvido," a realm of unconsciousness and absolute forgetfulness, becomes the only place where such a better image does not exist,

> *donde el amor, ángel, terrible,*
> *no esconda como acero*
> *en mi pecho su ala,*
> *sonriendo lleno de gracia aérea mientras crece*
>   *el tormento*

> where love, terrible angel,
> will not conceal like steel
> in my breast his wing,
> smiling full of airy grace while the
>   torment increases   (168)

and "donde termine este afán que exige un dueño a imagen suya, / sometiendo a otra vida su vida, / sin más horizonte que otros ojos frente a frente" ("where will end this desire that demands a master in its own image, / surrendering its life to another life, / with no more horizon than other eyes face to face") (168). The love experience is a transcendent version of forgetting that defies attempts to represent it. Only after love becomes a painful memory, a vision conjured by a freedom-denying force that limits love's landscape to "otros ojos frente a frente," does the demonic nature of desire express itself, to possess "el fondo del mismo amor que ningún hombre ha visto" ("the ground of love itself that no man has seen") (169), a transcendent image, "un dios en mis días / para crear mi vida a su imagen" ("a god in my days / to create my life in his image") (169), which no earthly image could satisfy.

Besides characterizing his erotic experience as a personal defeat, Cernuda's identification with fallen angels also marks a decisive step in the long process of his becoming a poet. Even though he may cast himself as "un ángel que arrojan / de aquel edén nativo" ("an angel that they throw out / from that native paradise") (174), condemned to walk the earth "errabundo mendigo, recordando, deseando; / recordando, deseando" ("as a wandering beggar, remembering, desiring; / remembering, desiring") (175), his remembrances are impotent only in the context of his failure to possess the absolute:

> Se buscaba a sí mismo,
> pretendía olvidarse a sí mismo;
> niño en brazos del aire,
> en lo más poderoso descansando,
> mano en la mano, frente en la frente.

> He was looking for himself,
> intending to forget himself;
> a child in the arms of the air,
> resting in the most powerful thing,
> hand in hand, face in face.   (175)

Cernuda's pursuit of love is similar to the existential goals affirmed by Salinas and Aleixandre. For Cernuda, however, such an ideal is cast in immoral terms, a primordial sin for which he is condemned: to become a poet, to see and remember the fragmentary images that remind him of his distance from love and the fullness of being. If this is a fall, into mortality and even nihilism (the belief in "la muerte de todo ... como tus ojos, como tus deseos, como tu amor" ["the death of everything ... like your eyes, like your desires, like your love"] [181]), the impotent creature who emerges is, like his counterpart in the biblical myth, something of a devil whose present is grounded in the memory of "aquel cuerpo de ángel que el amor levantara" ("that angel body that love raised") (177) and of the limitation of "mis ojos en el mundo, / dueños de todo por cualquier instante" ("my eyes in the world, / masters of everything for whatever moment") (178).

Cernuda emerges from these memories with a new understanding of the daimonic force he had earlier intuited and of his own intermediate status, as a medium, a special mortal with whom daimons, the gods' messengers, make contact. The pagan concept of an irrational, amoral force simultaneously angelic and demonic affecting mortals for good or ill, but usually for ill (see Soufas), is an apt metaphor for the type of experience that Cernuda has traversed first as an affirmative intuition-invocation and later negatively, via a loving body, as a direct presence. Cernuda's failure in love, however, is again attributable to his failure to discover a medium that meets his expectations. The ultimate consequence of such inadequacy is his estrangement from love's better image, the embittered affirmation that "El amor no tiene esta o aquella forma, / no puede detenerse en criatura alguna" ("Love does not have this or that form, / it cannot be contained in any creature whatsoever") (182). Although Cernuda acknowledges that he now shares the same space as other residents of the earth and that

> *[la tierra queda] con el deseo,*
> *con este deseo que aparenta ser mío y ni siquiera*
>   *es mío,*
> *sino el deseo de todos,*
> *malvados, inocentes,*
> *enamorados o canallas,*

> [the earth remains] with desire,
> with this desire that seems to be mine and is not
>   even mine,
> but rather the desire of everybody,
> villains, innocents,
> lovers or riffraff,   (183)

his recognition of the likeness of his image to that of others is only partial and short-lived. Cernuda does not fall so far or lose so much as those in whose midst he now recognizes himself. Along with a sense of loss, maturity brings the awareness that poetry will be his definitive vocation. Poetry cannot equal the absolute image that he has strived to possess in the final act of youth. It nevertheless affords the opportunity, in the aftermath of his amorous failure, to affirm a better image, his own mythic "imagen del poeta" ("image of the poet"). The sin of coveting an absolute image requires that he atone with a lifetime of reliving similar transgressions as he makes poetry, which becomes associated for the first time with the production of images.

If the poetry about adolescence is effectively dedicated to the invocation of an unseeable image through words, *Invocaciones a las gracias del mundo* (*Invocations to the Graces of the World*) (1934–35; known later simply as *Invocaciones*) is grounded in the divine memory of the unseeable, which makes Cernuda privy to special insights denied ordinary mortals. The overflow of words of *Un río, un amor* and *Los placeres prohibidos* that becomes a flood of memory in *Donde habite el olvido* now becomes a synthesis of the earlier means of production: privileged memories, better images, that Cernuda can see but not embrace. This posture becomes evident in "A un muchacho andaluz" ("To an Andalusian Boy"), which invokes his now spent youth in the image of an adolescent that emerges as "un resto de memoria [que] / levantaba tu imagen como recuerdo único" ("a remnant of memory [that] / raised your image like a unique remembrance") (188). Unlike the "dioses crucificados, / tristes dioses que insultan / esa tierra ardorosa que te hizo y deshace" ("crucified gods, / sad gods that insult / that burning earth that made you and unmakes you") (188)—a clear allusion to the Christian divinity sacrificed for the transgressions of ordinary mortals—this "muchacho que [surgió] / al caer de la luz" ("boy that [emerged] / on falling from the light") (187) fulfills a different role in Cernuda's system of values, which this and other better images collectively embody. The antithesis of "los ateridos fantasmas que habitan nuestro mundo" ("the numb phantoms that inhabit our world") (188), the adolescent offers an image worthy of veneration. Not unlike Christians, whose faith is grounded in the belief in immortality, Cernuda, inspired by the memory and example of the godlike adolescent, can also accept the burden of creating his own superior being and mythic poetic protagonist, the better image of himself. The memory of the adolescent, therefore, fulfills an almost religious function, as a "forma primera, . . . fuerza inconsciente de su propia hermosura" ("first form, . . . a force unconscious of its own beauty") (187).

If the strength of the adolescent is his unconsciousness and independence of inferior forms of love, then his undoing is his heightened expectations as a lover for whom only an absolute experience will suffice. The idyllic landscape that provides the setting for "El viento de septiembre entre los chopos" ("The Wind of September among the Poplars") provides a concrete image of what the adolescent searches for unconsciously during youth. As in the poetry of adolescence, it is not a precise image that draws the poet but rather "una sombra, / cuerpo de mi deseo" ("a shadow, / body of my desire") that communicates itself to him via the blind medium of words and sound ("Oigo caricias leves, / oigo besos más leves" ["I hear light caresses, / I hear lighter kisses"] [191]). Cernuda discovers an image of unmediated being, "arbórea dicha acaso / junto a un río tranquilo" ("arboreal happiness perhaps / next to a tranquil river") (191), embodied in a group of trees by a quiet river. The difference between the trees, the adolescent, and the now mature poet who continues to pursue such images is one of distance from the fullness of being, which the adolescent unconsciously possesses but loses in his desire to know it consciously as a form and with an image. The desire to know being, to be conscious of something that consciousness paradoxically destroys, brings its opposite. Consciousness means consciousness of one's mortality and ultimate insignificance in the context of a universe of images destined, like the eyes that gaze upon them, to disappear.

Although Cernuda has realized the diminished significance of his present life, equated with sighs in "No es nada, es un suspiro" ("It's Nothing, It's a Sigh"), such nothingness, proof of his longing and thus his absence from being, is nevertheless evidence of the existence of a transcendent presence not entirely unsympathetic to the plight of certain better mortals who have attempted demonic feats. Even though he realizes that such a force lies beyond his ability to comprehend it through the mediums he has embraced during youth, love and poetry ("nuestro amor" ["our love"] and the "palabra que creamos / en horas de dolor solitario" ["word that we create / in hours of solitary pain"] [193]), he also realizes that his sigh is the embodiment of a force now understood to be responsible for all his previous experiences, "el viento entre los chopos, / la bruma sobre el mar / o ese impulso que guía / un cuerpo hacia otro cuerpo" ("the wind among the poplars, / the mist over the sea, / or that impulse that guides / a body toward another body") (193). This force, daimonic power, which lies beyond the visible realm in a "margen invisible" ("invisible margin"), becomes the metaphor in adulthood for Cernuda's contact with a better reality, a divine medium that confers a temporary divinity on the poet who, in the making of an image, is able to produce an immortal version of an object of beauty, like its contemplator, threatened with destruction (see Harris, *Poetry* 66–67). Among such objects, of course, is Cernuda's own adult figure, whose full presence in being is no longer a possibility.

"Por unos tulipanos amarillos" ("Through Some Yellow Tulips") represents Cernuda's awareness of his new adult role as poet in the visitation of a daimonic "rubio mensajero" ("blond messenger") (194), described in terms suggestive of a sexual encounter, with whom "sellé el pacto, unidos el cielo con la tierra, / y entonces la vida abrió los ojos sin malicia, / con absorta delicadeza, como niño reciente" ("I sealed the pact, sky with earth united, / and then life opened its eyes without malice, / with absorbed delicacy, like a fresh child") (114). The final moment of the ecstasy is the creation of a poem inspired through "unos densos tulipanes amarillos / erguidos como dichas entre verdes espadas" ("some dense yellow tulips / standing up straight like happinesses between green swords") (194), as Cernuda declares:

> *mordí duramente la verdad del amor, para que*
>   *no pasara*
> *y palpitara fija*
> *en la memoria de alguien,*
> *amante, dios o la muerte en su día.*

> I bit hard the truth of love, so that it would not pass
> and beat securely
> in someone's memory,
> lover, god, or death in its day.   (195)

The ecstatic moment, however, exacts its price. In the aftermath of this experience with the "claro visitante" ("bright visitor"), "Dura melancolía" ("Harsh melancholy") replaces the initial joy, and thus becomes a burden, the "peso de una dicha hurtada al rígido destino" ("weight of a happiness stolen from an inflexible destiny") (195). At every opportunity, Cernuda is suggesting the superiority of his values, however difficult to endure, which seem even more divine when compared to the contemporary scene, which he surveys in "La gloria del poeta" ("The Glory of the Poet").

In this poem, Cernuda addresses a "Demonio hermano mío, mi semejante" ("Devil my brother, my fellow man") (196), the idealized image of himself in the role of poet, which he has accepted except for one detail, "el flamígero puñal codiciado del poeta" ("the fiery coveted dagger of the poet") (199), the final deformation of his "pecho sonoro y vibrante, idéntico a un laúd" ("sonorous and vibrant breast, identical to a lute"); now only death will be able to "hacer resonar la melodía prometida" ("make the promised melody ring") (199). In choosing the life of a poet, Cernuda has also chosen death, a better idea of death, which holds the promise of a final plenitude because it is chosen in full consciousness of death. Such a consciousness is lacking in Cernuda's fellow men, whom he evokes unflatteringly as

> ... *perdidos en la naturaleza,*
> *cómo enferman entre los graciosos castaños o los*
> *taciturnos plátanos,*
> *cómo levantan con avaricia el mentón,*
> *sintiendo un miedo oscuro morderle los talones;*
> *mira cómo desertan de su trabajo el séptimo*
> *día autorizado.*

> ... lost in nature,
> how they grow sick among the graceful chestnuts or
> the taciturn banana trees,
> how they greedily lift their chins,
> feeling a dark fear bite at their heels;
> look how they desert their work on the authorized
> seventh day.   (197)

The poet does not define his work in relation to conventional means of measurement—hours and days—but rather works for as long as he lives. In renouncing marriage as "la densa tiniebla conjugal" ("the dense conjugal darkness") and describing women as a "carga de suficiencia inconsciente" ("burden of unconscious complacency") (197), Cernuda is again proclaiming the superiority of his own sexual values. More threatening than the bourgeois institutions by which these mortals live, however, are their "interminables palabras" ("endless words") (197) and their "marmóreos preceptos / sobre lo útil, lo normal y lo hermoso" ("marmoreal precepts / on the useful, the normal, and the beautiful") (198), false images by which they enable themselves to "dictar la ley al mundo, acotar el amor, dar canon a la belleza inexpresable" ("dictate the law to the world, limit love, codify inexpressible beauty") (198). The ultimate expression of such a constricting value system invented by phantoms is, for Cernuda, none other than "el solemne erudito, oráculo de estas palabras mías ante alumnos extraños, / obteniendo por ello renombre, / más una pequeña casa de campo en la angustiosa sierra inmediata a la capital" ("the solemn scholar, oracle of my words before anonymous students, / obtaining renown from it, / plus a small country house in the distressed mountains near the capital") (198). The fate of Cernuda's better images, therefore, lies ultimately in the hands of others.

The culminating image of *Invocaciones*—the young sailor ("cifra de todo cuerpo bello" ["sum of every beautiful body"] [206]) of "El joven marino" ("The Young Sailor") who reenacts in mythic terms the final moment of youth in his reunion in death with the sea, as "el único ser de la creación digno de ti" ("the only being in creation worthy of you") (206)—also represents the moment of conferral of the "fiery coveted dagger of the poet." Just as the idea of the young sailor "despertaba en mí el deseo de la vida" ("awakened in me the desire for life"), so too his death "despierta en mí el deseo de la muerte" ("awakens in me the desire for death") (208). To desire death in the same terms in which this most beautiful of better images has experienced it is not a death wish so much as a willingness to embrace a destiny in which death is an inescapable conclusion. Cernuda can desire death since he understands it as the domain of an unquestionably superior value lost in the inevitable passage to the realm of life, mortal adult life. Cernuda, therefore, is again revaluing youth at the moment of declaring it lost forever. Life in bourgeois reality holds an attraction only because death now possesses a better image. It is worth enduring life's torments to experience that image again. The final mythic image of youth, the sailor and the sea "desposados el uno con el otro, / vida con vida, muerte con muerte" ("wedded one with the other, / life with life, death with death") (207), inspires what amounts to a faith in death. For one who has abandoned belief in the "sad god" of Christianity, the prospect of death necessarily means definitive disappearance. The sailor's exemplary death provides a better image to guide him to what must necessarily be the final expression of desire. Cernuda paradoxically loses everything as he affirms what amounts to the guiding values of maturity, conditioned on the remembrance of loss but nevertheless superior in every way to a bourgeois existence.

It is inadequate to characterize Cernuda's early poetry strictly in terms of the loss of innocence or the fall from an edenic state. Cernuda falls, into time and society, forced to acknowledge his place among the phantoms of the world and, ultimately, the end of youth. But as he underscores in "Palabras ante una lectura," his type of poetry requires "un estado de espíritu juvenil, y hasta no es raro que el poder de la juventud lo prolongue la poesía en el poeta más allá del tiempo asignado para aquélla" ("a state of youthful spirit, to the point that it is not odd that poetry may prolong the power of youth in the poet beyond the time assigned for it") (873). This is precisely the phenomenon in the first edition of *La realidad y el deseo.* The impotence and dreaming of adolescent desire have conspired to produce a better creature, a fallen angel, who becomes a poet. Cernuda loses his youth, as every mortal must, and his innocence as well, but he does so long after others who have perhaps not lamented its passing. By Cernuda's standards, his fall is certainly not to the level of his fellow humans, because he brings a set of alternative values that, while unable to restore him to the unconscious freedom of adolescence, are clearly thought of as superior. The images invoked in this final chapter of youth should be considered in a moral (or perhaps immoral) context as affirmations of an attitude to life that proceeds under unfavorable conditions, better images that together constitute an alternative personal ideology.

At the same time that Salinas is affirming what amounts to a statuesque ideal of existence, a frozen, silent space where being can be willed into conformity with one's vision of it, Cernuda is painfully acknowledging the limits of "sueños creados con mi pensamiento" ("dreams created with my thought") (208), likened in the concluding poem, "A las estatuas de los dioses" ("To the Statues of the Gods"), to the stone statues of the ancient gods that now lie "mutiladas y oscuras, / entre los grises jardines de las ciudades, / piedra inútil que el soplo celeste no anima" ("mutilated and dark, / among the gray gardens of the cities, / useless stone that the celestial breeze does not animate") (212). It is a final remembrance of Cernuda's own "tiempos heroicos y frágiles" ("heroic and fragile times") (212) that exist "lejos de los hombres, / allá en la altura impenetrable" ("far from men, / there in the impenetrable height") (213) but that nevertheless still inspire the poet "bajo el blanco embeleso lunático" ("beneath the white lunar rapture") to "[soñar] con vuestro trono de oro" ("[dream] of your throne of gold") (213). If the ancient gods and the values they embody have been reduced to the status of lifeless stone for modern culture, they possess an immeasurably higher value for Cernuda, for whom they and their "copero solícito" ("affectionate cupbearer"), the gods' eternal adolescent, represent another impotent beginning, again at an open window and in dreams. Although the first edition of *La realidad y el deseo* recounts a fall from adolescent grace, it also provides a cushion to such a fall in the better images, the alternative values of adulthood that emerge in the memory and image of youth. Cernuda's memories are of a mythic prehistory of better images that guide him to a mortal destiny, in poetry but also as poetry. The early poetry recounts a growing, and ultimately total, commitment to poetry, to the vocation of poet, and to a lifetime of struggle between desires and a reality for which there is no adequate image.

CHAPTER 5

Federico García Lorca

In contrast to Cernuda, whose ardent belief in a better existential reality allows him to affirm a viable image of himself as poet, Federico García Lorca in his poetry portrays the progressive failure of the human will and poetic imagination to establish a ground for the fullness of being. Lorca outlines the imagination's role in the semicritical lectures "La imagen poética de don Luis de Góngora" ("The Poetic Image of Luis de Góngora") and "Imaginación, inspiración, evasión" ("Imagination, Inspiration, Evasion") (see Laffranque 115–52). Although a poet is primarily a visual being "sereno frente a las mil bellezas y las mil fealdades disfrazadas de belleza que han de pasar ante sus ojos" ("serene in the face of the thousand beauties and the thousand uglinesses disguised as beauty that pass before his eyes"), he must not be overwhelmed "en su paisaje mental" ("in his mental landscape") by "las imágenes coloreadas, ni las brillantes en demasía" ("colored images, nor the excessively brilliant ones") (*Obras* 1044). Visual reality must become not an end but rather the pretext through which the imagination "fija y da vida clara a fragmentos de la realidad invisible donde se mueve el hombre" ("fixes and gives clear life to fragments of the invisible reality where man moves") (1065). The rational, visually oriented imagination is also the willful component of the artistic equation: "El poeta construye . . . una torre contra los elementos y contra el misterio. Es inatacable, ordena y es escuchado. Pero se le escapan casi siempre las mejores aves y las más refulgentes luces" ("The poet constructs . . . a tower against the elements and against the mystery. He is unassailable, he marshals and is listened to. But almost always the best birds and the most brilliant lights escape him")(1065). The imagination that "siempre opera sobre hechos de la realidad más neta y precisa" ("always operates upon matters of the most precise and clear reality") is ultimately an inadequate medium: "limitado por ella ... el poeta está en un triste quiero y no puedo a solas con su paisaje interior" ("limited by it ... the poet is in a sad 'I want to but can't' alone with his interior landscape") (1066).

Complementary and necessary to the imagination is poetic inspiration, which "ataca de plano muchas veces a la inteligencia y al orden natural de las cosas" ("often attacks the intelligence and the natural order of things flat out") (1069) and through which "la poesía pueda fugarse, evadirse, de las garras frías del razonamiento" ("poetry may escape and evade the cold claws of reasoning") (1069). Lorca characterizes this uncontrollable aspect picturesquely in "Teoría y juego del Duende" ("Theory and Game of the *Duende*"), where he describes a force that resembles Cernuda's daimonic power (see Binding 160–65; Stanton 10–13). In contrast to traditional agents of inspiration, such as the muse and the angel, the "duende," or sprite, "presupone siempre un cambio radical en todas las formas sobre planos viejos" ("always presupposes a radical change in all forms over the old planes") and is further characterized as "una comunicación con Dios por medio de los cinco sentidos" ("a communication with God by means of the five senses") (1102), again not unlike Cernuda's "zarza ardiente" ("burning bush"). It is the metaphor for Lorca's experience of a force that breathes into the vacant spaces of the human soul: "¿Dónde está el duende? Por el arco vacío entra un aire mental que sopla con insistencia sobre las cabezas de los muertos, en busca de nuevos paisajes y acentos ignorados" ("Where is the *duende*? Through the empty arch enters a mental air that blows with insistence over the heads of the dead, in search of new landscapes and unknown accents") (1109). The forces of inspiration impel the poet to transcend the rationality of his vision-dominated imagination in order to achieve a suprarational understanding, an "evasión" ("evasion"). The elements of poetic production described here do not differ significantly from the creative-destructive equations of Aleixandre or Cernuda. The difference lies in the significant incompatibility of these forces in Lorca. What in Aleixandre becomes a celebration of the aggrandizement of the human will in order to affirm his presence in being becomes in Lorca the recognition of the impotence of the will-imagination to establish hegemony over the landscapes and human forms it encounters. Lorca's poetry should be read, therefore, as the record of the poet's absence from being, a consequence of the debilitation of the imaginative vision by destructive inspiring forces. The poetry begins as the presentiment of such a negative potential.

The early poetry alludes to an emerging existential discord of considerable intensity. Perhaps the most noteworthy example from *Libro de poemas* (*Book of Poems*) (1921) is "¡Cigarra!" ("Cicada!"), nominally about the glorious death of a cicada "sobre el lecho de tierra / . . . borracha de luz" ("on the bed of earth / . . . drunk on light") (24), with which the young poet identifies intensely. The cicada has been "transfigurada / en sonido y luz celeste" ("transfigured / into sound and celestial light") (25) by the sunlight, a "Dios que desciende" ("God that descends") (24). The transfiguration, however, is purely an imaginative phenomenon. The cicada embodies Lorca's desire for a similar experience:

> *Sea mi corazón cigarra*
> *sobre los campos divinos.*
> *Que muera cantando lento*
> *por el cielo azul herido.*
>
> May the cicada be my heart
> on the divine fields.
> May it die slowly singing
> through the wounded blue sky.   (25)

The sun's light, which in the microcosm of the poem is a supreme force that embodies all of the positive qualities associated with the imagination, is an inadequate, idealized metaphor for a correspondingly intense force in the macrocosm that must necessarily supersede the imaginative vision. Such a light of plenitude is antithetical to consciousness and representation.[1] From the outset, ordinary light and the vision it affords the imagination become the measure of Lorca's distance from a transcendent existential experience. In "Encrucijada" ("Crossroads" or "Ambush"), a creative impasse characterized as "dolor de fuente ciega / y molino sin harina" ("pain of a blind fountain / and a mill without flour") (99) is suggestive of a dual estrangement from both a strong imagination and a beneficent inspiration (see also Zuleta 190). The poem recounts the loss of the ability to imagine the transfiguring light of "¡Cigarra!" as the moon appears "Por un monte de papel" ("Through a mountain of paper") (100), the consequence of failed attempts at poetic creativity. In "La luna y la muerte" ("The Moon and Death"), "La luna le ha comprado / pinturas a la Muerte" ("The moon has bought / paintings from Death") (114). The moon buys images from Death, an inspiring source of image production (a truer embodiment of the inspiring light of "¡Cigarra!") while the moon's inadequate light embodies the untenable product of the imaginative process, likened to a monetary transaction. Full, unmediated vision is possible only by obtaining death's images directly, without paying for them. Both modes of vision, whether free or paid for, however, require the destruction of consciousness.

Quite a similar existential equation brings Aleixandre, and also Cernuda, to much different understandings. The poetry of Aleixandre and Cernuda constitutes a progressive exposure to the poet's soul; Lorca, on the other hand, becomes aware very early of the irremediable gulf between vision-consciousness and the existential fullness he already knows can never be his. In "Deseo" ("Desire") he visualizes his desire as "Una enorme luz / que fuera luciérnaga / de otra" ("An enormous light / that was the glowworm / of another") framed "en un campo de / miradas rotas" ("in a field of / broken gazes") (117). In "Los álamos de plata" ("The Silver Poplars"), more despondent strategies emerge: "¡Hay que acostar al cuerpo / dentro del alma inquieta! / Hay que cegar los ojos con luz de más allá" ("One must put the body to bed / within the restless soul! / One must blind the eyes with a light from beyond") (118). Within the context of his understanding of vision and a "luz de más allá," these sentiments are admissions that he has no options, that he is trapped existentially and epistemologically. It is to this closure that "Manantial"

("Source") responds as Lorca inquires of "el negro secreto de la noche / y el secreto del agua" ("the black secret of the night / and the secret of the water"): "¿son misterios tan solo para el ojo / de la conciencia humana?" ("are they mysteries only for the eye / of human consciousness?") (125). His plea at the poem's conclusion is: "¡Señor, arráncame del suelo! ¡Dame oídos / que entiendan a las aguas!" ("Lord, uproot me from the ground! Give me ears / that understand the waters!") (127), which demonstrates a desire to discover other means to respond to his impasse.

Poema del cante jondo (*Poem of the Deep Song*) (1921) explores this alternative to vision that embodies itself in sound.[2] Rather than as autonomous protagonists, the Gypsy characters function as the props and scenery for an unseeable inspiring force that supersedes the vision-will. The poet understands in "La guitarra" ("The Guitar") that "Es inútil callarla. / Es imposible / callarla" ("It is useless to silence it. / It is impossible / to silence it") (158), that vision is incapable of circumscribing its range and realm. For example, in "Después de pasar" ("After Passing"), the original perspective, in which "Los niños miran / un punto lejano" ("The children look at / a far-off point"), cedes to a much wider area of activity in the concluding verses, in which "Las montañas miran / un punto lejano" ("The mountains look at / a far-off point") (162). The true landscape of these poems is not Andalucia but an inner "Tierra / de la muerte sin ojos / y las flechas" ("Land / of eyeless and arrowless death"), a realm of potential plenitude yet also an "ondulado / desierto" ("undulating / desert") (163). The title "Encrucijada" ("Crossroads") refers to the perspective formed by eyes that have perceived "Por todas partes ... el puñal / en el corazón" ("From all directions ... the dagger / in the heart") (170) of a murdered man, an image of death from a multiple vantage point that nevertheless underscores the impotence of those eyes to penetrate further. A more intense experience is recounted in "Sorpresa" ("Surprise") in another stabbing victim's "ojos / abiertos al duro aire" ("eyes / open to the hard air") (172). Here the man was presumably able to witness, if only momentarily and exclusively for himself, the presence and power of the medium of his destruction. The fact

that "Nadie / pudo asomarse a sus ojos" ("Nobody / could come
up to the window of his eyes") (172) suggests both his courage
and the power of a force that has expressed itself specifically at
the expense of vision.

The human will embodied in the imaginative vision is impotent to confront a force that supersedes it with a will of its own:
"Vine a este mundo con ojos / y me voy sin ellos" ("I came to
this world with eyes / and I will leave without them") (206).
These sentiments are dramatized in "Diálogo del Amargo"
("Amargo's Dialogue") in which Amargo, whose name is the
word for bitterness and who is initially a willful figure, boasts
"Yo le pregunté a la muerte" ("I inquired of death") (234) as a
rider overtakes him on the road. The horseman offers him a knife
as a gift, which Amargo refuses yet to which he is attracted since,
as the horseman tells him, even "los pescadores más humildes
de la orilla del mar se alumbran de noche con el brillo que
despiden sus hojas afiladas" ("the humblest fishermen on the
seashore are lit up at night by the brightness discharged by their
sharpened blades") (238). The temptation is to invest the knife
with added significance, an issue Amargo himself raises by his
insistence that "Un cuchillo no tiene que ser más que un cuchillo" ("A knife does not have to be more than a knife") (236).
Ultimately, the knife, again, becomes the symbol of an incomprehensible force that overwhelms the will as Amargo is killed. As
suggested in his mother's final song to the other women who
gather around her to mourn ("No llorad ninguna. / El Amargo
está en la luna" ["Nobody cry or swoon. / Amargo's in the moon"]
[241]), Amargo's ambivalence to the force that destroys him
leaves him "en la luna." His death is not the end of anything, only
the occasion for more song.

Primeras canciones (*First Songs*) (1922) is an apt title,
therefore, for the poetry that follows. The first of these
songs, "Remanso" ("Backwater"), sketches four possible backwater landscapes, each with its own tree and water: "estan-
cada" ("stagnant"), "cristalina" ("crystalline"), and "profunda"
("deep") are three. The final landscape—"Corazón. / (Agua de
pupila)" ("Heart. / (Water of the pupil)") (247)—is unexpected, yet again underscores the profound interpenetration

between the imagination and the physical landscapes on which the inner vision is projected. All four landscapes refer to Lorca since it is his pupil that characterizes the water in its various aspects, all suggestive of an existential impasse. The stagnant water suggests a cessation of movement and loss of vital energy, whereas the crystalline surface brings the temptation to self-absorption and self-desire, away from which the deep, mysterious, and more dangerous deep water seems the only possible direction. The following poem, "Remansillo" ("Little Backwater"), takes that deeper direction as Lorca portrays himself looking into a woman's eyes: "Me miré en tus ojos / pensando en tu alma" ("I looked at myself in your eyes / thinking of your soul") (248) only to discover instead the memory of his own desolate image reflected there.

A similar situation is portrayed in "Adán" ("Adam"), which retells the biblical story of creation of man and woman while also alluding to poetic creativity. As the poem begins, God has just taken Adam's rib, painfully ("Su voz deja cristales en la herida / y un gráfico de hueso en la ventana" ["His voice leaves crystals in the wound / and a graph of bone in the window"] [264]), in order to create Eve, to whom Adam remains indifferent. Instead, he dreams of "un niño que se acerca galopando / por el doble latir de su mejilla" ("a child that comes up galloping / through the double beating of his cheek") (264), the true embodiment of his own creative potential. In this "doble latir," there is another "Adán oscuro" ("dark Adam") who dreams a sterile dream, "neutra luna de piedra sin semilla / donde el niño de luz se irá quemando" ("neutral moon of seedless stone / where the child of light will slowly be consumed") (264). Besides presenting a more willful Adam, Lorca's version of the myth portrays an Adam tragically incapable of realizing his designs because of a self-destructive ambivalence that nullifies his creative potential. This idea is repeated more decisively in the concluding poem, "Canción" ("Song"), where the poet sees "dos palomas oscuras" ("two dark doves"), the sun and the moon, symbols of the discord within the imagination. Both are aspects of the same desire for existential fullness, which nevertheless competes against itself and brings instead estrangement from being. In the final verses, Lorca penetrates the shadows in order to see "dos palomas desnudas" ("two naked doves") but also sees that "la una era la otra / y las dos eran ninguna" ("one was the other / and the two were neither") (267).

Canciones (*Songs*) (1921–24) expands on the impasse re-counted in "Canción." In spite of the fact that a number of the protagonists of these poems are inanimate, the relationships they embody express perhaps even more clearly the imaginative anxieties of their creator. In "El canto quiere ser luz" ("The Song Wants to Become Light"), for example, the song that wants to become light is endowed with sentient and willful qualities. Yet the light, the song's goal, "no sabe qué quiere" ("does not know what it wants") (276), which calls into question the worthiness of the song's aspiration. The song, therefore, "En sus límites de ópalo, / se encuentra ella misma, / y vuelve" ("In its opal boundaries, / finds itself, / and turns back") (276). "Fábula" ("Fable"), a poem about "Unicornios y cíclopes" ("Unicorns and Cyclopes") (285), is also about "una pupila / y una potencia" ("a pupil / and a power"), the human will, which expresses its power via the light and the "eficacia / terrible" ("terrible / efficiency") of a dark power more than capable of destroying vision, which occasions the cry: "¡Oculta tus blancos, / Naturaleza!" ("Nature, / hide your targets!") (285; see Serrano Poncela). The sentiment is intensified in "Nocturnos de la ventana" ("Nocturnes from the Window"), which describes what can be contemplated by human eyes from an open window. In the third of these, the window becomes a "guillotina / invisible" ("invisible / guillotine") in which the poet, blinded by the ambivalence of his will, has placed "la cabeza sin ojos / de todos mis deseos" ("the eyeless head / of all my desires") (293). Likewise, "Canción de jinete (1860)" ("Rider's Song (1860)") is set in an even more stifling scenario of blindness under a "luna negra" ("black moon") as a dead horseman's "caballito negro" ("little black horse") contin-ues to carry him forward, even though no one—rider, horse, or poet—knows the answer to the question "¿Dónde llevas tu jinete muerto?" ("Where do you take your dead horseman?") (307).

The reply is voiced in the second "Canción de jinete" of the series, as the suggestion of continued, if useless, resistance to the destructive force, the horse's persistence in the darkness, cedes to a more resigned posture.[3] The second rider knows that "La muerte me está mirando" ("Death is watching me") and equally that "yo nunca llegaré a Córdoba" ("I will never get to Cordoba") (313): he will not be able to fulfill his destiny. He thus acknowledges the primacy of a destructive force that sees him but that he cannot see. The ascendancy of this force becomes manifest in the moon of "La luna asoma" ("The Moon Appears") at whose presence in the night sky "se pierden las campanas / y aparecen las sendas / impenetrables" ("the peal of the bells is lost / and then appear the impenetrable / paths") (339). The awareness of limitation in the face of the ultimate mystery of the human condition leads to a greater sense of isolation and weakness: "el mar cubre la tierra / y el corazón se siente / isla en el infinito" ("the sea covers the land / and the heart feels like / an island in infinity") (339). A "luna / de cien rostros iguales" ("moon / of a hundred equal faces") (339) reminds Lorca of the fragmentation of his being like so much "moneda de plata / [que] solloza en el bolsillo" ("silver coin / [that] sobs in the pocket") (339). His song, like his self, emerges from a fragmented perspective: "Ante una vidriera rota / coso mi lírica ropa" ("Before a broken glass / I sew my lyrical clothes") (342).

The section entitled "Trasmundo" ("World Behind") offers insights into the direction of Lorca's response to the challenge of an impasse that continues to grow at his expense, especially in "El niño mudo" ("The Mute Child"), about a child who "busca su voz. ... En una gota de agua" ("looks for his voice. ... In a drop of water") (361). The child's predicament and that of the poet are quite similar. The paradoxical goal of the search is not the recovery of the voice ("No la quiero para hablar; / me haré con ella un anillo / que llevará mi silencio / en su dedo pequeñito" ["I don't want it for speaking; / I'll make a ring with it, / which my silence will wear / on its little finger"] [361]) but a domesticated relationship (suggested by the ring) that will afford him autonomy over the things he does not say. His efforts fail as the "voz cautiva a lo lejos" ("captive faraway voice") becomes even more elusive when it acquires a "traje" ("dress") by which to distance itself further from the child. The range of the human will extends only to the physical landscape, whereas the voice, the human essence, remains the property of an entity independent of efforts even to make peace with it. Attempts to confront this force directly, as the succeeding poem, "El niño loco" ("The Crazy Child"), illustrates, result in a "broma" ("joke"), the separation of the "niño loco de su sombra" ("crazy child from his shadow") (362), his destruction.[4] This leads, in "Desposorio" ("Betrothal"), to the realization, by a hundred-year-old protagonist at the other extreme, that even the mute child's modest proposal is untenable: "Tirad ese anillo. Tengo / más de cien años. ¡Silencio!" ("Throw away this ring. I am / more than a hundred years old. Silence!") (363).

Equally bereft of a voice, Lorca is condemned to hear another that draws him farther away from his "primer deseo" ("first desire"), succinctly stated in "Cancioncilla del primer deseo" ("Little Song of First Desire"):

> *En la mañana viva,*
> *yo quería ser yo.*
> *Corazón.*
> . . . .
> *Y en la tarde caída*
> *quería ser mi voz.*
> *Ruiseñor.*

> In the living morning,
> I wanted to be me.
> Heart.
> . . . .
> And at nightfall
> I wanted to be my voice.
> Nightingale.   (369)

Being oneself means having a voice. As suggested in "Canción del naranjo seco" ("Song of the Dry Orange Tree"), having a voice means finding a place where "[puedo] vivir sin verme" ("[I can] live without seeing myself") (389). Lorca's vision is the terrible image of himself emptied of its content, an economy of poetic production based on an exorbitant exchange: the poet's essence for a never-ending cycle in which his autonomy is further undermined with every new and false image of the self. The concluding poem, "Canción del día que se va" ("Song of the Departing Day"), characterizes the poetic process as an untenable economic system. As Lorca tells the day, the temporal-empirical medium that quantifies being, a phenomenon that exists independently of such measurements:

> Te vas lleno de mí,
> vuelves sin conocerme.
> ¡Qué trabajo me cuesta
> dejar sobre tu pecho posibles realidades
> de imposibles minutos!

> You leave full of me,
> you return without knowing me.
> How much it costs me
> to leave upon your breast possible realities
> of impossible minutes!   (390)

The allusion is to the incompatibility of the two antagonistic dimensions of the poetic process, which produce an art grounded in empirical reality but at the mercy of "imposibles minutos," the antithesis of mimetic representational values. The "gran luz que sostiene / mi alma, en tensión aguda" ("great light that sustains / my soul, in acute tension") (390), the facilitating light of sensual reality, is now understood as something that is difficult. Lorca has become dissatisfied with representational values that lie at the heart of an existential impasse.

As Lorca matures, his dissatisfaction with empirically grounded representation intensifies. The long poem "Suite de los espejos" ("Suite of the Mirrors"), uncollected but written at the time of *Canciones,* examines mimetic principles and the problems they raise artistically and existentially. The initial segment, "Símbolo" ("Symbol"), presents Christ as mimesis personified, the embodiment of a noble but doomed way of life:

> Cristo
> tenía un espejo
> en cada mano.
> Multiplicaba
> su propio espectro.
> Proyectaba su corazón

en las miradas
negras.

Christ.
had a mirror
in each hand.
He multiplied
his own specter.
He projected his heart
into the dark
gazes.   (625)

In effect, Christ's activity is Lorca's. This segment consciously affirms the price he has paid for representing his absent "espectro" in the "miradas negras" of others, a destructive, fragmenting medium (see also Loughran 28–29; Zardoya 95–102). Lorca's Christ is never a presence but makes himself more of a specter by representing himself in an inadequate medium. This religious statement is actually an artistic manifesto that reflects Lorca's growing consciousness of the need to reformulate artistic premises that have led to a dead end. Like Christ, Lorca finds it exceedingly difficult to represent his heart to others. These ideas are complemented by the segment entitled "Los ojos" ("The Eyes"), in which human eyes are understood to contain "infinitos senderos" ("infinite paths") (633), infinite possibilities for diverting the will: "Las pupilas no tienen / horizontes. / Nos perdemos en ellas / como en la selva virgen" ("The pupils do not have / horizons. / We lose ourselves in them / as in the virgin wood") (633). The unstated complaint of this segment (and, indeed, many poems of the mid-twenties) is the insufficiency of mimetic images, impotent mirrors of a soul in the tenuous light of this fragmented medium.

"Oda a Salvador Dalí" ("Ode to Salvador Dalí") (1926), also uncollected, marks a turning point, or recalls a change, in Lorca's attitudes to the production of images.[5] This tribute to a still immature, presurrealist Dalí, with whom Lorca identifies artistically and personally, is not without its truthful critique of Dalí's "imperfecto pincel adolescente" ("imperfect adolescent brush") (776). Part of the reason for such honesty is perhaps that Lorca also recognizes himself and his own evolving attitude to art in

Vicente Aleixandre, Luis Cernuda, and Federico García Lorca in 1931

Dalí's paintings.[6] The already voiced dissatisfaction with empirical light, which forms the basis of perception, cognition, and
image production in traditional representation, and which exacts
an existential price in *Canciones* and "Suite de los espejos," is
confirmed in the fact that Dalí "Desnuda la montaña de niebla
impresionista" ("Undresses the mountain of impressionist fog")
(775). The difference between Lorca and Dalí is the latter's
willingness to act on what for Lorca have been only impotent
complaints and misgivings about a mode of art, here labeled
impressionism, the last of a long tradition of bourgeois forms
of expression. The greatest difference between Dalí and the
impressionists is not that he is attempting to represent things
that do not exist in nature but rather that the valuation of
the means to render these forms shifts from the possibilities
associated with light to those of line and solid form. As regards
"Los pintores modernos, en sus blancos estudios, / [quienes]
cortan la flor aséptica de la raíz cuadrada" ("The modern painters,
in their white studios, / [who] cut the aseptic flower of the square
root") (775):

> *Un deseo de formas y límites nos gana.*
> *Viene el hombre que mira con el metro amarillo.*
> *Venus es una blanca naturaleza muerta*
> *y los coleccionistas de mariposas huyen.*

> A desire for forms and limits overtakes us.
> The man comes who sees with a yellow ruler.
> Venus is a white still life
> and the butterfly collectors flee.   (775)

The new artist is a new man who sees reality according to
different values. Dalí's brush may be immature, but Lorca is
justified in praising his "ansias de eterno limitado" ("yearnings
for a limited eternity") (776), his desire to establish limits.

The new art does not reject visual reality but does demand
that it acquire substance. Lorca characterizes Dalí's imagination
in terms of touch as well as sight: "Tu fantasía llega donde llegan
tus manos, / y gozas el soneto del mar en tu ventana" ("Your
imagination reaches where your hands reach, / and you enjoy
the sonnet of the sea from your window") (776). And later:

Haces bien en poner banderines de aviso,
en el límite oscuro que relumbra de noche.
Como pintor no quieres que te ablanda la forma
el algodón cambiante de una nube imprevista.

You do well to put out warning flags,
on the dark border that shines at night.
As a painter you do not want your form to be softened
by the changeable cotton of an
        unforeseen cloud.   (777)

And again: "El pez en la pecera y el pájaro en la jaula. / No quieres inventarlos en el mar o en el viento. / Estilizas o copias después de haber mirado con honestas pupilas" ("The fish in the fishbowl and the bird in its cage. / You do not want to invent them in the sea or in the wind. / You stylize or copy after having looked with honest pupils") (777). These statements allude to the new values objects are understood to possess. Dalí "[ama] una materia definida y exacta" ("[loves] an exact and definite subject matter") and "la arquitectura que construye en lo ausente" ("the architecture that constructs where there was nothing") (777). His art is significant because his images also reveal the force and presence of Dalí in his art. Dalí imposes his gaze and his will on objects to give them a solidity and an outline they previously lacked. In this, he continues the work of the cubists while also refusing to make the artistic object an intellectual construct that must be reassimilated in the viewer's imagination to be understood. The very solidity and linearity of the object becomes evidence of a new sensibility. It heralds the possibility of going beyond the values of traditional art without abandoning the visual object and of affirming the presence of the artist in the act of representation.

Lorca recognizes a hidden center to Dalí, "la rosa del jardín donde vives ... / ... la rosa, siempre norte y sur de nosotros" ("the rose of the garden where you live ... / ... the rose, always north and south of us") (777), with which Lorca fully identifies. Although this hidden garden is "Tranquila y concentrado como una estatua ciega" ("Tranquil and concentrated like a blind statue"), it is also "Ignorante de esfuerzos soterrados que causa" ("Ignorant of buried forces that it creates") (778). This is a restatement of the balance of creative-destructive forces operant in Lorca's art from the outset. Lorca sees in Dalí an artist of very similar sensibility but also one for whom the artistic equation is less than tragic or, in the economic discourse that has become more frequent in the early poetry, one who produces an art that costs less existentially. Dalí is an artist who expresses his person in his art ("Digo lo que me dicen tu persona y tus caudros" ["I say what your person and your paintings tell me"] [778]), not one who grows more distant from that person in the manner of the early Lorca. The "Oda" helps to clarify Lorca's attitudes to the growing representational impasse of his early poetry, which he characterized as difficult and costly. That poetry produces images from an ordinary, unsteady source of light that indicates, much more than an insufficiency of form, a debilitated imagination. Lorca's association of Dalí's "person and paintings" with "tu pintura y tu vida" ("your painting and your life") (779) expresses his belief in the inseparability of his being and his poetry. Dalí's artistic intuitions are also existential intuitions, new means for Lorca to confront an intensifying artistic-existential impasse. The inspiration attributed to Dalí is evident in *Romancero gitano* (*Gypsy Ballads*) (1924–27). Lorca's Gypsies are his means to affirm, in the manner of his friend, a less costly economy of production and a somewhat more expansive will-imagination.

"Romance de la luna, luna" ("Ballad of the Moon, Moon") should be read as an allegory of Lorca's previous and present existential-artistic attitudes now embodied in the Gypsies. As creatures with "ojos entornados" ("half-opened eyes") (394), the Gypsies distrust the wide-open vision portrayed earlier in poems like "Sorpresa." In this poem, the child's death, communicated by the phrase "tiene los ojos cerrados" ("he has his eyes closed") (393), is the consequence of looking with widely opened eyes at the moon. The child greets the moon at the forge, a site of artistic production (Gypsies are traditionally blacksmiths and workers of metal), and warns her that "Si vinieran los gitanos, / harían con tu corazón / collares y anillos blancos" ("If the Gypsies were to come, / they would make with your heart / necklaces and white rings") (393), suggestive of the desire and the impasse of the earlier poetry. The Gypsies return to the forge to discover, more than the child's dead body, the absence of his essence. The child's willingness to help the moon brings him a death, represented as a loss of will and vision, which the Gypsy horsemen with "ojos entornados" are able to avoid. If the child re-creates the unproductive economy of the early poetry, the Gypsies offer a new medium of response to a destructive impasse that is also a consuming attraction. Lorca's Gypsies are creatures of line and solid form that embody his will for them to fight his battles, on terms more favorable than before, in landscapes of his choosing. The poems and protagonists of *Romancero gitano,* like Dalí's "pez en la pecera y el pájaro en la jaula" ("fish in the fishbowl and bird in the cage"), do not depend on the "niebla impresionista" ("impressionist fog") of ordinary visual reality and thus do not succumb, or succumb on more dignified terms, to the forces that threaten human integrity. Lorca's Gypsies operate in landscapes similar to Dalí's, which, although not destructive of the spectacle of vision, nevertheless become expressions of the artist's personal involvement with his represented objects. This, I believe, represents a turning point in Lorca's development as an artist. He is able here to transcend his dependence on empirical reality as he assigns form an existential value.[7] As a consequence he is in a position to confront "la rosa del jardín ... ignorante de esfuerzos soterrados que causa" ("the rose of the garden ... ignorant of buried forces that it creates"), the creative-destructive potential from which he has been estranged.

Lorca's Gypsy protagonists become his means to draw closer, if not to the fullness of being—never a real possibility—at least to the dynamic for his art. As expressions of his artistic will, the Gypsies enact a drama that, while establishing points of reference with empirical landscapes, corresponds primarily to "fragmentos de la realidad invisible donde se mueve el hombre" ("fragments of the invisible reality where man moves"). The Gypsies afford Lorca the means to direct the inspiring, form-destroying force to solid objects. The Gypsies of *Romancero gitano* are no longer the insubstantial creatures of song and sound of *Poema del cante jondo* but rather entities of line and mass, receptacles of a force against which Lorca's own person has proven an inadequate medium. The Gypsies thus free Lorca of some of his costly efforts.

If the child destroyed by the moon in "Romance de la luna, luna" allegorizes the past impotence, the Gypsies' defiance heralds a more organized response to the challenge of this force.[8] Such is also the case in "Preciosa y el aire" ("Preciosa and the Air") in which Preciosa is able to resist the wind, the embodiment of her fear of sex. The desire to avoid this sexual wind leads to the residence of "el cónsul de los ingleses" ("English consul"), a less than desirable refuge where Preciosa is offered "tibia leche" ("tepid milk") (397). Preciosa forsakes one existential possibility, the sexual desire that she fears, by refusing to return the glance of the "viento-hombrón" ("wind-man") as she also supplements this refusal by telling her story to "aquella gente" ("those people") (397), an uncomprehending audience that lives in houses with "tejas de pizarra" ("roof tiles of slate") and that has no framework for understanding a force that "furioso . . . muerde" ("furiously . . . bites") (397). Telling her story does not free Preciosa of her burden but does provide a momentary respite. In creating this ballad, Lorca has also continued to narrate his inner drama of resistance to a force he fears will destroy him (see Allen 33). Like all of Lorca's mature art, the poem takes place in two landscapes simultaneously. At one level, it tells an unlikely story. At a more profound level it recounts Lorca's artistic-existential discovery, a different voice, symbolized in Preciosa's storytelling, which objectifies an existential dilemma and makes it the occasion for art.

This greater objectivity regarding the impasse between the uncontrollable inspiring force and the imagination is embodied in the voice of the "juez con guardia civil" ("judge accompanied by Civil Guard") (399) of "Reyerta" ("Fight"). His judgment about the destruction as the result of "sangre contraria" ("contrary blood") is a legal-moral one ("aquí pasó lo de siempre" ["what took place here is what always happens"] [399]), which is also literary-critical. Lorca's art is the repeated spectacle of "sangre contraria," antagonistic forces that express themselves at the expense of one another. The difference between these poems and earlier, more costly formulations is that there is now room for another voice that, although incapable of altering this negative dynamic, momentarily evades some of the conse-

quences. The Gypsies and the "juez con guardia civil" are protagonists of a double drama, an existential bloodletting that is represented imagistically in a setting made conventional with the aid
of props or proxies, hollow Gypsy forms, for forces that defy
representation. The direct exchange of "sangre contraria" that
characterizes the earlier poetry is superseded by an imaginative
will aimed simply at channeling the destructive energy to a
different context or landscape. Like the judge accompanied by
Civil Guard, Lorca's attitude to his own existential tragedy is one
of understanding but also disapproval.

The complexity of these attitudes is confronted in "Romance
sonámbulo" ("Somnambular Ballad"), in which this new existential-artistic equation achieves its fullest development. The principals operate in radically different planes of experience, each of
which is necessary to explain the others. Although they possess
individualized physical forms, the postures they embody are not
unique. The father who greets his mortally wounded *compadre,*
the beloved of his dead daughter, who now occupies a green
realm, laments that "yo ya no soy yo, / ni mi casa es ya mi casa"
("I am no longer myself, / nor is my house any more my house")
(401). The young man, who spurned the daughter and the house,
returns bloodied from his dealings with the world. Desiring to
die "decentemente en mi cama" ("decently in my bed"), the
compadre proposes an exchange: "mi caballo por su casa, / mi
montura por su espejo, / mi cuchillo por su manta" ("my horse
for your house, / my saddle for your mirror, / my knife for your
blanket") (401). His desire to see his form reflected in a mirror
is reminiscent of an attitude, prominent in the earlier poetry, in
which the father no longer believes. The father has been unable
to maintain his house and its most precious possession, which
has languished in the *compadre's* absence. The principals are
defined in terms of landscapes to which the others do not have
access. The only real unity is that of the narrative voice that
contains them and is the only force capable of representing the
incompatible dimensions of experience. The narrative concludes with a double repression, the arrival of drunken Civil
Guards to take the *compadre* away (and thus to deny him his
death in bed) and a further reimposition of order by the narrative

voice, which shifts from the now familiar green realm of the Gypsy girl to a more conventional setting: "El barco sobre la mar. / Y el caballo en la montaña" ("The boat on the sea. / And the horse in the mountain") (403). This final shift in perspective and landscape underscores that the real content of the poem is a process of exchange. Lorca has exchanged what was previously enacted on his own person, his "house," for Gypsy actors who, although they do not resolve the continuing existential impasse, nevertheless are able to bring his personal tragedy into representable form.

"La casada infiel" ("The Unfaithful Married Woman") attempts to portray the dark power beyond images that demands a narrative.[9] The poem recounts an erotic experience that takes place outside the bounds of impressionistic light, where perception obeys different rules: "Se apagaron los faroles / y se encendieron los grillos" ("The street lamps were turned off / and the crickets were turned on") (406). Like Preciosa, the Gypsy fails to narrate an experience of plenitude, "el mejor de los caminos" ("the best of roads") (407), as a consequence of his sexual encounter with an unmarried virgin. Rather, he recounts what amounts to his own manipulation by a married woman whose deception taints the experience. The "casada infiel" is the real protagonist and the narrator's continuing obsession. The plenitude thought to be his actually belongs to the "casada infiel," and as a consequence elicits an attempt to redefine and devalue the experience, in now familiar terms of exchange, by assigning it to the category of prostitute and client: "Me porté como quien soy. / Como gitano legítimo. / La regalé un costurero / grande de raso pajizo" ("I conducted myself like the person I am. / As a legitimate Gypsy. / I gave her a large sewing box / of fine straw") (407). Yet the Gypsy who "no quise enamorarme" ("refused to fall in love") (407) has by now become obsessed with the false circumstances under which he achieved his glorious moment. By virtue of his recalling it for others, he exposes his lack of control and manliness, and he becomes a slave to a code of conventional conduct that further diminishes his stature. The Gypsy lover's truest desire is voiced by another female character, Soledad Montoya, of "Romance de la pena negra" ("Ballad of the

Dark Sorrow"), who declares: "Vengo a buscar lo que busco, / mi alegría y mi persona" ("I come to search for what I am looking for, / my happiness and my person") (408). Like the Gypsy lover, Soledad ("Solitude") is also "Soledad de mis pesares, caballo que se desboca" ("Soledad of my affliction, a runaway horse") (408), the simultaneous embodiment of an antithetical force-voice understood to affirm itself at the expense of one's person.

The two poems that feature Antoñito el Camborio introduce more serious themes, which dominate the rest of the volume. The second of these poems is perhaps where Lorca's new freedom to represent his imaginative obsessions most fully reveals itself. Antoñito is attacked, and killed, not by the Civil Guard but by his "cuatro primos" ("four cousins") who envy his shoes, medallions, and "este cutis amasado / con aceituna y jazmín" ("this skin kneaded / with olive and jasmine") (420). The agency of his death, however, is also ascribed to a preexisting discourse, "Voces antiguas que cercan / voz de clavel varonil" ("Ancient voices that surround / a voice of manly carnation") (419), an impersonal, seemingly "mythic" force that contradicts the narrator's explanation of the attack. There are two competing interpretations of Antoñito's destruction, one pathetically trivial, the other incomprehensible. There are also two incompatible interpretations of Antoñito's courage in the face of death. Antoñito's last words, hardly heroic, are for his companion Federico García to call the Civil Guards, presumably to denounce his cousins. The narrator, however, ennobles his death: "Tres golpes de sangre tuvo / y se murió de perfil. / Viva moneda que nunca se volverá a repetir" ("Three bloody blows he got / and he died in profile. / A living coin that will never be repeated") (420). The poem's contradictions underscore its real content, the will to endow with transcendence Antoñito's personal anecdote, which defies this desire. In complying with Antoñito's last will and fetching the Civil Guard, the character Federico García (Lorca considers this character to be himself, according to Binding 60) merely provides the ground for a poem like "Reyerta" in which the authorities arrive after the fact. Likewise, the narrator attempts to invest heroic qualities in an empty creature of line and mass summoned to life and destroyed by the poet, another

Federico García, who appeals to a different repressive agency. The creation of Antoñito is an attempt to transcend a cycle of unproductive exchanges, an existential inflation of false images of the self that have been costly and difficult for Lorca, and the recognition of the impossibility of such an undertaking. To become a "Viva moneda que nunca se volverá a repetir" is to end the consuming cycle that provides the dynamic for the poetry. The story told to the Civil Guards by Federico García underscores, however, the impossibility of such a closure. The poem is a failed attempt to impose form on something that defies transcendent explanation.[10]

The two poems that follow, "Muerto de amor" and "Romance del Emplazado," more clearly demonstrate Lorca's bifurcated attitude to ultimate experiences such as death. "Muerto de amor" ("Dead from Love") is about a Gypsy youth, mortally wounded in a fight over a woman, who wishes to publicize the event:

> *Madre, cuando yo me muera,*
> *que se enteren los señores.*
> *Pon telegramas azules*
> *que vayan del Sur al Norte.*

> Mother, when I die,
> let the ladies and gentlemen know.
> Send blue telegrams
> that go from the south to the north.   (422)

Although the gesture is pathetically comic, it also parodies Lorca's equally calculated gesture in *Romancero gitano* to provide form to a force that resists attempts to understand it. The intention is not to reverse the effects of this negative inspiration, but simply to endow it with physical and visual form. The absurdity of the Gypsy's last gesture of will succinctly characterizes Lorca's own tortured relationship with "los señores," official society. *Romancero gitano* is where Lorca begins to objectify his attitudes toward an audience, an integral aspect of the inspiring destructive force, to whom he knows he can never fully publicize his personal understanding of love, a killing impasse compounded by the ambivalence he feels toward his vision. As suggested by "Romance del Emplazado" ("Ballad of the Doomed

One"), the best to be hoped for is destruction on more favorable terms. The doomed man's knowledge of his fate, that "dentro de dos meses / yacerás amortajado" ("within two months / you will lie shrouded") (424), allows him to formulate a posture toward death that brings a certain "equilibrio a la muerte" ("equilibrium to death") (425). The difference between the Gypsy lover and the doomed man, however, is merely one of tone. Likewise, these characters afford Lorca a certain dramatic distance from the same forces more slowly but just as surely consuming him.

"Romance de la Guardia Civil española" ("Ballad of the Spanish Civil Guard"), which recounts the destruction of a Gypsy city, offers the fullest physical and visual portrayal of the inspiring force consuming the poet and his proxy-protagonists. The narrator explicitly equates the destruction of the Gypsies with his own person: "¡Oh ciudad de los gitanos! / ¿Quién te vio y no te recuerda? / Que te busquen en mi frente. / Juego de luna y arena" ("O city of the Gypsies! / Who that saw you does not remember you? / Let them look for you in my face. / Play of moon and sand") (430). Here the idea of dramatic distance all but disappears as an equivalent destruction is visited on both the Gypsies and their narrator, who represents them from a vantage point "donde joven y desnuda / la imaginación se quema" ("where young and naked / the imagination that is consumed") (429). The destroyers, who "Avanzan de dos" ("Advance by twos") (428), underscore physically their dual function. These representatives of arguably the most repressive of Spanish institutions are also overwhelming at an imaginative level:

> *Jorobados y nocturnos,*
> *por donde animan ordenan*
> *silencios de goma oscura*
> *y miedos de fina arena.*
> *Pasan, si quieren pasar,*
> *y ocultan en la cabeza*
> *una vaga astronomía*
> *de pistolas inconcretas.*

> Hunchbacked and nocturnal,
> wherever they emerge they ordain
> silences of dark rubber

and fears of fine sand.
They pass, if they want to pass,
and they hide in their heads
a vague astronomy
of inconcrete pistols.   (426)

Their repression is visited psychologically as well as physically.
The Gypsies' resignation in the face of their destruction affirms
the ultimate weakness of Lorca's characters, mediums through
which to respond to dark forces, imposed by both society and
self, which threaten an "imagination that is consumed." The
destruction of the Gypsy city acknowledges the fragility of Lorca's attempt to fashion a new poetic economy, which has ultimately failed to ameliorate the destructive effects of an inspiring
force unknowable despite the image assigned to it here.

The shift from Gypsy landscapes, over which the poet's imagination exerts at least some control, to "romances históricos"
("historical ballads") is a subtle acknowledgment of a loss of
creative will, a return to a more intimate personal history in
which the protagonists again embody the costlier economy of
production. "Martirio de Santa Olalla" ("Martyrdom of Saint
Olalla") features a painful mutilation—Olalla's breasts are sev-
ered—a variation on the earlier obsessive portrayals of the loss
of vision. "Burla de don Pedro a caballo" ("The Mocking of Don
Pedro on Horseback") is an allegory of the loss of potency and
manliness but also of expressive power. Pedro's mockery and
degradation is accompanied by "las palabras" ("the words")
(437), which accompany him to various watery abodes. The
words, the medium that has brought the Gypsies to life, share in
Pedro's loss of will. Like the child in "Romance de la luna,
luna," an infantilized don Pedro and the imaginative medium
that renders him become subject to a more powerful source of
production embodied in the involuntary croaking of the frogs:

Bajo el agua
están las palabras.
Limo de voces perdidas.
Sobre la flor enfriada,
está Don Pedro olvidado,
¡ay!, jugando con las ranas.

Beneath the water
are the words.
Slime of lost voices.
There, on the chilled flower,
is Don Pedro, forgotten,
ay!, playing with the frogs.   (438)[11]

Likewise, the incest of "Thamar y Amnón" ("Thamar and Amnon") essentially repeats the negative dynamic of the "Romance de la luna, luna":

Amnón estaba mirando
la luna redonda y baja,
y vio en la luna los pechos
durísimos de su hermana.

Amnón was looking at
the round, low moon,
and he saw in the moon the
hard, hard breasts of his sister.   (440)

This poem, however, offers no hope of defeating the power embodied in the moon. The volume concludes with a final gesture of willful impotence by David, the father of this ill-fated family, who "con unas tijeras / cortó las cuerdas del arpa" ("with a scissors / cut the strings of the harp") (442) to proclaim in silence the same message as the father of "Romance sonámbulo": "yo ya no soy yo, / ni mi casa es ya mi casa" ("I am no longer myself, / nor is my house any more my house").

Such is also Lorca's vulnerable state as he undertakes his most ambitious project, *Poeta en Nueva York* (*Poet in New York*) (1929–30), best read as an account of the imagination overwhelmed, which brings Lorca to New York "Tropezando con mi rostro distinto de cada día" ("Bumping into my face that is different every day") (471).[12] "1910" looks back to a time in the past to examine perhaps the first of these faces and the psychic moment from which the present impasse has originated, represented as a two-dimensional plane, a "blanca pared" ("white wall") of innocent existence[13] tainted not by golden sunlight but by the yellow urine of the "niñas," an allusion to the awareness of his sexuality but also to the content of his own pupils ("niñas") that, in images recalling the "Romances históricos," has left his eyes vulnerable ("en el seno traspasado de Santa Rosa dormida" ["in the pierced breast of sleeping Santa Rosa"]) and impotent ("en los tejados del amor, con gemidos y frescas manos, / en un jardín donde los gatos se comían a las ranas" ["in the rooftops of love, with cries and fresh hands, / in a garden where the cats ate up all of the frogs"] [448]). The consequences for his imagination, premised in *Romancero gitano* on the creation of poetic proxies to fight and suffer in his stead, are even more serious since now there are "en mis ojos criaturas vestidas ¡sin desnudo!" ("in my eyes creatures dressed, bereft of their naked form!") (448), bereft of their earlier, more substantial Gypsy form. Lorca's inability to dissociate his presence from these poems, to establish an aesthetic distance between himself and the New York landscape, is most suggestive of his imaginative collapse.

The poems about the blacks of Harlem, for example, become in reality elaborate masks for Lorca himself. As a characterization of the black condition, "Norma y paraíso de los negros" ("Norm and Paradise of the Negroes") is unsuccessful since besides the title there is very little to identify the blacks specifically as the poem's collective protagonist. The negros have adjusted to a destiny of unfulfillment by redefining the paradisiacal in terms of the norm. They have, in effect, lost the ability to imagine a better reality and thus have become embodiments of an imagination overwhelmed by dark forces. They become the antithesis of the childhood existence evoked in "Tu infancia en Mentón" ("Your Childhood in Mentón"). Closely paralleling the vocabulary of "Norma y paraíso," this white preadolescent paradise is the landscape where Lorca first acknowledges his own "norma de amor" ("norm of love") (452), an idealized homosexuality from which he has become alienated: "¡Amor de siempre, amor, amor de nunca! / ¡Oh sí! Yo quiero. ¡Amor, amor! Dejadme" ("Love of always, love, love of never! / Oh, yes! I love. Love, love! Leave me alone") (453). He is left with "el dolor de Apolo detenido / con que he roto la máscara que llevas" ("the pain of a suspended Apollo / with which I have broken the mask that you wear") (452), a reference to the spiritual crisis that has estranged him from his sexuality and robbed him of his masks, which created the distance necessary to shield himself from the raw forces that demand expression in the poetry.[14]

The negros become a living mask for Lorca's absent humanity. That they hate

> ... la sombra del pájaro
> sobre el pleamar de la blanca mejilla
> y el conflicto de luz y viento
> en el salón de la nieve fría
>
> ... the shadow of the bird
> above the high tide of the white cheek
> and the conflict of light and wind
> in the room of cold snow   (457)

makes more specific sense in relation to Lorca's hatred of his estrangement from his innocent "blanca mejilla," of his own long-standing existential-artistic hatred of the light of empirical representation, and of the wind of sexual desire, the negative dynamic underlying the poetry. If he temporarily distances himself from their effects in *Romancero gitano,* they have by now reasserted themselves. Subsequent images refer to "el salón de la nieve fría," the poet's (not the blacks') impotent inscape that, as in so many Lorca poems, replaces the original protagonist or landscape with another. The image of the blacks cedes to a weaker voice that loses contact with them in order to survey "el azul sin historia" ("the blue without history"), a landscape beyond consciousness where there resides "el desnudo del viento" ("the nude of the wind") and where "los durmientes borran sus perfiles bajo la madeja de los caracoles / y se queda el hueco de la danza sobre las últimas cenizas" ("the sleepers erase their profiles beneath the bundle of snails / and there remains the hollow of the dance over the last ashes") (458). The poem describes the ultimate destruction of all profiles, even those of the blacks, as the consequence not of their acts as protagonists but of Lorca's inability to maintain them in his poetic landscape. Lorca is not ideologizing the plight of the blacks but, as in the case of the Gypsies of *Romancero gitano,* is making use of their physical forms to ideologize himself, to characterize his own "blackening."

"Oda al Rey de Harlem" ("Ode to the King of Harlem") represents the same phenomenon, the disguising of the poet's shattered personality in a "Harlem dizfrazada" ("disguised Harlem")
(463). The king of Harlem is a proxy for Lorca's blackened
imagination weakened by the awareness that there is no landscape in which it can operate freely. The king, who, "Con una
cuchara, / arrancaba los ojos a los cocodrilos" ("With a spoon, /
plucked out the eyes of the crocodiles") (459), re-creates the
physical image of the limitations of Lorca's poetry. He exerts
ineffectual power over untamable, destructive creatures by attempting to divert vision from the site of its production. Liberated from their original mooring, however, the eyes become
invested with greater destructive potential, the clear evidence
of which is the king of Harlem's failure to become the poem's
true protagonist. Lorca's voice, not the king's, offers moral and
political advice to blacks seeking acceptance in white society,
likened to finding a crack in an invisible wall: "No busquéis,
negros, su grieta" ("Don't search, Negroes, for its crack") since
to do so is to "hallar la máscara infinita" ("discover the infinite
mask") (462). The political and economic oppression of the
blacks parallels exactly Lorca's diminished existential possibilities and loss of imaginative power. The "máscara infinita" is also
his, the ultimate devaluation of his person, the inflation of his
shattered image, which only landscapes filled with multitudes
can approximate, in a negative sense.

Thus in "Danza de la muerte" ("Dance of Death"), the "mascarón
. . . [que] viene del Africa a New York" ("great mask. . .[that] comes
from Africa to New York") is also a reference to Lorca, from the
"African," i.e., the southern part of Spain, and his displacement
from his human center and true form. Lorca's condemnation of an
"impúdica" ("shameless") North America is no less harsh than his
condemnation of his own immodesty since among those promi-
nently participating in the dance of death are homosexuals, "los
hombres fríos, / los que crecen en el cruce de los muslos y llamas
duras, / los que buscan la lombriz en el paisaje de las escaleras"
("the cold men, / those that grow in the intersection of the thighs
and the hard flames, / those that look for the earthworm in the
landscape of the stairs") (471). The great mask ultimately be-

comes an all-inclusive category. As it reaches Wall Street, it has become a symbol both of North American economic failure—the stock market crash and consequent Depression—and of Lorca's equal personal failure as the victim of the massive devaluation of his self-image. In "Paisaje de la multitud que vomita" ("Landscape of the Multitude That Vomits") the "ciudad entera se agolpó en las barandillas del embarcadero" ("entire city hit the railings of the wharf") to vomit and to embody physically the uncontrollable flood of images of the self that has overwhelmed Lorca's vision-imagination: "¡Ay de mí! ¡Ay de mí! ¡Ay de mí! / Esta mirada mía fue mía, pero ya no es mía" ("Oh, me! Oh, me! Oh, me! / This gaze used to be mine, but it's no longer mine") (474); this is the confession of an impotence unmediated by proxies such as the father of "Romance sonámbulo," whom these verses echo.

The succeeding poem, "Paisaje de la multitud que orina" ("Landscape of the Multitude That Urinates"), equates the poet's diminished capacity for vision with urination. As in the previous poem, in which vomiting is the metaphor for the loss of control of the production of words and image-ideas that pass through the medium of the throat, urination alludes to the effects of another yellow substance, empirical or impressionistic light. As these references suggest ("estas gentes que pueden orinar alrededor de un gemido / o en los cristales donde se comprenden las olas nunca repetidas" ["these people that can urinate around a cry / or on the glasses where the never repeated waves are understood"] [476]), the return to a dependence on such a medium as a consequence of the loss of imaginative power also marks the awareness of a political dimension to its oppressiveness. Such is also the vision in "La aurora" ("The Dawn"), in which "las monedas en enjambres furiosos / taladran y devoran abandonados niños" ("coins in furious swarms / drill and devour abandoned children") (485), possibly an allusion to the destructiveness of capitalism but more likely a reference to the escalating numbers of false self-images, like so many worthless coins, that are debasing the original, represented here and elsewhere as a young child or children, the presexual self.

"Poema doble del Lago Eden" ("Double Poem of Lake Eden") is exemplary of this estrangement. Although the poem is nominally set outside the city in a pastoral area, the final strophe makes explicit that the sentiments expressed in the poem have nothing to do with the landscape in which they are situated: "Así hablaba yo cuando Saturno detuvo los trenes / y la bruma y el Sueño y la Muerte me estaban buscando" ("I spoke this way when Saturn stopped the trains / and the mist and Dreams and Sleep were looking for me") (490). This is a reference to another time and place. Even this seemingly more affirmative moment—in which Lorca pictures himself talking to his "voz antigua" ("old voice") and declares his desire to "decir mi verdad de hombre de sangre / matando en mí la burla y la sugestión del vocablo" ("tell my truth of a man of blood / destroying in me the mockery and suggestiveness of the word") (490)—is a memory, not a response to his crisis but one of its causes. He has failed to destroy "la burla y la sugestión del vocablo" while creating a "double art" that juxtaposes, through an act of mockery, the existential dilemma to any convenient landscape. "Poema doble del Lago Eden" could have well carried another title and have just as easily been the introductory, or concluding, poem as the pastoral interlude it becomes here. Its content has nothing to do with Lake Eden, from which it is doubly removed. The poem is a juxtaposition of absences, a landscape that has never existed.[15]

Lorca is growing more distant from his "voz antigua," the vital, genuine center of his being, as he continues these mockeries of himself. Poems like "Vaca" ("Cow") and "Niña ahogada en el pozo" ("Girl Drowned in the Well"), which also nominally respond to experiences encountered during his stay in the countryside, are only loosely associated with the visual anecdote that supplies a unifying image for the poem. The wounded cow of "Vaca," which "Se tendió" ("stretched out") (497), is not one cow but rather "Las vacas muertas y las vivas . . . / [que] balaban con los ojos entornados" ("The dead and living cows . . . / [that] bleated with half-opened eyes") (497)—that is, all the proxy-protagonists of his imagination with half-opened eyes, especially his Gypsies, who have succumbed to an irresistible force (see García-Posada 277–78). "Niña ahogada en el pozo," subtitled "Granada y Newberg" ("Granada and Newberg"), represents simultaneously the consequences, and the cause, of the imagina-

tive impasse embodied in this image.[16] Everything has fallen into
the well, collapsed into the same plane. Like the drowned "niña,"
Lorca's own "niñas," his pupils and the more favorable economy
of production established in *Romancero gitano,* have succumbed to a confining chain of nonbeing forged from "Cada
punto de luz" ("Every point of light") (498). Rather than representing anything that occurs after his arrival in New York, these
poems make physical use of landscapes that, although they suggest a temporal narrative, actually depict a return to the costly
impasse that characterizes the early poetry. This vision continues
in "Muerte" ("Death"), where death is pictured as the effortless
end ("¡que grande, qué invisible, qué diminuto!, / sin esfuerzo"
["how big, how invisible, how diminutive!, / without effort"]
[503]) of a life that is all impotent effort and will:

> *¡Qué esfuerzo!*
> *¡Qué esfuerzo del caballo per ser perro!*
> *¡Qué esfuerzo del perro por ser golondrina!*
> *¡Qué esfuerzo de la golondrina por ser abeja!*
> *¡Qué esfuerzo de la abeja por ser caballo!*

> What effort!
> What effort for the horse to be a dog!
> What effort for the dog to be a swallow!
> What effort for the swallow to be a bee!
> What effort for the bee to be a horse!   (503)

An unproductive, circular exchange characterizes human willing, embodied in the non-image of the "hueco," especially in
"Nocturno del hueco" ("Nocturne of the Void"), where the
poet's diffuse essence is equated "Con el hueco blanquísimo de
un caballo. / Rodeado de espectadores que tienen hormigas en
las palabras" ("With the white hollowness of a horse. / Sur-
rounded by spectators that have ants in their words") (506).

The New York poetry has been the chronicle of Lorca's failure
to establish his presence in the New York landscape:

> *¿Qué voy a hacer? ¿Ordenar los paisajes?*
> *Ordenar los amores que luego son fotografías,*
> *que luego son pedazos de madera*
> *y bocanadas de sangre?*

What am I going to do? Put the landscapes in order?
Arrange loves that later are photographs,
that later are pieces of wood
and mouthfuls of blood?   (518–19)

The poems have become double exposures, landscapes that
provide the physical scenery for loves, Lorca's unfulfillable desires. His offer to be "comido / por las vacas estrujadas / cuando
sus gritos llenan el valle / donde el Hudson se emborracha con
aceite" ("eaten / by the stampeding cows / when their cries fill
the valley / where the Hudson gets drunk with oil") (519) is an
attempt to sacrifice his mocking voice in order to summon what
genuine vision remains in behalf of the multitudes like himself
and the multitudes within himself.[17] It is possible now only to
shed tears "como tiburones, / tiburones como gotas de llanto
para cegar una multitud" ("like sharks, / sharks like drops of
weeping to blind a multitude") (525), namely the double repressive multitude—the "miradas negras" of society and the multitude within—that defeats "la voluntad de la Tierra / que da sus
frutos para todos" ("the will of the Earth / that gives its fruits for
all") (527). Nevertheless Lorca contradicts himself in "Oda a
Walt Whitman" ("Ode to Walt Whitman"), where the idealized,
asexual homosexuality ascribed to Whitman (a "pájaro / con el
sexo atravesado por una aguja" ["bird / with its sex pierced by
a needle"][529]) is contrasted to the present-day carnal sexuality
of the "maricas de las ciudades" ("queers of the cities"), against
whom he raises his voice: "Que los confundidos, los puros, / los
clásicos, los señalados, los suplicantes / os cierren las puertas de
la bacanal" ("May the confused ones, the pure, / the classic, the
illustrious, the imploring ones / shut the doors of the bacchanal
on you") (532; Harris 61).[18] As both a "confundido" and one
who has entered "las puertas de la bacanal," Lorca nullifies his
earlier protest in the name of "la voluntad de la Tierra" since it
is nature's obvious will that this multitudinous minority exist.[19]
Even in protest, Lorca's self-estrangement is total. It is impossible
to "put the landscapes in order."

The succeeding "valses" recount the waltz of contradictory
forces and the reemergence of the voice of "mockery and suggestion." *Poeta en Nueva York* is not the unified expression of one

voice but of multiple contradictory voices, as emphasized in the concluding "Son de negros en Cuba" ("Song of Negroes in Cuba"), an almost parodic exposition of Lorca's failure to coordinate voices and landscapes. The intention to leave New York, reiterated in the obsessive refrain "Iré a Santiago" ("I will go to Santiago"), alternates with more specific references to the new landscape, both of which are ascribed to the blacks of Cuba. Through yet another act of mockery and suggestion, Lorca has made the poem into an impossibility. It does not make temporal sense in relation to the title, which suggests that the poet is already in Cuba, whereas the content represents his intention to go there. It is a final act of doubling. The willful voice "Iré a Santiago" is accompanied by its counterpart that sees a "ritmo de semillas secas" ("rhythm of dry seeds") (541) and "El mar ahogado en la arena" ("The sea drowned in the sand") (542), an impotent psychological landscape that no change of scenery can counteract. Whatever the actual Cuban landscape is like, Lorca knows beforehand that his arrival there has already been eclipsed by another dark and powerful medium he also carries with him, a "coche de agua negra" ("car of black water") (541).

Lorca writes very little poetry after *Poeta en Nueva York,* the definitive return to the earlier economy of production that exacts a substantial personal cost. It is not surprising that Lorca's greatest poem, "Llanto por Ignacio Sánchez Mejías" ("Lament for Ignacio Sánchez Mejías") (1935), raises the issue of being in relation to the ultimate destructive landscape, death. The return to the bull ring after retirement of Lorca's friend Sánchez Mejías also occasions Lorca's return to the vicious existential circle of his poetry. As has been the case throughout Lorca's mature poetry, the elegy to Sánchez Mejías is also an occasion to commemorate an attitude toward the writing of poetry and the creative spirit. "Llanto," Lorca's most profound meditation, is almost a manifesto on the possibilities of existence and his response through art to their destruction. If life is equated with being able to see, then Sánchez Mejías, like a number of Lorca protagonists who embody the desire to affirm life and being in the face of a more powerful adversary, goes to his death with his eyes open: "No se cerraron sus ojos / cuando vio los cuernos cerca" ("His eyes did not close / when he saw the horns close by") (554). Not unlike that of the boy of "Romance de la luna, luna," Sánchez Mejías's victimization by the "madres terribles" ("terrible mothers") (554)—the bull's horns, which also refer to the moon—is at the hands of a force that defies becoming an image and in the presence of which human will-imagination must necessarily fail to attain fullness and definitive presence. Lorca's ultimate response to his friend's blood, his now diluted presence, is: "¡¡Yo no quiero verla!!" ("I do not want to see it!!") (555). To see Sánchez Mejías's blood is to assume the same relation to his friend as to the vision-denying force that has destroyed him. The refusal to look at the blood is accompanied by the blood's transformation into song ("su sangre ya viene cantando" ["his blood already comes singing"] [555]). Sánchez Mejías's destroyed presence becomes refashioned into the words and images of the poem. His death brings Lorca to a definitive statement about the ultimate purpose of art in the face of a destiny of definitive absence from being, definitive nonbeing and disappearance ("También se muere el mar" ["Even the sea dies"] [557]), and definitive nonrecognition and loss of form:

> *No te conoce nadie. No. Pero yo te canto.*
> *Yo canto para luego tu perfil y tu gracia.*
> *La madurez insigne de tu conocimiento.*
> *Tu apetencia de muerte y el gusto de su boca.*
> *La tristeza que tuvo tu valiente alegría.*
>
> Nobody knows you. No. But I will sing of you.
> I sing your profile and grace for later.
> The distinguished maturity of your knowledge.
> Your appetite for death and the taste of its mouth.
> The sadness that your brave happiness bore.   (558)

Art is ultimately an impotent gesture but also the final defiant stronghold of the human will and spirit.

The poetry that follows "Llanto," however, suggests that Lorca's defiance here is perhaps his final gesture. The poems of *Diván del Tamarít* (1936) mark a retreat to earlier attitudes in order to underscore Lorca's continuing fragmentation of will and estrangement from being, as in "Casida del llanto" ("*Casida* of Lament"), an explicit reference to "Despedida" ("Good-bye") in *Canciones* and the entreaty "Si muero, / dejad el balcón abierto." ("If I die, / leave the balcony open") (364). Here the poet is also willfully gesturing, but for a different purpose: "He cerrado mi balcón / porque no quiero oír el llanto" ("I have closed my balcony / because I do not want to hear the cry") (590). The presence of the lament has drowned out his song, his will to form. "Gacela de la huida" ("*Gacela* of Escape") also clearly recalls "¡Cigarra!" in *Libro de poemas,* but in the human context of existential loss and separation:

> *Como me pierdo en el corazón de algunos niños,*
> *me he perdido muchas veces por el mar.*
> *Ignorante del agua voy buscando*
> *una muerte de luz que me consuma.*

> Just as I lose myself in the heart of some children,
> I have been lost many times by the sea.
> Ignorant of the water, I go searching for
> a death of light that will consume me.   (583)

Although the sentiments are the same, the attitudes toward this "muerte de luz" have changed. It is no longer a hope for final transcendence but rather a means of escape from an economy of existence that has yielded diminishing returns. The final sign of the collapse is the "Casida de las palomas oscuras" ("*Casida* of the Dark Doves"), which is simply a transcription of "Canción," the final poem of *Primeras canciones,* about antithetical forces that cancel each other out, a fitting finale for a poetry grounded in an "absent soul": "Por las ramas del laurel / vi dos palomas desnudas. La una era la otra / y las dos eran ninguna" ("In the branches of the laurel / I saw two naked doves. One was the other / and the two were neither") (598).

CHAPTER 6

Rafael Alberti

Of all the poets associated with a Generation of 1927, none lends more credence to the concept than Rafael Alberti, who was initially much beholden to the influence and guidance of his contemporaries, especially Lorca.[1] Somewhat in the manner of Lorca's "Oda a Salvador Dalí," Lorca himself becomes the subject of three sonnets of veneration, collectively entitled "A Federico García Lorca, poeta de Granada" ("To Federico García Lorca, Poet of Granada"), in the initial section of *Marinero en tierra* (*Sailor on Land*). Most significant for Alberti is Lorca's exemplary creative will in the face of a sterile existence: "mirad al dulce amigo / sobre las altas dunas reclinado" ("look at the gentle friend / reclined on the high sand dunes") (*Poesía* 22). In the final sonnet, a larger-than-life Lorca "en largo ciervo de agua convertido" ("transformed into a long, watery stag") (22) embodies the medium itself as Alberti also characterizes the representational possibilities of poetry, understood imagistically and sensually but also as surpassing pictoriality and corporeal solidity: "Deja que escriba, debil junco frío, / mi nombre en esas aguas corredoras" ("Let me write, cool weak reed, / my name in those running waters") (23). Alberti's sympathy with Lorca is paralleled by the consciousness with which he embraces an artistic medium in which he hopes to discover a more profound truth, "mi nombre," in the rapid current of life. Alberti begins his poetic vocation with an acute sense of existential diffuseness, but, unlike Lorca and other contemporaries, he comes to poetry as a consequence of his dissatisfaction with a previous vocation, painting, to which he calls attention in *La arboleda perdida* (*The Lost Grove*): "la pintura como medio de expresión me dejaba completamente insatisfecho, no encontrando manera de meter en un cuadro todo cuanto en la imaginación hervía" ("painting as a medium of expression was leaving me completely unsatisfied, unable to find a means of putting in a picture everything that was boiling in my imagination") (144; see also Jiménez-Fajardo 18–19). The willingness to embrace new representational mediums goes far in explaining Alberti's distinctiveness as a poet. His search for his "nombre" is inextricably wed to his search for an adequate medium in which to write and read it.[2]

One of Alberti's first poems, a three-part poem entitled "Balcones" ("Balconies"), collected in *Primeros poemas* (*First Poems*) (1922), exemplifies this attitude. In *La arboleda perdida*, Alberti claims to have been inspired by the long-remembered image of a twelve- or thirteen-year-old girl he once observed named Sofía who "contemplaba abstraída ante un atlas geográfico tras los cristales" ("was contemplating absent-mindedly before an atlas beyond the windowpanes") (155; see Tejada 126–34; Jiménez-Fajardo 29–31). The poem makes no specific reference to this anecdote but rather converts Sofía reading the atlas into a "Mariposa en el túnel, / sirenita del mar" ("Butterfly in the tunnel, / little siren of the sea") (7), a creature of the poet's imaginative world, a better geography, which Alberti, distanced from that space, wishes to read. By the poem's conclusion, her final transformation is even more decisive: "eres la luz / que emerge de la luz" ("you are the light / that emerges from the light") (8). As in the Lorca sonnets, Sofía embodies the poetic medium itself understood as a productive principle that takes Alberti beyond the impressionistic light of pictorial representation to an inner light that emerges as a response to this perceived inadequacy. This is both the starting point and the principle of continuity for Alberti's aesthetics and his attitude toward life, his personal ideology. Already aware of the limitations of the pictorial medium, Alberti consciously chooses the "luciérnaga del valle" ("glowworm of the valley") (6), the inner light embodied in Sofía, in the hope that poetry will bring him in closer proximity to "la inmovilidad de su perfil" ("the immobility of her profile") (*Arboleda* 155) and thus, in turn, closer to the immobile center of his being. Even in this poem, there is an awareness that this center, if it exists at all, is already growing distant. The first request of Sofía, and indicative of the relationship Alberti establishes with poetry, is "Ora por el lucero perdido" ("Pray for the lost star") (6), a request to intercede on behalf of something no longer present.

Alberti's dissatisfaction with pictoriality does not imply an abandonment of the image but does signal a different value, a secondary role for it in relation to the desire to read the interior geography of being. In "Del poeta a un pintor" ("From the Poet to a Painter"), which is dedicated to the painter Gregorio Prieto but could just as easily refer to himself,[3] Alberti outlines how this new mode of production—described as both an ascent from an earlier time of "sueño" ("dreaming") and a descent into the world, "al mar de nuestra vida, ya esmeralda y sereno" ("to the sea of our life, already emerald and serene")—is to proceed: "por los súbitos lampos, sobre el carro de trueno" ("via sudden flashes, on the wagon of thunder") (20). His medium is not to be a diffuse empirical light but the sudden flash that briefly illumines the darkness and that leaves after-the-fact evidence of its presence, in sound. Alberti's source of lighting is a discontinuous flash comparable to the brief presence of light during the process of photography, which becomes a more powerful manifestation of light by virtue of its penetration of a completely darkened space. The difference between Alberti's representational medium and the camera obscura is that the photographic process produces an image, whereas Alberti begins with an image in order to produce additionally a "carro de trueno," a sonorous trace of the flash that, nevertheless, possesses a substantiality that the "súbitos lampos" do not: words that persist and allow the poet to "recordar al toque final de la retreta / la clara faz del alba, su voz hecha corneta / de cristal largo y fino" ("remember at the final call for retreat / the clear face of the dawn, its voice made a trumpet / of long and fine crystal") (21). The switch from painting to poetry is not value free but ideologically motivated. The symbolic medium of words does not exist to reproduce mimetic images of the world; rather, images from the world provide the building blocks that allow statements to be made about, and from, the poet's own camera obscura, his private geography, in which the images of raw reality are made to serve another purpose.[4]

The physical posture of one of Alberti's best-known poetic protagonists, La Húngara—an entertainer who travels about the countryside in her "carro verde" ("green wagon") (161) in *El alba del alhelí (The Dawn of the Wallflower)*, pictured at one point "en la ventana del carro, / mirándote a un espejito / y con un peine en la mano" ("in the window of the wagon, / looking at yourself in a little mirror / and with a comb in your hand") (164)—further serves to illustrate the nature of Alberti's early attitude toward image production. La Húngara, like Alberti, has the choice of looking directly out the window of her cart to nature but chooses instead to look at and to groom herself in the mirror. In either direction, facing the empirical outside or turning her back to that scene, she will see an image of herself framed by the outside reality, either as a larger frame to her mirror or as a frame within her mirror. La Húngara neither affirms nor rejects ordinary reality but values more highly her own image framed against the natural backdrop. Her physical relationship to the empirical realm in this brief tableau is indicative of Alberti's relationship to raw reality. As in Lorca, pictoriality is not rejected, merely relegated to the background in favor of the true focus, the image of the self that emerges from the empirical medium, the landscape reflected in the mirror. The image of the world as the end of art, which leads Alberti to despair of painting, becomes merely the starting point. Alberti's icons affirm an additional purpose, representing being (helping him read and write "mi nombre"). More than simple objective correlatives of the poet's emotions (see Debicki), Alberti's landscapes are photographic reproductions of an interior geography. He attempts, through primarily verbal means, if not to affirm the presence of being "por los súbitos lampos" at least to be attentive to the "carro de trueno," the solid body of sound, the by-product of this desire that is the poem. Alberti's poetry is grounded in his distancing from the images of ordinary reality, which in turn become the mediums through which he represents his distance from being.

Alberti's awareness of his separation from his human center motivates the early poetry. The impotent sentiments expressed in the prefatory "Sueño del marinero" ("Dream of the Sailor") permeate *Marinero en tierra* (1924), which, despite its apparent exuberance, already shows consciousness of limitations on the human will (see especially Salinas de Marichal 15). The sailor's dream is to be "almirante de navío, / para partir el lomo de los mares" ("ship's admiral, / to part the back of the seas") (15), to be in command of a vessel, a medium, that proceeds through the waters of the sea, the "mar de nuestra vida" ("sea of our life"). The ship-medium, however, proves to be "una verde sirena" ("a green siren") (15) with whom he is in love and who reciprocates by making him more and more dependent on her, "atado a los cabellos finos / y verdes de [su] álgida melena" ("tied to the fine, green hair / of [her] cold, flowing mane") (16), as she diverts him from his dream of autonomy. The poem recounts the loss of a primary desire, a medium that would have ensured existential autonomy, obviating altogether the need for words and images. The poems of the third section, which herald the presence of a new sailor, a "marinero en tierra," are the logical consequences of the failure of the earlier dream. The original sailor and the voice that emerges from him to ride the sea with the green siren have suffered defeats in their attempts to dominate the "mar de nuestra vida," which the landlocked sailor now visualizes in terms of his diminished perspective, as a duality, a reality and its remembrance: "El mar. La mar. / El mar. ¡Solo la mar!" ("The sea. The sea. / The sea. Only the sea!") (59). The bifurcation of the sea into masculine and feminine aspects (the alternation of the articles *el* and *la*) is also an acknowledgment of the division of reality into an empirical-visual realm, "la mar" (in the manner of Alberti's first unsatisfying painterly vocation), and a realm where empirical rules do not apply, "el mar." "El mar," the projected site of full being, is never a real possibility. The question to his father, the agent of his engendering, "¿Por qué me desenterraste / del mar?" ("Why did you unearth me / from the sea?") is the same as asking why he has come into consciousness, why he would want to partake of a destiny that diminishes him and makes him a "marinerito en tierra."[5]

His insignificance in the landlocked medium is emphasized in "Salinero" ("Salt-Maker") by the new occupation, salt-maker, dedicated to the generation of a by-product of the sea-that-is-being. Such an occupation, which closely parallels Alberti's poetic vocation, only intensifies feelings of absence from a vital center and elicits impotent gestures:

> *Branquias quisiera tener,*
> *porque me quiero casar.*
> *Mi novia vive en el mar*
> *y nunca la puedo ver.*
>
> I would like to have gills,
> because I want to marry.
> My beloved lives in the sea
> and I can never see her.   (61)

"La mar" and the empirical values it embodies become progressively more threatening, as in "Chinita" ("My Little Dear One"), where he voices the hope that "la mar nunca te trague, / chinita de mi cantar" ("may the sea never devour you, / little dear one of my song") (63). Whereas "el mar" communicates at a distance, the visual phenomenon of "la mar" is always present to detour the desire to affirm "el mar." "El mar muerto" ("The Dead Sea") acknowledges the death of this inner sea that no one else has understood ("No lo sabe nadie, nadie. / ¡Mejor que nadie lo sabe!" ["Nobody knows, nobody. / It's better that nobody knows!"] [66]), the consequences of which are also experienced in the inability to see "la mar" from "los balcones de mi casa" ("the balconies of my house") (67). These mournful gestures are followed in "Pirata" ("Pirate") by the emergence of the pirate who wishes to steal "la aurora de los mares" ("the dawn from the seas") (68), the visual image of the sea, in order to gain dominion over "la mar." While the gestures certainly seem more willful, the pirate is a much weaker protagonist than even the salt-maker since his goal is power over the light, a given in earlier moments. In "Desde alta mar" ("From the High Seas") the goal becomes simply to "ir andando por la mar al puerto" ("go walking through the sea to port") (69), where the phenomenon experienced in "el mar" now occurs with "la mar": "Fuera de la mar, /

me perdí en la tierra" ("Out of the sea, / I got lost on land") (70).
Whereas "el mar" simply disappears without anyone's noticing
its passing, "tierra" and "la mar" complement each other. "La
mar" is a medium that leads its gesturing pirate astray on land,
which is its extension in the realm of ordinary reality.

This is underscored in "Verano" ("Summer"), a dialogue between a mother and her son, who returns from the cinema,
which exemplifies two possible attitudes toward the empiricism
embodied in cinematic representation. The son states:

> —*Del cinema al aire libre*
> *vengo, madre, de mirar*
> *una mar mentida y cierta,*
> *que no es la mar y es la mar.*

> —From the cinema into the open air
> I come, mother, from looking at
> a deceptive and certain sea,
> which is not the sea and is the sea.   (70)

The son is undermining the distinction between "la mar" as a physical presence in nature and as a represented simulacrum in the
movie house, suggesting that the image of "la mar" is also its effective essence. He is affirming a position that does not recognize the
primacy of one type of image over another. Images that originate
in nature as well as those empirically reproduced are fundamentally alike in that they are not considered ends in themselves. Images in nature are no more present than are cinematic images. The
son thus wishes to go out in the open air to test his hypothesis. The
mother replies that this is not necessary:

> —*Al cinema al aire libre,*
> *hijo, nunca has de volver,*
> *que la mar en el cinema*
> *no es la mar y la mar es.*

> —To the cinema to the open air,
> son, you never have to return,
> for the sea in the cinema
> is not the sea and the sea is.   (70)

The mother establishes that there is a fundamental difference
between natural and represented images, one of being. The

direct visual spectacle of "la mar" is assigned a definitive value. In the context of Alberti's associations with "la mar," however, the mother's words are an invitation to affirm the naturalness of visual reality, whereas the son in his hypothesis understands that images everywhere must be seen as absent phantoms of a reality that transcends the empirical value system.[6]

These sentiments are echoed in "Elegía del niño marinero" ("Elegy for the Child Sailor"), in which the death of the child sailor is represented in terms of an erosion of the child's will to affirm "el mar" over "la mar." A voice, somewhat reminiscent of the mother of "Verano," asks the sailor "tan guapo y tan pinturero" ("so handsome and so swanky," an indirect allusion to Alberti himself):

> ¿Qué harás, pescador de oro,
> allá en los valles salados
> del mar? ¿Hallaste el tesoro
> secreto de los pescados?

> What will you do, fisher of gold,
> there in the salty valleys
> of the sea? Did you find the secret
> treasure of the fish?   (75)

The plea to abandon "el mar," however, is to exchange something of greater value for something of lesser value, the substantiality of "el mar" for the phantom image "la mar":

> Deja, niño, el salinar
> del fondo, y súbeme el cielo
> de los peces y, en tu anzuelo,
> mi hortelanita del mar.

> Abandon, child, the salt mine
> at the bottom, and bring up to me the sky
> of the fishes and, on your hook,
> my little maiden gardener of the sea.   (76)

The elegy becomes simply a clever means of acknowledging Alberti's diminishing expectations of the sea of being.[7] He fishes from this sea lesser approximations of the earlier inspiration to become a sailor. The siren of the "Sueño del marinero" has become a domesticated gardener. In "Dime que sí" ("Tell Me

Yes"), an unresponsive female sailor becomes the object of an impotent entreaty: "Dime que he de ver la mar, / que en la mar he de quererte" ("Tell me that I will see the sea, / that in the sea I will love you") (81). His seeking to know her in "la mar" (and not "el mar") further emphasizes his desperation to find her in any medium, no matter how insubstantial or uncontrollable: "Dime que he de ver el viento, / que en el viento he de quererte" ("Tell me that I will see the wind, / that in the wind I will love you") (81).

This impotence is expressed, as in Lorca, by the loss of imaginative vision. Alberti consciously understands that "Colgadura, no muralla, / pone a tu calle la mar" ("Hangings, not a wall, / the sea places on your street") (82): the images from ordinary reality, like false hangings that tempt him to accept them as finalities, although individually unable to undermine him, have collectively become "Una ciudad marinera / [que] quiere a tu casa arribar" ("A marine city / [that] wants to put into port at your house") (82). The reply "Di que no, con tu bandera" ("Say no, with your flag") (82), with the semaphore (verbal-visual) signals of the poetic medium, indicates that Alberti is acutely aware both that he is ineffective in altering the course of his distancing from "el mar" and that his willful efforts serve only to produce more "colgaduras" to threaten his "casa." He laments through the vehicle of his sailor's suit:

> *¡Traje mío, traje mío,*
> *nunca te podré vestir,*
> *que al mar no me dejan ir!*
> . . . .
> *Mi madre me lo ha encerrado,*
> *para que no vaya al mar.*

> My suit, my suit
> I will never be able to wear you,
> since they don't let me go to the sea!
> . . . .
> My mother has locked it up,
> so that I won't go to the sea.   (86)

The more highly valued medium, "el mar," has been exchanged for one of lesser value, which becomes intolerable, "una mar muerta, / [que] la empujó un mal viento" ("a dead sea, / [that] a bad wind propelled") (87). The concluding poems concern themselves with what direction Alberti's "ojos tristes, sin rumbo" ("sad eyes, without direction") (87) will take. He is aware that "detrás de la celosía" ("behind the lattice")—the "colgadura"— of empirical images, there are "Ojitos que estáis mirando" ("Little eyes that you are watching") (89), other if lesser manifestations of the medium beyond vision. They are visualized as "mi niña virgen del mar / [que] borda las velas nevadas" ("my virgin daughter of the sea / [who] embroiders the snow-covered sails") (89) and a "sirenilla cristiana" ("little Christian siren") who "gritando su pregonar" ("shouting her goods") (91) sells the earlier priceless commodities from "los naranjos del mar" ("the orange trees of the sea") in exchange for lesser fruits of labor. Like Lorca, Alberti is aware that the poetic medium is exacting its price, that he is emptying himself in the act of producing images. This is also expressed in "El rey del mar" ("The King of the Sea"), where he confronts another who wants to be king of the sea: "Que él quiere ser rey del mar / y que yo también quiero serlo" ("He wants to be king of the sea / and I also want to be") (92). By the volume's conclusion not only has the possibility of life on the high seas disappeared but Alberti is consciously aware of the threat to his landlocked voice: "Si mi voz muriera en tierra, / llevadla al nivel del mar / y dejadla en la ribera" ("If my voice dies on land, / carry it to the sea / and leave it on the coast") (95). His imagination begins to fail him since it can project a return only to the point of origin of his impotence, the shore, not to the sea.

Alberti's recourse is to look to what remains of the earlier energizing vitality, which assumes female form late in *Marinero en tierra,* in order to continue to map his interior geography. In a form appropriate to the physical terrain in which they function (the "tierras altas" ["high terrain"] of Castilla, the "litoral del norte" ["north coast"], and back again in circular progression), the principals of *La amante* (*The Lover*) (1925), the poet and his lover (a landlocked version of the "sirenilla cristiana"), continue the earlier quest (see González Martín 69). As in the efforts to affirm "el mar," the "amante" also exacts a price. Exchanging

"mi casa, amante, / por ir al campo a buscarte" ("my house,
lover, / in order to go to the countryside to look for you") (104)
brings the experience of a lover "muy malherida / bajo del rosal,
mi vida" ("very badly wounded / beneath the rose bush, my life")
(104), a telling description of the inner geography. Thus begin
considerations of the economic conditions obtaining in this
landscape: "Aquí nadie vende nada. / Dime lo que quieres, di. /
No sé qué comprarte" ("Here nobody sells anything. / Tell me
what you want, speak. / I don't know what to buy you") (107).
Since he has nothing of sufficient value to offer her, the lover
remains unresponsive. The only response is from the "galga del
río Duero" ("greyhound of the river Duero"), which barks in the
night. Embodying Alberti's incipient awareness of a definitive
breach between his desire to know the inner geography and the
meager responses to these efforts, he shouts to the unresponsive
"Castellanos de Castilla" ("Castilians of Castilla") who "nunca
habéis visto la mar" ("have never seen the sea"):

> *¡Alerta, que en estos ojos*
> *del Sur y en este cantar*
> *yo os traigo toda la mar!*
>
> *¡Miradme, que pasa el mar!*
>
> Watch out, for in these eyes
> from the south and in this song
> I bring you the whole sea!
>
> Look at me, the sea is going by!   (108–09)

Such gesturing contrasts with the impotent posture in "Ruinas"
("Ruins"), in which the crying poet asks a child for "un vasito de
agua" ("a little glass of water") (109) as he laments the loss of
his "dulce galga" ("sweet greyhound") (112) killed by deer. A
sense of blindness accompanies this loss, an overwhelming of
the will comparable to waters "Que van ciegas, ciegas, ciegas, /
dándose hombros y frente; / mi amiga, contra las piedras" ("That
go blindly, blindly, blindly, / striking head and shoulders, / my
friend, against the rocks") (116), and also a complementary
deafness to the lover who expresses herself through "Los niños
de la amiga" ("The children of the friend"), a language ("¡A, B,
C, D!" [111]) he cannot understand. Alberti thus manifests his

personal dilemma in terms of an incompatibility between the mediums of eye and ear through which poet and lover are attempting to communicate: Alberti experiences a loss of will and vision as utterances from the lover fall on uncomprehending ears. As he returns in the poem "El mar" to the sea self-consciously comparing "mis marecitas del Sur / ante las mares del Norte" ("my little seas from the south / to the seas of the north") all he can do is "llorar, / como una niña, ante el mar" ("cry, / like a girl, before the sea") (123).

Alberti's weakness is underscored in "Mi lira" ("My Lyre"), which refers to protagonists prominent in *Marinero en tierra.* The earlier siren and the king of the sea have been superseded by new agents identified with the productive means of poetry: "La reina de las sirenas / y el hijo del rey del mar, / mi lira" ("The queen of the sirens / and the son of the king of the sea, / my lyre") (124), suggesting a further shift in the existential equation in favor of unconscious and uncontrollable forces. What was earlier a welcoming sea now becomes the source of unwelcome "fruits," such as the

> *¡Fiera cigala del mar!*
>
> *Del mar que yo te robé,*
> *al agua gris de la ría,*
> *al agua gris te arrojé.*
>
> *¡Y el agua tan gris, amante,*
> *tan gris, que murió de sed!*
>
> Ferocious sea crab!
>
> From the sea that I stole you,
> to the gray water of the estuary,
> to the gray water I threw you.
>
> And the water was so gray, lover,
> so gray, that it died of thirst!   (126)

The return to Madrid is to an awareness of loss symbolized in "Madrigal del peine perdido" ("Madrigal of the Lost Comb") by the loss of the lover's comb. The grooming instrument that helps the lover, but also the poet, maintain a surface appearance of orderliness and control falls into "el mar, huerto perdido" ("the sea, lost garden") beyond conscious control: "va y viene, amante, tu peine, / por los cabellos, mi vida, / de una sirenita verde" ("there comes and goes, lover, your comb, / through the hair, my life, / of a little green siren") (132). By the time this "buen amante andaluz" ("good Andalusian lover") bids his beloved "Niña del pecho de España, / ¡mis ojos!" ("Daughter of the breast of Spain, / my eyes!") (136) good-bye, he is also aware that "Por esas ojeras yo / me estoy quedando sin vida" ("Through those rings around the eyes I / am growing lifeless") (133). The attempt to represent the force embodied in the lover through visual means has further estranged him from his desire. His circular journey through the Castilian and Cantabrian geography has been accompanied by a linear drift, symbolized in the downward trajectory of the lover's comb, into more threatening territory.

The loss of existential presence becomes a principal theme of *Dos estampidas reales* (*Two Grand Stampedes*) (1925). The shepherdess of the "Estampida real del vaquero y la pastora" ("Grand Stampede of the Herdsman and the Shepherdess") complains that "al sol que te conocí / mi roja color perdí / yo, / vaquero mío, por ti" ("to the sun in which I met you / I / lost my red color, / my herdsman, because of you") (140), voicing a double complaint about inadequate mediums of light that have inverted the normal expectations. The shepherdess could as well be the lover whose true potential Alberti has failed to know for the same reasons. This is accompanied by the "Estampida celeste de la Virgen, el Arcangel, el lebrel y el marinero" ("Celestial Stampede of the Virgin, the Archangel, the Greyhound, and the Sailor"), a title representing a scale of descending existential value, in which the archangel intercedes to the Virgin on behalf of the sailor, who asks "quiero, con mi lebrel, / que me nombres timonel, / al sol, de tu cañonero" ("I want, with my greyhound, / that you name me helmsman, / to the sun, of your gunboat") (142). The dog's bark, the sonorous embodiment of the will, is all that remains of the sailor's earlier dream. Their new domain, the "banda azul de la mar / bordada en el firmamento" ("blue strip of sea / embroidered in the firmament"), the sky, is a distant reflection of "la mar," itself a distant reflection of "el mar." What is represented superficially as a gift from heaven actually becomes a paradoxical gift *of* heaven, the wrong medium, a most negative

Federico García Lorca and Rafael Alberti in 1927

exchange to which *El alba del alhelí* (*The Dawn of the Wall-flower*) (1925–26) makes explicit and continued reference. Indeed, the "Prólogo" proposes an exchange:

> *Todo lo que por ti vi*
> *—la estrella sobre el aprisco,*
> *el carro estival del heno*
> *y el alba del alhelí—,*
> *si me miras, para ti.*

> All that I saw through you
> —the star over the sheepfold,
> the summer hay wagon,
> and the dawn of the wallflower—,
> if you look at me, for you.   (149)

As in the sailor's supplication to the Virgin, Alberti is again calling on the medium that allowed him his earlier vision ("Todo lo que por ti vi") to manifest itself as a direct presence. Since the volume is entitled *El alba del alhelí,* presumably part of the treasure that he wishes to bestow is the poems themselves, the inference being that the otherness addressed in the prologue has not been experienced in a satisfactory manner. Alberti's earlier dilemma has intensified. He has progressively less to exchange for what he truly desires, a redistribution of the forces in the representational equation. The desire for a better economy of production parallels the emergence of the decentering influence of sexual desire (symbolized in the "alhelí," the rose, and the carnation) which makes it difficult to amass sufficient existential capital. As the infant Jesus, who represents yet another Albertian persona at the dawn of his awareness that his divine and mortal possibilities nullify each other, succinctly states it: "¿Cómo vivir sin dinero? / —¡Vendedor, / que se muere mi alba en flor!" ("How to live without money? / —Seller, / my flowering dawn is dying!") (154). The apparently more prosperous situation that obtains with La Húngara, whom he could, like the lover, also follow "Por toda España ... vendiendo caballos malos, / vida, por caballos buenos" ("Throughout Spain ... selling bad horses, / life, for good ones") (162), is tempered by the possibility that this declaration refers to a perpetrated fraud as much as to a time when the medium of exchange was in his favor. With both La Húngara and the young Jesus, the stories abruptly end, leaving the narrator in confusion, as in La Húngara's departure: "¿Por qué vereda se fue? / ¡Ay, aire, que no lo sé!" ("Through what path did she leave? / Oh, air, I do not know!") (165).

The next persona to emerge is "El pescador sin dinero" ("The Penniless Fisherman"), of an entirely different seafaring occupation from that of the sailor, berated by an accusing voice that tells him, "Ya te lo has tirado todo. / Y ya no tienes amigo" ("You've thrown it all away. / And you have no friend") (165), seconded by the fisherman's own lament: "¡Oh campo mío en la mar, / ya no te podré comprar, / que me quedé sin dinero!" ("O my field in the sea, / I won't be able to buy you, / since I am penniless") (166). Given the context of these statements, the fisherman presents evidence of a deteriorating poetic economy.[8] This friendless figure is succeeded by further instances of abandonment, as in "La novia" ("The Bride"), in which the bride is left "sin mi amante, / yéndome a casar" ("without my lover, / on the way to get married") (168), a pattern repeated in a number of variant forms, including "El lancero y el fotógrafo" ("The Lancer and the Photographer"), which recounts a verbal exchange between a lancer who wants his picture taken and a photographer. The lancer, somewhat in the spirit of the earlier sailor, wants to be photographed "con mi traje de lancero, / con mi casco y su plumero" ("with my lancer's suit, / with my helmet and its plume") (169). The photographer tells him "Quietecito, quietecito / con la lanza, el caballero, / que va a salir, volandero, / de esta casa, un pajarito" ("Be still, be still / with your lance, sir, / because from this house / is going to fly a birdie") (169), presumably a reference to the birdie that traditionally accompanies the portrait-maker. The child, however, becomes obsessed with the birdie ("¡Pues lo quiero!" ["I want it!"] [169]) and thus fails to have his full likeness captured ("¡Qué mal lancero!" ["What a bad lancer!"]): he confuses a false medium for the true medium. Neither party has anything to show for his efforts except the failure to produce a viable exchange of images, which also re-creates the conditions of production in *El alba del alhelí.* The dawn of the desire to experience a liberating medium as a direct presence becomes corrupted into another form of transaction: "¡Salid a los miradores / a comprar amor, que pasa / la luna vendiendo amores!" ("Come out to the balconies, because the moon passes / selling love!") (176).

The second section, entitled "El negro alhelí" ("Black Wallflower"), begins with "La mal cristiana" ("The Bad Christian Woman"), in which a female protagonist decides that it is necessary to confess her sin of omission: she has fallen asleep beneath her lover's window. Desire has been overwhelmed by a more powerful medium that keeps the lovers separated. This leads in "La maldecida" ("The Accursed Woman") to a more somber vision of the beloved:

> *quiero verte siempre enlutada.*
> . . . .
> *Porque me robas los ojos*
> *y me asesinas los labios,*
>
> . . . .
> *Porque me pisas el pecho,*
> *porque me sorbes la sangre,*
>
> . . . .
> *¡vuélvete cangrejo negro*
> *y que te traguen las aguas!*
>
> I want always to see you in mourning.
> . . . .
> Because you steal my eyes
> and you murder my lips,
>
> . . . .
> Because you step on my breast,
> because you suck up my blood,
>
> . . . .
> change into a black crab
> so the waters can swallow you!   (186–87)

In "La encerrada" ("The Confined Woman"), Alberti's helplessness is expressed in the confinement of the beloved, attributed to her will and not that of her mother, who holds the key to her room:

> *¿Para qué tanto esconderte*
> *y siempre esa mano sola,*

como una mano cortada,
para regar los claveles?

¿Por qué no quieres
que yo te vea la cara?

Why so much hiding yourself
and always that solitary hand,
like a cut hand,
to water the carnations?

Why don't you want
me to see your face?   (188)

The one-handed watering of the carnations expresses in iconic
shorthand the inadequacy of the lover's response, stemming in
part from rumors "que yo no vengo por ti, / que vengo por tus
dineros" ("that I do not come for you, / I come for your money")
(189). Such uncontrollable gossip is another indication of weakness and a further distancing from the better geography of being.
Indeed, if given the chance the beloved would not marry this
suitor ("Soñando estoy / un traje para mi boda. / —¿Conmigo? /
—No" ["I am dreaming about / a gown for my wedding. / —With
me? / —No"] [192]). At another point, Alberti's deteriorating
position is represented as a loss of vision at the hands of irresistible destructive forces ("Vinieron, vida, vinieron / los negros
quebrantahuesos / y me sacaron los ojos. / ...Y no veía" ["They
came, life, / the black ospreys came / and they scratched out my
eyes. / ... And I did not see"] [196]), a diminishment of will and
a further self-estrangement.

New personae, the prisoner of "El prisionero" and the foreigner of "El extranjero," embody alienated roles but, ironically,
also mark the intuitions of the emergence of a new representational paradigm. The narrative voice, in a familiar pattern, intercedes with the prisoner's female jailer not for his freedom but,
more modestly, for his being able to walk the streets so that he
may see again: "Que vean sus ojos los campos / y, tras los campos,
los mares, / el sol, la luna y el aire" ("May their eyes see the
fields / and, beyond the fields, the seas, / the sun, the moon, and
the air") (196). The trajectory of vision included in the request,
however, parallels the cycle already completed, which has re-

sulted in the imprisonment. It offers no solution but rather restates the prisoner's "crime." His physical circumstance, which denies him the light, leaves him isolated from the medium of vision but, for the first time, open to one that expresses itself in sound:

> —*Oído, mi blando oído,*
> *¿qué sientes tú contra el muro?*
>
> —*La voz del mar, el zumbido*
> *de este calabozo oscuro.*
>
> —Ear, my soft ear,
> what do you hear against the wall?
>
> —The voice of the sea, the buzz
> of this dark prison.   (199)

This intuition about the peculiar language of "el mar" leads in "El extranjero" to a logical conclusion: "Mi lengua natal, ¿de qué / me sirve en tierras extrañas?" ("My native language, what / good does it do me in foreign lands?") (200). It does him no good at all. A voice in the second section reacts to "Un extranjero / [que] me quiere a mí" ("A foreigner / [that] loves me"): "Yo no, porque considero / que no le voy a entender / cuando me diga: ¡Te quiero!" ("Not I, because I consider / that I am not going to understand him / when he tells me: I love you!") (200–01). More than to an amorous pretender, this protagonist is reacting to a new medium that involuntarily imposes itself and speaks a different language.

Despite the rejection of this foreign language, which exists independently of any image Alberti can manufacture, succeeding poems recount a steady undermining of the vision-dominated medium. "Torre de Iznajar" ("Tower of Iznajar") represents a prisoner content to remain in his prison ("Prisionero en esta torre, / prisionero quedaría" ["A prisoner in this tower, / a prisoner I would remain"] [206]) since it has "Cuatro ventanas al viento" ("Four windows to the wind") (206), objective means of verifying his presence there. The poem recounts the unexplainable disappearance of these windows and the subsequent realization that both the prisoner and his female friend have been effaced: "—¿Quién llora al Oeste, amiga? / —Yo, que voy muerta a tu entierro" ("—Who cries to the west wind, friend? / —I, who go dead to your funeral") (207). The reliance on vision as a primary medium has resulted in the failure of his love, the failure to find himself in his geography: "Mis ojos, mis dos amores, / se me han caído a la fuente. / Ya para mí estará ausente / la estrella de los albores" ("My eyes, my two loves, / have fallen into the fountain. / And for me will be missing / the star of the dawn") (208). All that remains to him, as he phrases it in his burlesque self-portrait "El tonto de Rafael" ("Silly Rafael"), is "el cretino eco fiel" ("the faithful cretinous echo"), the absent, irrational remnant of a desire that leaves him a "Tonto llovido del cielo / del limbo, sin un ochavo" ("Fool rained from the sky / of limbo, without a dime") (214).

In more dramatic terms in the third section, Alberti recounts the wind of irrational forces overwhelming the will that "Se ha llevado al mar, volando, / la ropa del tendedero" ("Has carried away to the sea, flying, / the clothes from the line") leaving him "en esta barca, bogando, / ... por la mar buscando / la ropa del marinero" ("in this boat, rowing, / ... through the sea looking for / the clothes of the sailor") (224). "Barcos extranjeros" ("Foreign ships") now weigh anchor at this once peaceful landscape. The initial response, to look at them ("¡Pronto, corre a verlos!" ["Quick, run and see them!"] [225]), cedes to a desire to listen ("Busco por la orilla / una concha blanca" ["I search along the shore for / a white shell"] [225]) and the awareness of the need to break the impasse of understanding by embracing a new expressive medium. This is underscored in "La marinera, el pastor, el marinero y la pastora" ("The Woman Sailor, the Shepherd, the Sailor, and the Shepherdess"), in which old players return to beg each other for an object in exchange "antes que me muera" ("before I die") (228), to which the reply is always "No, que no" ("No, no") (228). The strongly resisted suggestion is to abandon the earlier medium, the voice-that-has-been-eyes. As he turns to one of his most trustworthy consorts, the "sirenilla marinera" ("sailor siren") who has grown and now possesses a "voz de mujer" ("voice of a woman"), Alberti asks her a question that is its own answer: "¿quién querrá hacerme a mí ver / que estoy viviendo engañado / no creyéndote mentira?" ("who will want to make me see / that I am living deceived / by not believing you to be a lie?") (230). Remaining as he is or going onward requires the death ("Capaz soy yo de matarme" ["I am quite capable of killing myself"] [231]) of the earlier geography. The only question is under what conditions such a death will occur.

The original title of *Cal y canto* (figuratively, *Resistance*) (1926—27) was *Pasión y forma* (*Passion and Form*) (Salinas de Marichal 150), perhaps even more suggestive of the struggle and the growing existential-artistic impasse recounted in *El alba del alhelí*. Alberti resists the inexorable emergence of a more powerful representational paradigm centered around hearing, which overwhelms his efforts to gain dominion over himself via the production of images. In "Busca" ("Search"), for example, he asks his "can decapitado" ("beheaded dog"), a reference to the earlier greyhound that symbolizes his psychosexual energy: "¿Por dónde tú, si ardiendo en la marea / va, vengador, mi can decapitado?" ("Where do you travel, if you go burning in the tide, / avenger, my beheaded dog") (241). This force has been lost in an unknown, threatening medium. In "Amaranta," a poem named after its female protagonist, the means of this decapitation become more precise. The "Rubios, pulidos senos de Amaranta, / por una lengua de lebrel limados" ("Golden, polished breasts of Amaranta, / smoothed over by the tongue of a greyhound") (243) become symbols of an alternating light that has provided the dynamic for the earlier poetry. Here, however, the breasts are simply conduits that direct attention to a new productive locus "por el canal que asciende a tu garganta" ("through the canal that ascends to your throat") (243). Amaranta becomes an attractive-destructive force that illumines the greyhound only to imprison him "como un ascua impura, / entre Amaranta y su amador" ("like an impure coal, / between Amaranta and her lover") (243). The lover is Alberti, an equal party in the destruction (see Salinas de Marichal 157).

The destructive process continues in "El arquero y la sirena" ("The Archer and the Siren") as a siren "atenta al hilo y no a la puntería" ("attentive to the bowstring but not to the aim") embodies an idea of representation "En diez espejos rota" ("Broken into ten mirrors") (248). This is resisted in "Oso de mar y tierra" ("Bear of Land and Sea") with a new image-landscape, a

Bar en los puertos y en las interiores
ciudades navegadas de tranvías,
tras la nereida azul que en los licores

cuenta al oído y canta al marinero
coplas del mar y de sus valles frías.

Bar in the ports and in the interior
cities navigated by trolley cars,
beyond the blue Nereid that in the liquors

tells stories to the ear and sings to the sailor
verses from the sea and its cold valleys.   (250)

As the earlier paradise of "el mar" "Rompe, hirviendo, el Edén, hecha océano" ("Bursts, boiling, Eden, become ocean") (251), Alberti portrays his attempt to forestall the collapse of his representational structure with a new protagonist dependent on an artificial medium: "Dios desciende al mar en hidroplano" ("God descends to the sea in a hydroplane") (251). The unviability of such means is underscored in the "Sueño de las tres sirenas" ("Dream of the Three Sirens"), in which, among other human inventions, the hydroplane appears again in "redondo vuelo" ("circular flight") (252; see Salinas de Marichal 166–73). Alberti is confronted with an unwanted identity, the falsest of images, from which his creative means cannot save him, the narcissistic sailor of the poem "Narciso": "Narciso, tú, la insignia en el sombrero, / del club alpino, *sportman,* retratado / en el fijo cristal del camisero" ("Narcissus, you, the insignia on your hat, / of the alpine club, sportman, portrayed / in the fixed crystal of your outfitter") (254). To be associated with such an image suggests yet another unprofitable exchange of false identities and a further loss of imaginative power.

"Romeo y Julieta" ("Romeo and Juliet") suggests a continuing deterioration of Alberti's position as he loses his "Precipitada rosa" ("Cast-down rose") (262), the remains of his psychosexual energy replaced by a "rosa mecánica" ("mechanical rose"), an image as threatening as that in "Narciso." The poem "Romance que perdió el barco" ("Ballad That Lost the Boat") marks the end of the sailor as a character in the poetry while it underscores the inseparability in Alberti of the medium and its content. The demise of the sailor, who emerged from a specific mode of image production, is also the demise of the ideology that brought that mode to life. Yet as Alberti surveys his wrecked Paradise ("¡Ni mar, ni buque, ni nada!" ["No sea, or boat, or anything!"] [268]), "ángeles albañiles" ("bricklaying angels") have already descended to begin a new production that proceeds inexorably against his will:

> *—Angeles, ¿qué estáis haciendo?*
> *Derribada en tres mi frente,*
> *mina de yeso, su sangre*
> *sorben los cubos celestes,*
> *y arriba, arriba y arriba,*
> *ya en los columpios del siete,*
> *los ángeles albañiles*
> *encalan astros y hoteles.*

> —Angels, what are you building?
> My face has crumbled in three,
> a mine of plaster, the celestial cubes
> suck up its blood,
> and up, up, up,
> already in the swings of seventh heaven,
> the bricklaying angels
> whitewash stars and hotels.   (268–69)

The angels' medium is the same "puño de cal [que] paralizaba / mi lengua, pies y manos" ("fist of lime [that] paralyzed / my tongue, feet, and hands") (272), the by-product of a paralyzed will. *Cal y canto* marks the appearance of another productive medium thrice removed from a primary source. Images earlier conceived as verbal supplements to visual reality now emerge as by-products of a mode of production that expresses itself in sound, not as song but in the uncontrollable utterances that erupt from the throat. As the primary organ of perception shifts from eye to ear, the throat becomes the means by which Alberti continues to communicate with his inner geography. The empty echoes resisted in *El alba del alhelí* now become an all-inclusive medium in the "Soledad tercera" ("Third Solitude") as Alberti in the role of "joven caminante" ("young traveler") continues to flounder. This tribute to Góngora is a stylization of what has just befallen him, a youth who "vio, música segura, / volar y, estrella pura, / diluirse en la Lira, perezoso" ("lazily saw, sure music, / fly and, pure star, / become watered down in the Lyre") (275).[9]

The fifth section represents a further attempt to acknowledge the presence of the new force-medium. "Madrigal al billete del tranvía" ("Madrigal to the Trolley Car Ticket") acknowledges the presence, in the trolley ticket, of a "flor nueva" ("new flower," in contrast to the natural flowers that symbolized Alberti's psychosexual energy). Although the trolley car physically transports the traveler to a destination after the ticket is purchased, this verbal by-product of the previous exchange is the guarantor of the ride and may thus be considered the true medium of transportation. In comparison with other failed means of transport, the ticket represents another attempt to find an adequate medium to penetrate the alternative geography, his inner center: "Huyes, directa, rectamente liso, / ... a ese centro / cerrado y por cortar del compromiso" ("You flee, directly, straightly smooth, / ... to that closed / and yet to be cut center of commitment") (283). Alberti places the ticket in a "libro que viaja en la chaqueta" ("book that travels in my jacket") (283) to underscore its symbolic role as a plane medium, a language beyond desire ("no arde en ti la rosa ni en ti priva / el finado clavel" ["in you the rose does not burn nor in you does / the dead carnation deprive"] [283]) that leads to an idealized destination where the language of desire and convention ("El giratorio idioma de los faros, los vientos, detenidos" ["The gyrating language of the lighthouse beacons, the winds, stopped"] [283]) is definitively transcended. That this is clearly wishful thinking is confirmed later by another medium-that-is-a-by-product, a telegram, which underscores its unviability: "Un triángulo escaleno / asesina a un cobrador" ("a scalene triangle / assassinates a ticket seller") (292). A trolley car ticket seller is killed along with the dashed hope for an easy ride to the destinations that await.

The new poetic landscapes become cityscapes, confining and more desolate locales yet still within the Albertian geography. "Venus en ascensor" ("Venus in an Elevator") allegorizes the trajectory of his lifeless desire embodied in a mannequin Venus, a "niña, de madera / y de alambre" ("girl, of wood /

and wire") (287), as it traverses the various levels of Alberti's psychic department store in an elevator that passes a "Despacho de poesías" ("Poetry office") and a level where "Se perfila el sonido" ("Sound shows its profile") (287), exactly the phenomenon fast becoming Alberti's exclusive means of expression. The ascent produces no change in Venus, only an inventory of the store's dubious contents. The next section, "A Miss X, enterrada en el viento del oeste" ("To Miss X, Buried in the West Wind"), repeats the previous sentiments but in a much more diffuse medium. If Venus the "niña" travels by elevator in a well-defined poetic inscape, the lost and "buried" "Miss X niña" (299), of essentially the same essence, has, paradoxically, already disappeared, the only traces of her being vague memories of her superficial bourgeois milieu ("El barman, ¡oh, qué triste!" ["The barman, oh, how sad!"]) that quickly fade: "Ya nadie piensa en ti" ("Nobody thinks of you anymore") (299). Miss X fulfills the ultimate potential of Narcissus and his false way of life.

"Platko" was inspired by newspaper headlines and photographs of a Hungarian soccer goalkeeper who, in the national championship match between Barcelona and San Sebastián played on May 20, 1928, demonstrated exceptional courage in defense of the goal, for which he received a bloody head wound.[10] The poem, however, is only nominally about this soccer player. It equates the photograph and story of the bleeding goalie with the means by which Alberti has become informed about the state of his defense of his own inner space. The "Platko lejano" ("far-off Platko") of the poem bears only a superficial resemblance to the flesh and blood individual who distinguished himself in 1928. Like Platko the political symbol, the literary Platko represents the final trace of Alberti's will to resist repression, which persists only in its resonance in the memory:

> *¡Oh Platko, Platko, Platko,*
> *tú, tan lejos de Hungría!*
>
> *¿Qué mar hubiera sido capaz de no llorarte?*
>
> *Nadie, nadie se olvida,*
> *no, nadie, nadie, nadie.*

O Platko, Platko, Platko,
you, so far from Hungary!

What sea would have been capable of not weeping
    for you?

Nobody, nobody forgets,
no, nobody, nobody, nobody.   (303)

It is as nobody, an existential nullity, that an image in a newspaper also embodies Alberti's present condition of being. It is appropriate that the volume should conclude with "Carta abierta" ("Open Letter"), which declares itself a letter, and a fragment at that. Gone is the power to make images in the old manner, in the spirit of Platko: "mi alma ... bate el *record* continuo de la ausencia" ("my soul ... beats the extended record for absence") (308). He can only look back on his old self, which, in a cruel parody of his earlier desire, is now pictured at the center of the *absence* of being: ". . . tú, desde tu rosa, / desde tu centro inmóvil, sin billete, / muda la lengua, riges rey de todo. . . . / Y es que el mundo es un álbum de postales" ("you, from your rose, / from your immobile center, without a ticket, / your tongue mute, you rule as king of everything. . . . / And the world is an album of postcards") (308). By now his capitulation to the new medium is complete:

> *Vi los telefonemas que llovían,*
> *plumas de ángel azul, desde los cielos.*
> *Las orquestas seráficas del aire*
> *guardó el auricular en mis oídos.*

> I saw the telephone calls that rained,
> feathers of a blue angel, from the skies.
> The telephone receiver held
> the seraphic orchestras to my ears.   (308)

A medium has imposed itself against his will, making Alberti its instrument: "¿Quién eres tú, de acero, rayo y plomo? / —Un relámpago más, la nueva vida" ("Who are you, of steel, thunderbolt, and lead? / —One lightning flash more, the new life") (309).

In the context of the evolution of Alberti's poetry, *Sobre los ángeles* (*Concerning the Angels*) (1927–28) is simply a further exploration of a medium that expresses itself in a new language relayed by "carteros [quienes] no creen en las sirenas" ("postmen [who] do not believe in the sirens") (308), by angels. The angels, however, are of the same substance as the "ángel muerto, vigía" ("dead angel, lookout") (317) lamented in the initial poem, the dead remains of the earlier, vision-centered medium. The angels emerge as a much fainter "luz que emerge de la luz" ("light that emerges from the light"), by-products of a now untenable poetic-existential economy that nevertheless herald the new if unwanted medium.[11] Alberti entitles the prologue "Entrada" ("Entrance"), for it is something of a Dantean entrance to a hellish realm where, "muerta en mí la esperanza" ("hope dead in me"), he languishes hoping to find "ese pórtico verde" ("that green portico") (318), a means of escape from this foggy, insubstantial medium that has invited him as its involuntary guest (see Salinas de Marichal 241). Alberti has been evicted from his earlier residence, as the title "Desahucio" ("Eviction") indicates, and the angels ("ángeles malos, crueles, / quieren de nuevo alquilarla" ["bad, cruel angels / want to rent it again"] [321]) project their tormenting images toward him. Alberti must attempt to comprehend them in a light-denying medium (see especially Gagen; Morris, "Imagery").

The first angel, in "Angel desconocido" ("Unknown Angel"), is an image of Alberti himself dressed in the fashionable clothes of his alienation, as depicted earlier in "Narciso," tormented because

> *Zapatos son mis sandalias.*
> *Mi túnica, pantalones*
> *y chaqueta inglesa.*
> *Dime quien soy.*
>
> Shoes are my sandals.
> My tunic, pants,
> and English jacket.
> Tell me who I am.   (322)

It suggests that his present emptiness is a consequence of acts committed against the essence that inhabited his body: "Yo te arrojé de mi cuerpo, / yo, con un carbón ardiendo" ("I hurled you from my body, / I, with a burning coal") (322), a likely reference to his will-desire, a heat that has generated no light and that has destroyed the old geography ("Llevaba una ciudad dentro. / La perdió" ["He carried a city within. / He lost it"] [325]). The consequence is a will overwhelmed that leaves him "Sin ojos, sin voz, sin sombra" ("Without eyes, voice, shadow") (325), incapable of producing voluntarily the images that, like "fría luz en silencio / de una oculta ventana" ("cold light in silence / of a hidden window") (327), now appear involuntarily to do the will of the new medium. In the first of a number of such appearances, in "El ángel bueno" a "good angel" reveals another of the causes of his downfall: his desire to maintain a fixed position, to remain his static self forever (see Vivanco 193). The angel's words re-create the pride that has defeated him: "¡Oh anhelo, fijo mármol, / fija luz, fijas aguas / movibles de mi alma!" ("O longing, fixed marble, / fixed light, fixed movable waters / of my soul!") (328). Alberti's sin has been to make the mapping of his geography an exclusive end, leaving him will-less and, as related in "Juicio" ("Judgment"), the beneficiary-victim of a judgment: "el fallo de la luz [que] hunde su grito, / juez de sombra, en tu nada" ("the failure of the light [that] buries its scream, / a judge of shadow, in your nothingness") (329), the emergence of these angels. With each new angel, however, Alberti begins to understand. In "El ángel desengañado" ("The Undeceived Angel") he receives what amounts to an invitation ("ven a mi país" ["come to my country"] [332]) to penetrate this new realm further: "Te esperan ciudades, / sin vivos ni muertos, para coronarte" ("Cities await you, / without living or dead people, to crown you") (332). This is rejected with a counterinvitation in "Invitación al aire" ("Invitation to the Air"), a healthier sign of true disabusal that visualizes the new medium as a selfish version of the old, a "Sombra que nunca sales / de tu cueva" ("Shadow, you who never leaves / your cave") (333). It has emerged from the air, a realm of light, space, and sound, without returning "el silbo / que al nacer te dio el aire" ("the hiss / that on being born the air gave you") (333).

The second section begins with the invocation of an avenging "Angel de luz, ardiendo" ("Angel of light, burning") to vanquish his "subterráneo ángel de las nieblas" ("subterranean angel of the fogs") (339) but then to leave him alone: "¡Quémalo, ángel de luz, / quémame y huye!" ("Burn him, angel of light, / burn me and flee!") (340). The paradox of Alberti's dilemma is that in his struggle to recover from his fall he can avail himself only of the very means that have resulted in his defeat. To invoke the "angel of light" is to fall even deeper. The poem "5" recalls in more intimate, sensory detail the process of becoming estranged from being, described previously as a loss of light: "Era su luz la que cayó primero" ("It was his light that fell first") (340). This pattern of repetition suggests that, rather than being a traditional temporal progression, the various sections of *Sobre los ángeles* retrace and repeat the same experience of loss and impotence. The progression in *Sobre los ángeles,* therefore, is as much backward as it is forward. The cry in "Entrada" ("Entrance") is "¡Atrás, atrás!" ("Backward, backward!") (318), suggesting that the first section may represent a sort of purgatory while the second section seems by far the deepest and most hellish. The emphasis here is on the process of loss, which in turn leads to further insights about the productive medium that emerges from these ashes.[12]

Exerting a much more intense and direct effect on Alberti in this section, the angels force him to relive the process by which "la voz y los albedríos" ("the voice and the wills") (342) have been defeated and to face the consequences. The "ángeles de la prisa" ("hurrying angels"), an energizing force, make him aware of "los ángeles crueles" ("the cruel angels") who cannot fly. In "Engaño" ("Deception") the new medium that emerges as a consequence of the loss of will appears as a producer of words:

> *Alguien detrás, a tu espalda,*
> *tapándote los ojos con palabras.*
>
> *Detrás de ti, sin cuerpo,*
> *sin alma.*
> *Ahumada voz de sueño*
> *cortado.*

> Somebody behind, at your back,
> covering your eyes with words.
>
> Behind you, bodyless,
> without a soul.

Smoked voice of
interrupted dream. (344)

These "palabras, vidrios falsos" ("words, false glasses") have effaced his earlier identity, ascribed, in "El ángel ángel" ("The Angel Angel") to the presence of "el mar" ("Y el mar fue y le dio un nombre" ["And the sea was and it gave him a name"] [343]). Alberti senses in "El ángel del misterio" ("The Angel of Mystery") that "en las almenas grita, muerto, alguien / que yo toqué, dormido en un espejo" ("in the battlements shouts, dead, someone / who I touched, asleep in a mirror") (350), the remains of his earlier name now attempting to communicate to him in "Ecos del alma hundida en un sueño moribundo" ("Echoes of the soul sunken in a moribund dream") (351). The "ángeles mudos" ("silent angels"), who want to but cannot ask the question "¿Cómo tú por aquí y en otra parte?" ("How can you be here and in another place?") (352), and are paralleled by "Hombres, mujeres, mudos, [que] querrían ver claro" ("Men, women, silent, [who] would want to see clearly"), suggest a further penetration of the new medium that in "Alma en pena" ("Soul in Torment") is expressed even more forcefully: "te conozco aunque ataques diluido en el viento" ("I know you even though you attack diluted in the wind") (353). This brings him in "El ángel avaro" ("The Greedy Angel") to the objective image of his bankrupt self:

> *Ese hombre está muerto*
> *y no lo sabe.*
> *Quiere asaltar la banca,*
> *robar nubes, estrellas, cometas de oro,*
> *comprar lo más difícil: el cielo.*
> *Y ese hombre está muerto.*

> That man is dead
> and he doesn't know it.
> He wants to assault the bank,
> rob clouds, stars, golden comets,
> buy the most difficult thing: the sky.
> And that man is dead. (355)

This lowest point, however, is immediately followed in "Los ángeles sonámbulos" ("The Sleep-Walking Angels") by another revelation, the objective image of the medium into which he has fallen, characterized politically as a rebellion against "un rey en tinieblas" ("a king in darkness") (355), the earlier self from which he has descended. It has been a rebellion of both eye and ear, the "ojos invisibles de las alcobas" ("invisible eyes of the bedrooms") (355), the stifling inner vision that has over-whelmed Alberti's "pupilas muertas" ("dead pupils") with false images (including the angels), and "también los oídos invisibles de las alcobas" ("also the invisible ears of the bedrooms"), which "se agrandan contra el pecho" ("aggrandize themselves against the breast") and which "bajan a la garganta" ("descend to the throat") (356) to expose this king that the poet can no longer be: "Un rey es un erizo sin secreto" ("A king is a hedgehog without a secret") (356). This portrait of a medium that has superseded mimetic representation brings Alberti full circle, to the utter defeat of his earlier self and system of representation and to the threshold of a new existential-artistic paradigm.[13]

The third section marks yet another step backward in a circu-lar progression that leads even deeper to the mythical paradise from which the present conflict emerges. The "Tres recuerdos del cielo" ("Three Memories of Heaven") are approximations of what Alberti's existential prehistory ("Todo anterior al cuerpo, al nombre y al tiempo" ["Everything before the body, name, and time"] [359]) might have been like. The first memory offers an ideal vision in which it is possible to "[mirarse] sin verse" ("[look at yourself] without seeing yourself") (359), a medium of pres-ence that underscores the inadequacy of the conscious human vision irremediably distanced from, and thus incapable of repre-senting, the existential fullness (pure vision unconscious of it-self) from which he has emerged. The second remembrance corresponds to a slightly later time, yet before the emergence of the king alluded to earlier, "Cuando tú abriste en la frente sin corona ... Cuando tú, al mirarme en la nada, / inventaste la primera palabra" ("When you opened in the crownless face ... When you, on looking at me in nothingness, / invented the first word") (360). As alluded to in the "Tercer recuerdo" ("Third Memory"), this pair of ideal mediums weds to produce an off-spring, "nuestra luna primera" ("our first moon") (361), a secondary medium grounded in the interdependence of words and images whose product is consciousness, at a distance from the unmediated presence that is being. Alberti is now able to understand the rest of the story: "que el mar verdadero era un muchacho que saltaba desnudo, / invitándome a un plato de estrellas y a un reposo de algas" ("that the true sea was a boy who jumped naked, / inviting me to a plate of stars and to a repose of algae") (361). He has been sated and put to sleep by his extended love affair with his youthful self. This image lies at the heart of his crisis. He begins to realize that it is possible, through a voice-dominated medium, to affirm "que más de una ventana puede abrir con su eco otra voz, si es buena" ("that more than one window can open another voice with its echo, if it is good") (363). He thus begins to associate responsibility for his "descenso de la vía láctea a las gargantas terrestres" ("descent from the Milky Way to the terrestrial throats") (365) with the word *niño,* his earlier self, which leads to the judgment: "Para ir al infierno no hace falta cambiar de sitio ni postura" ("To go to hell it is not necessary to change place or position") (366).

Alberti is now able to undertake further exploration of a hitherto unknown and unknowable geography. Such is the theme of "Expedición" ("Expedition") and "Los ángeles colegiales" ("The School Angels"), where basic truths about his recuperating condition begin to be understood. This continues in "Novela" ("Novel"), which recounts the death of "un monarca" ("a monarch") (368), the ruler over his youth who refused to cede to a new and more mature regime, whose passing is now viewed as a self-victimization: "un suicida lento de noviembre / había olvidado en mi estancia. / Era la última voluntad de un monarca" ("a slow November suicide / I had forgotten in my room. / It was the last will of a monarch") (368). "Invitación al arpa" ("Invitation to the Harp") affirms that the new medium itself holds the key to the recovery of his powers as a poet: "Una voz desde el olvido mueve el agua dormida de los pianos" ("A voice from forgetfulness moves the sleeping water of the pianos") (370). What has seemed an oppressive medium may become instead an opportunity to understand its positive potential. Alberti raises his voice, as voice, to ask that he be heard ("Oídme.

... Oídme aún. Más todavía" ["Hear me. ... Hear me more. Still more"] [371]): "Porque siempre hay un último posterior a la caída de los páramos" ("Because there is always a last thing after the fall of the wastelands") (372). Now he simply desires "un poco de distancia: / la mínima para comprender un sueño" ("a little bit of distance: / the minimum to understand a dream") (374), which leads finally to a willingness to accept his fall in affirmative terms: "una rosa es más rosa habitada por las orugas / que sobre la nieve marchita de esta luna de quince años" ("a rose is more a rose inhabited by the caterpillars / than over the withered snow of this fifteen-year-old moon") (377). The present, in all its non-angelic ugliness, is finally preferable to the geography that has produced it. It has left Alberti, like the "ángel superviviente" ("surviving angel"), wounded, wingless but with a voice.

Sermones y moradas (*Sermons and Dwellings*) (1929–30) recounts the emergence of a new poetic voice that uses the irrational language of *Sobre los ángeles* but in a worldly context. The self-critical fall from a false paradise of prolonged youth reverses the focus of the poetry. Rather than write for himself, Alberti begins to examine his mistaken assumptions in a more public fashion. He feels compelled to tell others, to give sermons that amount to palinodes, about his disastrous existential experience: "En frío, voy a revelaros lo que es un sótano por dentro" ("Coldly, I am going to reveal the meaning of a basement from within") (383). Perhaps the most important revelation is his realization that his earlier vision-dominated mode of production is now useless in his new geography—the world of men, women, and politics—something he now claims to have known "desde el primer día que la luz se dio cuenta de su inutilidad en el mundo" ("from the first day that the light became aware of its uselessness in the world") (386). This is also the subject of "Adiós a las luces perdidas" ("Goodbye to the Lost Lights"), in which he remembers that "le dieron la vida los espejos que recogen el frío de esos ojos que se deshacen" ("the mirrors that gather the cold of those eyes that come undone gave him life") and asks for "olvido y lágrimas para las luces que se creen ya perdidas definitivamente" ("forgetfulness and tears for the lights

that believe themselves definitively lost") (390). "Se han ido"
("They Have Left") continues the self-criticism as Alberti recalls
that his crisis has been inspired by "las hojas" ("the leaves"),
perhaps a reference to the pages on which his poetry has been
written, "derrotadas por un abuso de querer ser eternas" ("defeated by an abuse of wanting to be eternal") (390), a negative
desire not to change that has finally led to a new realization:

> *Había que expatriarse involuntariamente,*
> *dejar ciertas alcobas,*
> *ciertos ecos,*
> *ciertos ojos vacíos.*

> It was necessary to expatriate oneself involuntarily,
> to leave certain bedrooms,
> certain echoes,
> certain empty eyes.   (391)

Accompanying his expulsion from his earlier paradise, however, is the realization that he has denied himself the experience
of a wider medium, the world itself: "Tenías tú que vivir más de
una media vida sin conocer las voces que ya llegan pasadas por
el mundo" ("You had to live more than half a life without knowing the voices that already come, passed on by the world")
(391). The conclusion is a positive one: "Hace ya treinta años
que ni leo los periódicos: mañana hará buen tiempo" ("It's been
thirty years since I have read the newspapers: tomorrow the
weather will be good") (391). Alberti is becoming aware of
a new commitment to the worldly counterpart of the word-
dominated medium of his crisis. As he states in "Yo anduve toda
una noche con los ojos cerrados" ("I Wandered a Whole Night
with My Eyes Closed"): "Ya a mí no me hace falta para nada
comprobar la redondez de la Tierra" ("I no longer have any
need to verify the roundness of the Earth") (393). That he has
discovered "de pronto el origen del desfallecimiento de toda
una familia" ("suddenly the origin of a whole family's weakness")
(398) does not mean that he has found the proper context
for his newer and more mature voice. In "Muro" ("Wall"), for
example, he remains as vulnerable as ever: "un hombre baja por
tabaco y en la segunda esquina le hiela su cigarro la muerte. /

Tres calles largas salen a buscarme. / No estoy" ("a man goes
down for tobacco and on the second corner death freezes his
cigar. / Three long streets go out to look for me. / I'm not there")
(403). The absent existence alluded to here has become a double
absence, but in a positive sense. Conscious of his mortality,
Alberti has abandoned his youthful paradise for a life in temporality and history. He is also absent from his earlier preoccupation
with affirming his existential presence. What remains, however,
is to fill this void.

Alberti's growing up is also a growing away from the poet he
has been. The "desfallecimiento de toda una familia," his stock of
protagonists nullified in his encounter with the voice-dominated
medium, becomes in *Yo soy un tonto y lo que he visto me ha
hecho dos tontos* (*I Am One Fool and What I Have Seen Has
Made Me Two Fools*) (also 1929) the occasion to bid farewell
to the "tonto" he has been as a consequence of "lo que he visto"
("what I have seen"), a self-critical reference via Calderón to the
vision-dominated earlier poetry. This volume may certainly be
read as referring to the movie stars (Charlie Chaplin, Harold
Lloyd, Buster Keaton, and others) listed in the titles of these
poems.[14] However, since the physical geography of Alberti's
early poetry amounts to little more than a convenient construct,
a nonmoving picture in which to set his poems, it is equally
plausible to understand that, instead of sailors or sirens, he
chooses slapstick comedians to embody physically the poetic
content, a prolonged act of self-criticism. Alberti can no longer
take seriously his earlier mode of production or the poet he has
been. This culminates in "Charles Bower, inventor," where, in
effect, Alberti-Bower, the "Difunto inventor" ("Dead inventor")
that the "tonto" Alberti once was, signs his own poem, something
of a last will and testament.

The poem begins with a lament by Bower-Alberti (Bower is
a very minor light in comparison with the other stars, an effective
non-image, a persona who fails to play the part) over "La defun-
ción ante mi chaleco de los más poéticos bosques" ("the demise
before my waistcoat of the most poetic forests") (431), the
earlier geography now lost forever. The title "inventor" may
refer to the willfully produced earlier poetry premised from the

outset on a paradigm of vision, "la creación de un fantasma" ("the creation of a phantom") (432). The poem concludes with the signature and new title "Charles Bower. / Difunto inventor" ("Charles Bower. / Dead inventor") (432). The act of signing his name marks the precise moment when Bower gives up his identity completely to another force, which adds the definitive critique. An entire paradigm of production dedicated to reading and writing "mi nombre" is declared dead. At this point, it remains for him to take the next step. It should come as no surprise that Alberti understands his becoming a political activist, a "poeta en la calle" ("poet in the street"), in terms of his having rejected his earlier vision-dominated paradigm in favor of a world- or street-centered paradigm grounded in "palabras" ("words").

From the outset of the "poetry in the street," which Alberti himself maintains begins with the long poem "Con los zapatos puestos tengo que morir" ("I Must Die with My Shoes On") (1930), also referred to as "Elegía cívica" ("Civic Elegy"), there is an attempt to link the political poetry to the earlier writing, to suggest that this mode is the logical consequence of having affirmed a new poetic paradigm. If the earlier poetry is conceived as a "luz que emerge de la luz" ("light that emerges from the light"), then the political poetry becomes a "voz pública" ("public voice") that emerges from the inner voices that bring him out of the interior geography and into the street. "Elegía cívica" becomes a political poem by virtue of Alberti's including it under the genre of poetry in the street. The poem could also have easily been placed in *Sermones y moradas* and, indeed, makes more sense in terms of its being understood as a poem in which Alberti is groping to find the voice that will shortly make him a poet in the street. In a recent study of Alberti's political poetry, Nantell considers the poem flawed as a political poem because Alberti interrupts it at various points (see also Connell; Cano Ballesta). He "forgoes investigating the causes of the social disorder in favor of listing, with surrealist rhetoric and hermetically private images, aspects of his own malaise" (Nantell 28). This is correct if "Elegía cívica" is to be read only as a political poem; "Elegía cívica" is better read, however, as a poem that establishes the ground for a poetry in the street precisely because it focuses

equally on "aspects of his own malaise." Thus when Alberti calls
out to an Aurelio and declares "que tus ojos de asco los hemos
visto derramarse sobre una muchedumbre de ranas en cualquier
plaza pública" ("that we have seen your eyes of loathing spill out
on a multitude of frogs in any public plaza") (*Calle* 22) the
remark can be taken to refer to the street or, much more aptly,
to the phenomenon of his own malaise. A vision-dominated
medium has rained down on a "multitude of frogs" and has
provided the best possible medium to provide sustenance to the
cacophony of voices (croaking of frogs is used by Lorca to
refer to the involuntary production of sound-voice-language),
precisely the "surrealistic rhetoric" (see especially Ilie) that
informs the poetry from *Cal y canto* onward. None of the images
of "Elegía cívica" is "hermetically private," especially the most
often-cited verse: "Oíd el alba de las manos arriba" ("Listen to
the dawn of the raised hands") (23), which seems to suggest
that Alberti is throwing in his lot with the clenched-fist salute of
international communism. The verb *oír,* the essence of Alberti's
new artistic paradigm, suggests that he is alluding to much more:
not simply the fact of his political conversion but also the process. Unlike Louis Aragon, who rejects surrealism to "return to
reality," Alberti is suggesting in this image that it has been the
adoption of a new medium, heard initially indoors, that has led
him to new strength (via the process of hearing) and has brought
him to the threshold of a political affirmation. "Elegía cívica" is
further evidence of a consistent attitude in Alberti toward the
mediums of art that have guided his life.

In *Poeta en la calle* (*Poet in the Street*), Alberti makes self-
conscious use of references that in an earlier context are negative
in order to suggest, to himself if nobody else, both the distance
he has come and the growth he has achieved. In "Un fantasma
recorre Europa" ("A Phantom Crosses Europe"), he uses the
phantom, earlier the symbol of his vision-dominated paradigm
of production and of the youthful self under the spell of such
image-making, to bring forth something positive: "Un fantasma
recorre Europa, el mundo. / Nosotros le llamamos camarada" ("A
phantom crosses Europe, the world. / We call him comrade")
(30). From the false phantoms of his earlier life there now

emerges the antithesis of a phantom, the embodiment of the comradeship Alberti enjoyed earlier at the Residencia de Estudiantes as a member of a new poetic generation. Comradeship is transferred to a wider medium. As "La familia" ("The Family") suggests, the new mode of poem-making brings Alberti to a new sense of family and belonging:

> *Hace falta estar ciego,*
> *tener como metidas en los ojos raspaduras de vidrio,*
> *cal viva,*
> *arena hirviendo,*
> *para no ver la luz que salta en nuestros actos,*
> *que ilumina por dentro nuestra lengua,*
> *nuestra diaria palabra.*

> It is necessary to be blind,
> to have placed, like cheap shots, glass filings in
>   your eyes,
> quicklime,
> boiling sand,
> in order not to see the light that leaps into our acts,
> that from within illumines our tongue,
> our daily word.   (55)

On the eve of the Spanish Civil War, Alberti is no longer at war with himself. The light is no longer antithetical to "nuestra lengua, / nuestra diaria palabra." Both have now united to struggle against a greater foe.

Conclusion

Poetry and Politics

These readings have been grounded in the ideological assumption that the words and images that constitute poetic form must not be considered separable from the belief system, the ideology, of a poet. Form provides the opportunity to represent a complete idea of the world that comes into being by virtue of its dialectical relationship with the value-laden words and images of reality that belong to a specific historical milieu and value standard. The labels "aesthetic" and "apolitical" as applied to Spain's modernist poetry have served only to limit the scope of critical inquiry and to suggest that the only level at which it is appropriate to speak of ideology is the political level. Such an assumption is itself ideologically motivated, as I maintained in the introduction, which examined the significant theoretical discussions over the past half century about the existence of a Generation of 1927. The image of a close-knit group of friends and collaborators supportive of each other in a variety of ways during the years preceding the Spanish Civil War is insufficient to account for the variety of distinct attitudes toward art and reality represented in their poetry. To consider that these poets share a common poetics is also to advocate a notion of artistic production fundamentally different from other aspects of cultural and historical experience as well as to ascribe too great a role to the human will as a determinant of literary form. Long-discredited "doctrines of will" so popular in Europe in the late twenties and thirties continue to underpin the Hispanic literary-historical consciousness, which suggests the need for an ongoing examination and critique of the methodological basis for Spanish literary history of the contemporary era. The concept "Generation of 1927" has hindered the breaking of new critical ground by virtue of the severe restrictions it has placed on the premises under which this poetry may be legitimately studied.

The term *modernism,* applied to most European poets of the early decades of this century, evokes the idea of a very loose, pluralistic grouping based primarily on the rejection of the representational premises of realism-naturalism. This very broad, all-inclusive concept, which applies equally to Spanish poetry, is much simpler and ultimately more descriptive of the general evolution of these poets than is their association with the many specific schools and tendencies that arose during that time. The significant differences among these poets stem from the varied ends to which their sustained anti-realist production, and not their adhesion to a momentary tendency, leads them. That only Cernuda and Guillén (who invoke respectively surrealism and imagism) acknowledge any appreciable sympathy with other European aesthetic movements suggests that these poets are conscious of processes at work in their poetry that transcend school affiliations, including nationalistic ones such as the neo-popularism under which Lorca and Alberti are often grouped. Even at its most seemingly conventional (for example, Salinas's early poetry), there is an intense dissatisfaction with ordinary reality and its modes of representation. The term *modernism* encompasses all the phases of the evolution of this production during the twenties and thirties: it posits a negative unifying concept (rejection of the representational premises of realism-naturalism) while it allows for individual interpretations of the direction that this rejection will take, positions toward art (which encompass all "isms") and existence in both an ontological and social sense that make these poets distinctive and interesting.

The poetry of Guillén, Salinas, and Aleixandre, up to 1936, is largely dedicated to the creation of alternatives to ordinary reality, private worlds that I have characterized as landscapes of will. All three poets seek an expanded consciousness or understanding and place the highest value on the affirmation of existential fullness or presence. This is accomplished by redefinitions of value relationships in the act of contemplating landscapes (Guillén), by the creation of an alternative realm where the values of full being will manifest themselves (Salinas), or by penetrating to the very ground of being to confirm one's presence there (Aleixandre). Although repeated in individual poems in Guillén, the quest for existential presence is an extended process that requires significant epistemological adjustments, typically expressed in the form of an intellectual violence perpetrated on the ordinary reality from which this poetry departs. Alongside belief in the possibility of representing the presence of being stands a theory of form and language that makes words and images into the very materials of being. Guillén's words and images fuse their separate functions as the site of consciousness effectively becomes the poem itself, understood as an activity of making present. The deepest meaning of Salinas's beloved is in the role of an alternative productive principle, the origin and site of atemporal being toward which desire, through poetry, is invariably moving him. If ordinary reality is composed of words and images, of temporal movement and sound, then the ideal realm where all can be willed present becomes its dark, silent, motionless antithesis. Aleixandre undertakes a similar quest for understanding but through more outwardly violent and irrational means as he penetrates to the center of the otherness that is being.

Compelled by forces greater than themselves to abandon private landscapes, Cernuda, Lorca, and Alberti deny the possibility of representing the fullness of being in their poetry in order to confront the world. Forced to acknowledge their irremediable distance from a full existence, they discover new standards by which to define themselves in the form of temporality and history and, ultimately, politics. The profoundly idealistic Cernuda, who, perhaps more than anyone, desires to experience an atemporal alternative reality where he can be himself, is forced to reformulate his idealism in the form of a better image, the vocation of poet, in an attempt to continue his commitment to an alternative existence in the inhospitable realm of ordinary reality. He comes to the reluctant understanding that his mission as poet requires him to deal with the world in its ugliness as well as to seek ways to affirm its fleeting and threatened beauty. Lorca's unrelenting existential impasse—a struggle between "dark forces" within himself and in the "miradas negras" ("dark glances") of society, the real content of his poetry—makes it impossible to sustain the more favorable economy of production affirmed in *Romancero gitano. Poeta en Nueva York* marks the terrible recognition that he cannot continue to seek refuge in the private worlds of his imagination. This is also the message of Alberti's poetry. Whereas Lorca never visualizes an escape from his anguish and alienation, Alberti, by virtue of a fundamental openness to his medium, is able to redeem, in political commitment, what he comes to understand as a wasted youth. In distinct contrast to the privileged status of the eye and the image of Guillén (and to a lesser extent Salinas and Aleixandre) these poets progressively affirm mediums based on a paradigm of hearing, the involuntary language of words and sounds that echo from an existential center, which they possess no means of fully knowing. If this produces an arrogant nostalgia in Cernuda and a deepening sense of tragedy in Lorca, in Alberti it leads eventually to a completely new aesthetic and existential formulation, the emergence of a new poet dedicated to the affirmation of a collective will in history greater than his own.

These differences in aesthetic and philosophical-existential contexts of the twenties and thirties become more significant still in the context of the political ideologies in which poetry is also grounded. The leftist political commitment of Alberti has been richly documented, as has been Luis Cernuda's temporary adhesion to communism and his strong initial support of the Second Republic during the Spanish Civil War before despairing of the conflict and opting for exile in England. Gibson and others have clarified the context of Lorca's assassination, a great part of the motivation for which must be understood as a direct consequence of Lorca's prominence as a supporter of the Second Republic. Lorca's poetry and drama in the supercharged political context of the thirties offer substantial political connotations, another contributing factor in his identification as a target for political elimination. As is particularly evident in Alberti but also in Lorca and Cernuda, this leftism is not accidental or ancillary to the poetry but emerges as a direct consequence of an aesthetic-existential position. The same poetry that leads these poets to painful discoveries about themselves also brings them into contact with forces that cannot be explained by recourse to bourgeois models of epistemology or consciousness. Even if these forces are given apolitical names such as "poder daimón-ico," "duende," or "el mar"—"daimonic power," "sprite," or "the sea"—these poets are describing forces that transcend the individual will-consciousness and a destiny grounded in autonomous desire.

The poetry, if not the actual politics, of Guillén, Salinas, and Aleixandre is influenced by rightist thinking. The values espoused in their poetry should not be considered bourgeois or petit bourgeois, as Cernuda, Rodríguez, and others have suggested. Engaged in its own way in a rather systematic critique of middle-class values, this poetry nevertheless evolves differently from that of younger, leftist, and more politically active poetic colleagues. Although Salinas and Guillén also leave Spain along with Cernuda and Alberti as a consequence of the Spanish Civil War, the reasons for their departure are quite different. The conservative Salinas feared assassination by leftists in the early days of the Civil War, and when he arrived in the United States in August, 1936 for a teaching position at Wellesley College, he adopted, according to Newman, an "ambiguous position" (156) regarding the war. It is clear that the private visions developed in their poetry do not bring Salinas, Guillén, and Aleixandre to the same social understanding or public commitment as other poets in their circle, who become dispersed forever as a consequence of an ideological conflict that eventually spread throughout Europe and the world.

This examination of one of the most significant literary milieus of the Spanish twentieth century has accounted for the production of literary form via subjective, interested, "better" images of reality that, while rarely articulating an overtly political position, nevertheless construct a complete system of beliefs and values, a personal ideology that demands to be studied as such. Whereas the ideological concept known as the Generation of 1927 has fostered an incomplete and limiting notion of literary history that has hindered the wider acceptance of these poets in the world community, the present study has taken a different critical direction in order to establish more relevant and universal criteria by which to open this poetry to appreciation in a wider context of historical and aesthetic understanding.

Notes

Introduction

1. For a different opinion, see Cate-Arries.
2. For an erroneous reading of Ortega's alleged role in shaping the concept of the literary generation, see Rodríguez 234–35.
3. I prefer this term to avant-garde; Bürger, however, establishes a sharp distinction between the social roles of modernist and avant-garde artists, which I find unconvincing.
4. For background discussions, see Pound and Fenollosa; Steiner 24, 99; Mitchell 29; Hulme; Bürger 20–34; Jameson; Poggioli 60–78, 174–207.

Chapter 1: Jorge Guillén

1. See Matthews 32–34; for an opposite view, see Havard 54–60.
2. See Macrí 35–36 for a different view.
3. For opposite views, see Matthews 21; Macrí 35.
4. Debicki 230–31 provides a more standard interpretation.
5. For a different view, see Frutos, "Existencialismo."
6. Most readings interpret this as a real woman; see Matthews 48–50.
7. For a different view, see Miller.
8. For a more philosophically oriented discussion, see Frutos, "Existencialismo" 199–206.
9. For a different view, see Blecua.

Chapter 2: Pedro Salinas

1. See Feal Deibe 16; Zardoya 106–12.
2. For a different interpretation, see Allen 29–31.
3. For a different view, see Stixrude 61–79.
4. For a different view, see Debicki.
5. For background discussion, see Villegas.
6. For a different view, see Feal Deibe 119–26.

Chapter 3: Vicente Aleixandre

1. See Alonso 285–87; Bousoño 64–65; Galilea 82–83.
2. For a different view, see Olivio Jiménez 10–11.
3. For a different view, see Ilie 43.
4. For a discussion, see Granados 177–81.

Chapter 4: Luis Cernuda

1. Harris, *Poetry* 66; Muñoz 116–17.
2. For a discussion, see Harris, *Poetry* 67–74; Soufas.
3. For a discussion, see Harris, *Perfil* 91–98; Capote Benot, *Período* 45–71.
4. See Molina; Olivio Jiménez for a discussion.
5. For a different opinion, see Harris, *Poetry* 30.
6. See Onís 230–37.

Chapter 5: Federico García Lorca

1. For a different view, see Allen 34–44.
2. For a more traditional reading, see Stanton.
3. Francisco García Lorca provides the most detailed analysis of this poem.
4. Binding 102–14 has detected self-referential homosexual overtones in this and the previous poem.
5. Lee provides a cogent discussion of this poem.
6. For accounts of the Lorca–Dalí friendship, see Gibson 367–79, 464–587; Auclair 136–43; Rodrigo; Rojas 234–65.
7. For more standard views concerning Lorca's Gypsies, see López-Morillas; Ramos-Gil 123.
8. For discussions of the mythic qualities of the moon, see Correa 39–82; Ramos-Gil 231–58.
9. For an interesting yet erroneous reading of this poem, based on stereotyped ideas about Spanish existential attitudes, see Eich 17–42; see also Alonso; Berenguer Carisomo 47–63.
10. Poems such as this raise questions about the desirability of interpreting Lorca's poetry from a mythic perspective, as in Correa, which seems an oversimplification.
11. For interpretations in a similar vein, see Cobb 69; Glasser.
12. Although I quote from the Spanish first edition by Bergamín, as it appears in the *Obras Completas,* I have attempted to make my discussion compatible with the considerable debate about the problematics of this text, especially among Eisenberg, García-Posada, and Martín.
13. For a succinct discussion of this theme, see Harris 23–35.
14. Garciá-Posada 68–71 provides a succinct summary of the amorous theme in this volume.
15. For a cogent statement on Lorquian ambiguity, see Predmore 4–32.

16. For a different view, see Allen 45–60.
17. For an unconvincing discussion of the idea of sacrifice in this volume, see Saez.
18. For a concise discussion of love and sex in Lorca, see Martínez Nadal 87–111.
19. Binding's apologetic interpretation of Lorca's "double attitude" (132–42) fails to understand Lorca's lifelong ambivalence to his sexuality.

Chapter 6: Rafael Alberti

1. For Alberti's opinions on his poetic milieu, see *Arboleda* 250; for a discussion of Lorca's influence, see Tejada 36–49.
2. A somewhat similar idea is developed in more formal terms by Jiménez-Fajardo.
3. For a history of this title, see Tejada 217.
4. For a much different view of image production in the early poetry, see Manteiga 17–41.
5. Spang 50 especially has noted the "el/la mar" division; for a discussion of the sea theme in *Marinero,* see Correa.
6. For a different view, see Tejada 355–57.
7. See Zardoya 402 for a different view.
8. For a different view, see González Martín 72.
9. For a discussion, see Spang 66–70.
10. See Morris, "Forgotten" 16–17. Morris overlooks the immense political symbolism of this game since the Barcelona goalie, defending against the blue and white, i.e., monarchist-colored, uniforms of the Real Sociedad de San Sebastián, becomes an immediate symbol of republican opposition to the monarchy.
11. For surveys of theories underlying the motivations for the volume, see Salinas de Marichal 204–12; Onís 154–65.
12. This view contrasts with those of Bowra 250–53; Jiménez-Fajardo 50–51; Morris, *Sobre.*
13. For a different view of this poem, see Jiménez-Fajardo 57.
14. For discussions, see Welles; Morris, *Darkness.*

Sources

Preface

Alonso, Dámaso. "Una generación poética." *Obras completas.* Vol. 4. Madrid: Gredos, 1975. 653–76.

Althusser, Louis. *Lenin and Philosophy.* Trans. Ben Brewster. London: New Left, 1971.

de Man, Paul. *Blindness and Insight: Essays in the Rhetoric of Contemporary Criticism.* 2nd ed., rev. Introduction by Wlad Godzich. Minneapolis: U of Minnesota P, 1971, 1983.

Derrida, Jacques. *Of Grammatology.* Trans. Gayatri C. Spivak. Baltimore: Johns Hopkins UP, 1976.

Eagleton, Terry. *Criticism and Ideology.* London: New Left, 1976.

Goya, Francisco de. *Los Caprichos. The Complete Etchings of Goya.* Introduction by Aldous Huxley. New York: Crown, 1943.

Jameson, Fredric. *Fables of Aggression: Wyndham Lewis, the Modernist as Fascist.* Berkeley: U of California P, 1979.

Jiménez-Fajardo, Salvador. *Multiple Spaces: The Poetry of Rafael Alberti.* London: Tamesis, 1985.

Locke, John. *Essay Concerning Human Understanding.* Ed. P. H. Nidditch. Oxford: Oxford UP, 1975.

Macherey, Pierre. *Pour une théorie de la production littéraire.* Paris: Maspero, 1970.

Marx, Karl. *The German Ideology.* Trans. R. Pascal. New York: International, 1947.

Mitchell, W. J. T. *Iconology: Image, Text, Ideology.* Chicago: U of Chicago P, 1986.

Wimsatt, William K. *The Verbal Icon.* 2nd ed. New York: Noonday, 1958.

Introduction

Alonso, Dámaso. "Una generación poética (1920–36)." *Obras completas.* Vol. 4. Madrid: Gredos, 1975. 653–76.

Azorín. "La generación de 1898." *Clásicos y modernos. Obras completas.* Vol. 12. Madrid: Caro Raggio, 1919. 233–55.

Blanco Aguinaga, Carlos. *Juventud del 98.* 2nd ed. Barcelona: Editorial Crítico, 1978.

Bürger, Peter. *Theory of the Avant-Garde.* Trans. Michael Shaw. Minneapolis: U of Minnesota P, 1984.

Cano, José Luis. *La poesía de la generación del 27.* Madrid: Guadarrama, 1973.

Cate-Arries, Francie. "Poetics and Philosophy: José Ortega y Gasset and the Generation of 1927." *Hispania* 71 (1988): 503–11.

Caturla, María Luisa. *Arte de épocas inciertas.* Madrid: Revista de Occidente, 1944.

Cernuda, Luis. *Estudios sobre poesía española contemporánea.* Madrid: Guadarrama, 1957

Debicki, Andrew P. *Estudios sobre poesía española contemporánea.* Madrid: Gredos, 1968.

Diego, Gerardo. *Poesía española: Antología.* Madrid: Signo, 1934.

Gaos, José. "Sobre sociedad e historia." *Filosofía de la filosofía e historia de la filosofía.* Mexico City: Fondo de Cultura Económica, 1947.

Gaos, Vicente. *Antología del grupo poético del 1927.* Madrid: Anaya, 1965.

González, Angel. *El grupo poético de 1927. Antología.* Madrid: Taurus, 1979.

Gullón, Ricardo. "La generación poética de 1925." *Insula* 117 (1955): 3, 12.

———. "Recuerdo de los poetas." *At Home and Abroad: New Essays on Spanish Poets of the Twenties.* Ed. Salvador Jiménez-Fajardo and John C. Wilcox. Lincoln, Neb.: Society of Spanish and Spanish American Studies, 1983. 11–22.

Heidegger, Martin. *Being and Time.* Trans. John Macquarie and Edward Robinson. New York: Harper, 1962.

Hulme, T. E. "Romanticism and Classicism." *Speculations: Essays on Humanism and the Philosophy of Art.* Ed. Herbert Read. New York: Harcourt, 1924.

Jameson, Fredric. *Fables of Aggression: Wyndham Lewis, the Modernist as Fascist.* Berkeley: U of California P, 1979.

Krauss, Rosalind. "The Photographic Conditions of Surrealism." *October,* no. 19 (1981): 3–34.

Laín Entralgo, Pedro. *Las generaciones en la historia.* Madrid: Instituto de Estudios Políticos, 1945.

Mitchell, W. J. T. *Iconology: Image, Text, Ideology.* Chicago: U of Chicago P, 1986.

Morris, C. B. *A Generation of Spanish Poets: 1920–36.* Cambridge: Cambridge UP, 1971.

Onís, Carlos Marcial de. *El surrealismo y cuatro poetas de la generación del 27.* Madrid: José Porrúa, 1974.

Ortega y Gasset, José. *El tema de nuestro tiempo. Obras completas.* Vol. 3. Madrid: Revista de Occidente, 1955.

———. *Ensayos sobre la generación del 98.* Madrid: Revista de Occidente, 1981.

———. *En torno a Galileo. Obras completas.* Vol. 5. Madrid: Revista de Occidente, 1951.

Petersen, Julius. "Las generaciones literarias." *Filosofía de la ciencia literaria.* Trans. Carlos Silva. Mexico City: Fondo de Cultura Económica, 1946. 137–93.

Poggioli, Renato. *The Theory of the Avant-Garde.* Cambridge, Mass.: Harvard-Belknap, 1968.

Pound, Ezra, and Ernest Fenollosa. *The Chinese Written Character As a Medium for Poetry.* San Francisco: City Lights, 1936.

Rodríguez, Juan Carlos. "Poesía de la miseria, miseria de la poesía (notas sobre el 27 y las vanguardias)." *La norma literaria.* Granada: Universidad de Granada, n.d. 234–71.

Rozas, Juan Manuel. *El 27 como generación.* Santander: Isla de los Ratones, 1978.

———, and Gregorio Torres Nebrera. *El grupo poético del 27.* 2 vols. Madrid: Cincel, 1980.

Salinas, Pedro. *Literatura española: Siglo XX.* Mexico City: Séneca, 1941.

Steiner, Wendy. *The Colors of Rhetoric.* Chicago: U of Chicago P, 1982.

Chapter 1: Jorge Guillén

Alvar, Manuel. *Visión en claridad: Estudios sobre "Cántico."* Madrid: Gredos, 1976.

Blanch, Antonio. "Jorge Guillén y Paul Valéry." *La poesía pura española.* Madrid: Gredos, 1976. 284–303.

Blecua, José Manuel. "El tiempo en la poesía de Jorge Guillén." *Jorge Guillén.* Ed. Biruté Ciplijauskaité. Madrid: Taurus, 1975. 183–88.

Casalduero, Joaquín. *"Cántico" de Jorge Guillén y "Aire nuestro."* Madrid: Gredos, 1974.

Ciplijauskaité, Biruté, ed. *Jorge Guillén.* Madrid: Taurus, 1975.

Debicki, Andrew. *La poesía de Jorge Guillén.* Madrid: Gredos, 1973.

Diego, Gerardo. *Poesía española: Antología.* Madrid: Signo, 1934.

Frutos, Eugenio. "The Circle and Its Rupture in the Poetry of Jorge Guillén." *Luminous Reality: The Poetry of Jorge Guillén.* Ed. Ivar Ivask and Juan Marichal. Norman: U of Oklahoma P, 1969. 75–81.

———. "El existencialismo jubiloso de Jorge Guillén." *Jorge Guillén.* Ed. Biruté Ciplijauskaité. Madrid: Taurus, 1975. 189–206.

Guillén, Jorge. *Cántico.* 2nd ed. Madrid: Cruz y Raya, 1936.

———. "Una generación." *El argumento de la obra.* Barcelona: Sinera, 1969. 7–42.

Havard, Robert G. *Cántico.* London: Grant and Cutler, 1986.

Ivask, Ivar, and Juan Marichal, eds. *Luminous Reality: The Poetry of Jorge Guillén.* Norman: U of Oklahoma P, 1969.

Kern, Stephen. *The Culture of Time and Space.* Cambridge: Harvard UP, 1983.

MacCurdy, G. Grant. *Jorge Guillén.* Boston: Twayne, 1982.

Macrí, Oreste. *La obra poética de Jorge Guillén.* Barcelona: Ariel, 1976.

Matthews, Elizabeth. *The Structured World of Jorge Guillén.* Liverpool: Francis Cairns, 1985.

Miller, Martha Lafollete. "'Transcendence through Love in Jorge Guillén's *Cántico:* The Conciliation of Inner and Outer Reality." *MLN* 92 (1977): 312–25.

Poulet, Georges. "Jorge Guillén y el tema del círculo." *Jorge Guillén.* Ed. Biruté Ciplijauskaité. Madrid: Taurus, 1975. 241–46.

Silver, Philip. "Poulet, Guillén y la imaginación poética española." *Revista de Occidente* 38 (1972): 79–85.

Xirau, Ramón. "Lectura a 'Cántico.'" *Jorge Guillén.* Ed. Biruté Ciplijauskaité. Madrid: Taurus, 1975. 129–40.

Zardoya, Concha. "Jorge Guillén y Paul Valéry." *Poesía española del siglo XX.* Vol. 2. Madrid: Gredos, 1974. 168–219. 4 Vols.

Chapter 2: Pedro Salinas

Allen, Rupert C. *Symbolic Experience: A Study of Poems by Pedro Salinas.* University: U of Alabama P, 1982.

Debicki, Andrew P. "La metáfora en algunos poemas tempranos de Salinas." *Pedro Salinas.* Ed. Andrew P. Debicki. Madrid: Taurus, 1976. 113–18.

Diego, Gerardo. *Poesía española: Antología.* Madrid: Signo, 1934.

Feal Deibe, Carlos. *La poesía de Pedro Salinas.* 2nd ed. Madrid: Gredos, 1970.

González Muela, Joaquín. "Poesía y amistad: Jorge Guillén y Pedro Salinas." *Pedro Salinas.* Ed. Andrew P. Debicki. Madrid: Taurus, 1976. 197–206.

Guillén, Jorge. Prologue. *Pedro Salinas: El diálogo creador.* By Alma de Zubizarreta. Madrid: Gredos, 1969. 9–19.

Havard, Robert G. "Pedro Salinas and Courtly Love: The 'amada' in *La voz a ti debida:* Woman, Muse, and Symbol." *Bulletin of Hispanic Studies* 56 (1979): 123–44.

Palley, Julian. *La luz no usada: La poesía de Pedro Salinas.* Mexico City: Andrea, 1966.

Salinas, Pedro. *Poesías completas.* 2nd ed. Ed. Soledad Salinas de Marichal. Barcelona: Barral, 1975.

———. *La realidad y el poeta.* Ed. Soledad Salinas de Marichal. Barcelona: Ariel, 1976.

Stixrude, David L. *The Early Poetry of Pedro Salinas.* Madrid: Princeton U Dept. of Romance Languages, 1975.

Villegas, Juan. "El amor y la salvación existencial en dos poemas de Pedro Salinas." *PMLA* 85 (1970): 205–11.

Zardoya, Concha. "La 'otra' realidad de Pedro Salinas." *Poesía española del siglo XX.* Vol 2. Madrid: Gredos, 1974. 106–48. 4 vols.

Chapter 3: Vicente Aleixandre

Aleixandre, Vicente. *Obras completas.* Prologue by Carlos Bousoño. Madrid: Aguilar, 1968.

Alonso, Dámaso. "La poesía de Vicente Aleixandre." *Poetas españoles contemporáneos.* Madrid: Gredos, 1952. 281–317.

Bousoño, Carlos. *La poesía de Vicente Aleixandre.* 3rd ed. Madrid: Gredos, 1977.

Carnero, Guillermo. "*Ambito* dentro de la obra de Vicente Aleixandre." *Vicente Aleixandre: A Critical Appraisal.* Ed. Santiago Daydi-Tolson. Ypsilanti, Mich.: Bilingual, 1981. 94–103.

Colinas, Antonio. *Conocer Vicente Aleixandre y su obra.* Barcelona: Dopesa, 1977.

Daydi-Tolson, Santiago, ed. *Vicente Aleixandre: A Critical Appraisal.* Ypsilanti, Mich.: Bilingual, 1981.

Galilea, Hernán. *La poesía superrealista de Vicente Aleixandre.* Santiago, Chile: Espejo de Papel, 1971.

Granados, Vicente. *La poesía de Vicente Aleixandre (formación y evolución).* Madrid: Planeta, 1977.

Ilie, Paul. "Descent and Castration (Aleixandre)." *The Surrealist Mode in Spanish Literature.* Ann Arbor: U of Michigan P, 1968. 40–56.

Molho, Mauricio. "La aurora insumisa de Vicente Aleixandre." *Vicente Aleixandre.* Ed. José Luis Cano. Madrid: Taurus, 1977. 139–43.

Novo Villaverde, Yolanda. *Vicente Aleixandre, poeta surrealista.* Santiago de Compostela: Universidad, 1980.

Olivio Jiménez, José. *Vicente Aleixandre.* Madrid: Júcar, 1981.

Puccini, Darío. *La palabra poética de Vicente Aleixandre.* Barcelona: Ariel, 1979.

Schwartz, Kessel. *Vicente Aleixandre.* New York: Twayne, 1970.

Volek, Emil. "Entre el *id* y la utopía mística: la oscura revelación y la modernidad en la poesía de Vicente Aleixandre." *Cuatro claves para la modernidad: Análisis semiótico de textos hispánicos.* Madrid: Gredos, 1984. 19–87.

Chapter 4: Luis Cernuda

Aguirre, J. M. *Primeras poesías* de Luis Cernuda." *Luis Cernuda.* Ed. Derek Harris. Madrid: Taurus, 1977. 215–27.

Capote Benot, José María. *El período sevillano de Luis Cernuda.* Prologue by F. López Estrada. Madrid: Gredos, 1971.

———. *El surrealismo en la poesía de Luis Cernuda.* Sevilla: Universidad de Sevilla, 1976.

Cernuda, Luis. *La realidad y el deseo.* Ed. Miguel J. Flys. Madrid: Castalia, 1982.

———. *Prosa completa.* Ed. Derek Harris and Luis Maristany. Barcelona: Barral Editores, 1975.

Delgado, Agustín. *La poética de Luis Cernuda.* Madrid: Editora Nacional, 1975.

Gil de Biedma, Jaime. "El ejemplo de Luis Cernuda." *Luis Cernuda.* Ed. Derek Harris. Madrid: Taurus, 1977. 124–28.

Goytisolo, Juan. "Cernuda y la crítica literaria española." *El furgón de cola.* Paris: Ruedo Ibérico, 1967. 86–97.

Harris, Derek, ed. *Luis Cernuda.* Madrid: Taurus, 1977.

————. *Luis Cernuda: A Study of the Poetry.* London: Tamesis, 1973.

————, ed. *Perfil del aire.* London: Tamesis, 1971.

Jiménez-Fajardo, Salvador. *Luis Cernuda.* Boston: Twayne, 1978.

Molina, Ricardo. "La conciencia trágica del tiempo, clave esencial de la poesía de Luis Cernuda." *Luis Cernuda.* Ed. Derek Harris. Madrid: Taurus, 1977. 102–10.

Muñoz, Jacobo. "Pensamiento poético en Luis Cernuda." *Luis Cernuda.* Ed. Derek Harris. Madrid: Taurus, 1977. 111–23.

Olivio Jiménez, José. "Emoción y trascendencia del tiempo en la poesía de Luis Cernuda." *La caña gris* (Valencia) 6–8 (1962): 54–83.

Onís, Carlos Marcial de. "Luis Cernuda." *El surrealismo y cuatro poetas de la generación del 27.* Madrid: José Porrúa, 1974. 209–44.

Paz, Octavio. "La palabra edificante." *Papeles de Son Armadans* 36 (1964): 41–82.

Silver, Philip. *"Et in Arcadia Ego": A Study of the Poetry of Luis Cernuda.* London: Tamesis, 1965.

Soufas, C. Christopher, Jr. "Cernuda and Daimonic Power." *Hispania* 66 (1983): 167–75.

Summerhill, Stephen J. *"Un río, un amor:* Cernuda's Flirtation with Surrealism." *Journal of Spanish Studies, Twentieth Century* 6 (1978): 131–57.

Valdés, Jorge H. "La aportación de *Egloga, elegía, oda* a la evolución poética de Luis Cernuda." *At Home and Beyond: New Essays on Spanish Poets of the Twenties.* Ed. Salvador Jiménez-Fajardo and John C. Wilcox. Lincoln, Neb.: Society of Spanish and Spanish American Studies, 1983. 97–112.

Valender, James. *Cernuda y el poema en prosa.* London: Tamesis, 1984.

Chapter 5: Federico García Lorca

Allen, Rupert. *The Symbolic World of Federico García Lorca.* Albuquerque: U of New Mexico P, 1972.

Alonso, Dámaso. "Federico García Lorca y la expresión de lo español." *Obras completas.* Vol. 4. Madrid: Gredos, 1975. 758–66.

Auclair, Marcelle. *Vida y muerte de García Lorca.* Mexico City: Ediciones Era, 1972.

Berenguer Carisomo, Arturo. *Las máscaras de Federico García Lorca.* Buenos Aires: Editorial Universitaria, 1969.

Binding, Paul. *Lorca: The Gay Imagination.* London: GMP, 1985.

Cobb, Carl. *Federico García Lorca.* Boston: Twayne, 1967.

Correa, Gustavo. *La poesía mítica de Federico García Lorca.* Madrid: Gredos, 1970.

Durán, Manuel, ed. *Lorca.* Englewood Cliffs, N.J.: Prentice-Hall, 1962.

Eich, Christoph. *Federico García Lorca: Poeta de la intensidad.* Madrid: Gredos, 1970.

Eisenberg, Daniel. *Poeta en Nueva York: historia y problemas de un texto de Lorca.* Barcelona: Ariel, 1976.

García Lorca, Federico. *Obras completas,* 2 vols. Ed. Arturo del Hoyo. 20th ed. Madrid: Aguilar, 1978.

————. *Poeta en Nueva York: Tierra y luna.* Crit. ed. Eutimio Martín. Barcelona: Ariel, 1981.

García Lorca, Francisco. "Córdoba, lejana y sola." *Federico García Lorca.* Ed. Ildefonso-Manuel Gil. Madrid: Taurus, 1980. 275–86.

García-Posada, Miguel. *Lorca: Interpretación de "Poeta en Nueva York."* Madrid: Akal, 1981.

Gibson, Ian. *Federico García Lorca. De Fuente Vaqueros a Nueva York (1898–1929).* Barcelona: Grijalbo, 1985.

Gil, Ildefonso-Manuel, ed. *Federico García Lorca.* Madrid: Taurus, 1980.

Glasser, Doris Margaret. "Lorca's 'Burla de don Pedro a caballo.' " *Hispania* 47 (1964): 295–301.

Harris, Derek. *Federico García Lorca: Poeta en Nueva York.* London: Grant and Cutler–Tamesis, 1978.

Laffranque, Marie. *Les idées esthétiques de Federico García Lorca.* Paris: Centre de Recherches Hispaniques, 1967.

Lee, Cecilia Castro. "La 'Oda a Salvador Dalí': Significación y trascendencia en la vida y creación de Lorca y Dalí." *Anales de la literatura española contemporánea* 11 (1986): 61–78.

López-Morillas, Juan. "García Lorca y el primitivismo lírico: reflexiones sobre el *Romancero gitano.*" *Federico García Lorca.* Ed. Ildefonso-Manuel Gil. Madrid: Taurus, 1980. 311–26.

Loughran, David K. *Federico García Lorca: The Poetry of Limits.* London: Tamesis, 1978.

Martínez Nadal, Rafael. *Cuatro lecciones sobre Federico García Lorca.* Madrid: Fundación Juan March, 1980.

Predmore, Richard L. *Lorca's New York Poetry: Social Injustice, Dark Love, Lost Faith.* Durham, N.C.: Duke UP, 1980.

Ramos-Gil, Carlos. *Claves líricas de García Lorca.* Madrid: Aguilar, 1967.

Rodrigo, Antonina. *Lorca–Dalí: Una amistad traicionada.* Barcelona: Planeta, 1981.

Rojas, Carlos. *El mundo mítico y mágico de Salvador Dalí.* Barcelona: Plaza y Janés, 1985.

Saez, Richard. "Ritual Sacrifice in Lorca's *Poet in Nueva York.*" Manuel Durán, ed. *Lorca.* Englewood Cliffs, N.J.: Prentice-Hall, 1962. 108–29.

Serrano Poncela, Segundo. "Lorca y los unicornios." *Federico García Lorca.* Ed. Ildefonso-Manuel Gil. Madrid: Taurus, 1980. 201–06.

Stanton, Edward F. *The Tragic Myth: Lorca and Cante Jondo.* Lexington: UP of Kentucky, 1978.

Zardoya, Concha. "Los espejos de Federico García Lorca." *Poesía española del siglo XX.* Vol. 3. Madrid: Gredos, 1974. 75–119. 4 vols.

Zuleta, Emilia de. "La poesía de Federico García Lorca." *Cinco poetas españoles.* Madrid: Gredos, 1971. 168–272.

Chapter 6: Rafael Alberti

Alberti, Rafael. *La arboleda perdida.* Barcelona: Seix Barral, 1975.

———. *Poesía (1924–1967).* Ed. Aitana Alberti. Madrid: Aguilar, 1972.

———. *El poeta en la calle.* Ed. Aitana Alberti. Madrid: Aguilar, 1978.

Bowra, Cecil M. "Rafael Alberti, 'Sobre los ángeles.' " *The Creative Experiment.* New York: Grove, 1948. 250–53.

Cano Ballesta, Juan. "La poesía revolucionaria: Rafael Alberti" and "Rafael Alberti, poeta revolucionario (1934–36)." *La poesía española entre pureza y compromiso.* Madrid: Gredos, 1972. 112–28, 195–200.

Connell, Geoffrey W. "The End of a Quest: Alberti's *Sermones y moradas* and Three Uncollected Poems." *Hispanic Review* 33 (1965): 290–309.

Correa, Gustavo. "El simbolismo del mar en *Marinero en tierra.*" *Rafael Alberti.* Ed. Manuel Durán. Madrid: Taurus, 1975. 111–17.

Debicki, Andrew P. "El 'correlativo objetivo' en la poesía temprana de Rafael Alberti." *Estudios sobre la poesía española contemporánea.* Madrid: Gredos, 1968. 224–61.

Durán, Manuel, ed. *Rafael Alberti.* Madrid: Taurus, 1975.

Gagen, Derek. "'Thy Fading Mansion': The Image of the Empty House in Rafael Alberti's *Sobre los ángeles.*" *Bulletin of Hispanic Studies* 64 (1987): 225–36.

González Martín, G. Pablo. *Rafael Alberti.* Madrid: Júcar, 1974.

Ilie, Paul. "Surrealist Rhetoric (Alberti)." *The Surrealist Mode in Spanish Literature.* Ann Arbor: U of Michigan P, 1968. 121–30.

Jiménez-Fajardo, Salvador. *Multiple Spaces: The Poetry of Rafael Alberti.* London: Tamesis, 1985.

Manteiga, Robert C. *The Poetry of Rafael Alberti: A Visual Approach.* London: Tamesis, 1978.

Morris, C. Brian. "Forgotten Idols: Miss X and Charley Bowers." *Siglo XX / 20th Century* 3 (1985–86): 15–23.

———. "Parallel Imagery in Quevedo and Alberti." *Bulletin of Spanish Studies* 36 (1959): 135–45.

———. *Rafael Alberti's "Sobre los ángeles": Four Major Themes.* Hull: U of Hull, 1966.

———. *Surrealism and Spain (1920–1936).* Cambridge: Cambridge UP, 1972.

———. *This Loving Darkness: The Cinema and the Spanish Writers, 1920–36.* Oxford: Oxford UP, 1980.

Nantell, Judith. *Rafael Alberti's Poetry of the Thirties: The Poet's Public Voice.* Athens: U of Georgia P, 1986.

Onís, Carlos Marcial de. "Rafael Alberti." *El surrealismo y cuatro poetas de la generación del 27.* Madrid: José Porrúa, 1974. 151–207.

Salinas de Marichal, Solita. *El mundo poético de Rafael Alberti.* Madrid: Gredos, 1968.

Spang, Kurt. *Inquietud y nostalgia: La poesía de Rafael Alberti.* Pamplona: Universidad de Navarra, 1973.

Tejada, José Luis. *Rafael Alberti, entre la tradición y la vanguardia.* Madrid: Gredos, 1976.

Vivanco, Luis Felipe. "Rafael Alberti en su palabra acelerada y vestida de luces." *Rafael Alberti.* Ed. Manuel Durán. Madrid: Taurus, 1975. 181–204.

Welles, Marcia. "Lorca, Alberti and 'los tontos del cine mudo.' " *At Home and Beyond: New Essays on Spanish Poets of the Twenties.* Ed. Salvador Jiménez-Fajardo and John C. Wilcox. Lincoln, Neb.: Society of Spanish and Spanish American Studies, 1983. 113–25.

Zardoya, Concha. "La técnica metafórica altertiana." *Poesía española del siglo XX.* Vol. 3. Madrid: Gredos, 1974. 399–445. 4 vols.

Conclusion: Poetry and Politics

Cernuda, Luis. "Pedro Salinas." *Estudios sobre la poesía española contemporánea.* Madrid: Guadarrama, 1957. 197–206.

Gibson, Ian. *La represión nacionalista en Granada en 1936 y la muerte de Federico García Lorca.* Paris: Ruedo Ibérico, 1971.

Newman, Jean Cross. *Pedro Salinas and His Circumstance.* San Juan, P.R.: Inter American UP, 1983.

Rodríguez, Juan Carlos. "Poesía de la miseria, miseria de la poesía (notas sobre el 27 y las vanguardias)." *La norma literaria.* Granada: Universidad de Granada, n.d. 234–71.

Other Works Consulted

General Works

Bodini, Vittorio. *Los poetas surrealistas españoles.* Barcelona: Tusquets, 1971.

Bousoño, Carlos. *Teoría de la expresión poética.* 5th ed. 2 vols. Madrid: Gredos, 1970.

——. *El irracionalismo poético (el símbolo).* Madrid: Gredos, 1977.

Brihuega, Jaime. *Manifiestos, proclamas, panfletos y textos doctrinales. Las vanguardias artísticas en España. 1910–1931.* Madrid: Cátedra, 1979.

——. *La vanguardia y la República.* Madrid: Cátedra, 1982.

Buckley, Ramón, and John Crispin. *Los vanguardistas españoles (1925–1935).* Madrid: Alianza Editorial, 1973.

Cabrera, Vicente. *Tres poetas a la luz de la metáfora: Salinas, Aleixandre y Guillén.* Madrid: Gredos, 1975.

Cano, José Luis. *Antología de los poetas del 27.* Madrid: Espasa-Calpe, 1982.

Connell, Geoffrey N. *Spanish Poetry of the "Grupo Poético de 1927."* Oxford: Pergamon, 1977.

Corbalán, Pablo. *Poesía surrealista en España.* Madrid: Centro, 1974.

Darmangeat, Pierre. *Antonio Machado, Pedro Salinas, Jorge Guillén.* Madrid: Insula, 1969.

Dehennin, Elsa. *La résurgence de Góngora et la génération poétique de 1927.* Paris: Didier, 1962.

Díez de Revenga, Francisco Javier. *La métrica de los poetas del 27.* Murcia: Universidad de Murcia, 1973.

Geist, Anthony J. *La poética de la generación del 27 y las revistas literarias: De la vanguardia al compromiso (1918–36).* Barcelona: Labor-Guadarrama, 1980.

González Muela, Joaquín, and Juan Manuel Rozas. *La generación poética de 1927.* Madrid: Alcalá, 1974.

Ilie, Paul. *The Surrealist Mode in Spanish Literature.* Ann Arbor: U of Michigan P, 1968.

——, ed. *Documents of the Spanish Vanguard.* Chapel Hill: N.C. Studies in the Romance Languages, 1969.

Laín Entralgo, Pedro. *La generación del noventa y ocho.* 4th ed. Madrid: Espasa-Calpe, 1959.

Marco, Joaquín. "¿Generación del 27? Algunos problemas pendientes." *Insula.* 368–69 (1977): 28.

Marías, Julián. *El método histórico de las generaciones.* Madrid: Revista de Occidente, 1967.

Morris, C. B. *Surrealism and Spain: 1920–36.* Cambridge: Cambridge UP, 1972.

Neira, Julio. *"Litoral,"* *la revista de una generación.* Santander: Isla de los Ratones, 1978.

Rojo Martí, María del Rosario. *Evolución del movimiento vanguardista. Estudio basado en "La gaceta literaria" (1927–1932).* Madrid: Fundación Juan March, 1982.

Romero, Hector, ed. *Nuevas perspectivas sobre la "Generación del 27."* Miami: Universal, 1983.

Siebenmann, Gustav. *Los estilos poéticos en España desde 1900.* Madrid: Gredos, 1973.

Zuleta, Emilia de. *Cinco poetas españoles.* Madrid: Gredos, 1971.

Works on Specific Poets

Jorge Guillén

Bernáldez Bernáldez, José M. "Jorge Guillén, la poesía como existencia." *Cuadernos hispanoamericanos* 318 (1976): 626–33.

Blecua, José Manuel, and Ricardo Gullón. *La poesía de Jorge Guillén: Dos ensayos.* Zaragoza: Heraldo de Aragón, 1949.

Bobes Naves, María del Carmen. *Gramática de "Cántico" (análisis semiológico).* Barcelona: Planeta, 1975.

Cervantes, Alfonso. "Empirical Observation and Speculation in Jorge Guillén's *Cántico." Journal of Spanish Studies: Twentieth Century* 6 (1978): 97–106.

Ciplijauskaité, Biruté. *Deber de plenitud, la poesía de Jorge Guillén.* Mexico City: Sepsetentas, 1973.

Close, L. J. "Guillén and the Aristotelian Tradition." *Studies in Modern Spanish Literature and Art.* Ed. Nigel Glendinning. London: Tamesis, 1972. 45–64.

Costa, Luis. "La expresión vital: Jorge Guillén y José Ortega y Gasset." *At Home and Beyond: New Essays on Spanish Poets of the Twenties.* Ed. Salvador Jiménez-Fajardo and John C. Wilcox. Lincoln, Neb.: Society of Spanish and Spanish American Studies, 1983. 37–52.

Dehennin, Elsa. *"Cántico" de Jorge Guillén: Une Poésie de la clarté.* Brussels: Presses Universitaires de Bruxelles, 1969.

Gil de Biedma, Jaime. *El mundo y la poesía de Jorge Guillén.* Barcelona: Seix Barral, 1960.

González Muela, Joaquín. *La realidad y Jorge Guillén.* Madrid: Insula, 1962.

Havard, Robert G. "La metafísica de *Cántico:* Jorge Guillén, Ortega, Husserl y Heidegger." *Sin Número* 14 (1984): 54–71.

————. "The Early *décimas* of Jorge Guillén." *Bulletin of Hispanic Studies* 48 (1971): 111–27.

Olson, Paul R. "Language and Reality in Jorge Guillén." *Hispanic Review* 34 (1966): 149–54.

Pinet, Carolyn E. "The Sacramental View of Poetry and the Religion of Love in Jorge Guillén's *Cántico.*" *Hispania* 62 (1979): 209–18.

Polo de Bernabe, José Manuel. *Conciencia y lenguaje en la obra de Jorge Guillén.* Madrid: Alfar, 1977.

Rodríguez, Israel. *La metáfora en las estructuras poéticas de Jorge Guillén y Federico García Lorca.* Madrid: Hispanova, 1977.

Ruiz-de-Conde, Justina, et al., eds. *Homenaje a Jorge Guillén* (Wellesley College, Department of Spanish). Madrid: Insula, 1978.

Sibbald, K. M. *Hacia "Cántico": Escritos de los años veinte.* Barcelona: Ariel, 1980.

————. "Some Early Versions of the Poems of *Cántico* 1919–1928: Progress towards *claridad.*" *Bulletin of Hispanic Studies* 50 (1973): 23–44.

————. "T. S. Eliot and Jorge Guillén: Towards a 'Revolutionary' Classicism." *At Home and Beyond: New Essays on Spanish Poets of the Twenties.* Ed. Salvador Jiménez-Fajardo and John C. Wilcox. Lincoln, Neb.: Society of Spanish and Spanish American Studies, 1983. 87–96.

Pedro Salinas

Baeza Betancourt, Felipe. *La amada más discreta: Ensayos sobre "La voz a ti debida" de Pedro Salinas.* Las Palmas, Canary Islands: El Museo Canario, 1967.

Cabrera, Vicente. " 'Suicidio hacia arriba' de Pedro Salinas." *Romance Notes* 13 (1971): 221–25.

Cirré, José F. *El mundo lírico de Pedro Salinas.* Granada: Don Quijote, 1982.

Costa Viva, Olga. *Pedro Salinas frente a la realidad.* Madrid: Alfaguara, 1969.

Crispin, John. *Pedro Salinas.* Boston: Twayne, 1974.

Debicki, Andrew P. "La visión de la realidad en la poesía temprana de Pedro Salinas." *Estudios sobre poesía española contemporánea.* Madrid: Gredos, 1968. 56–83.

————. "The Play of Difference in the Early Poetry of Pedro Salinas." *MLN* 100 (1985): 265–80.

Dehennin, Elsa. *Passion d'absolute et tension expressive dans l'oeuvre poétique de Pedro Salinas.* Gent: Rijksuniversite Gent, 1957.

Feal Deibe, Carlos. *La poesía de Pedro Salinas.* 2nd ed. Madrid: Gredos, 1970.

————. "'Thou Wonder, and thou Beauty, and thou Terror': La poesía amorosa de Pedro Salinas." *MLN* 94 (1979): 283–300.

Friedman, Edward H. "Poetic Duality in Pedro Salinas's *Seguro azar.*" *Language Quarterly* 16 (1977): 51–52, 60.

Guillén, Jorge. "Pedro Salinas." *MLN* 82 (1968): 135–48.

Havard, Robert G. "The Reality of Words in the Poetry of Pedro Salinas." *Bulletin of Hispanic Studies* 51 (1974): 28–47.

_____. "The Ironic Rationality of *Razón de amor*: Pedro Salinas: Logic, Language, and Reality." *Orbis Literarium* 38 (1983): 351–70.

Helman, Edith. "A Way of Seeing: 'Nubes en la mano' by Pedro Salinas." *Hispanic Review* 45 (1977): 359–84.

Marichal, Juan. "Pedro Salinas: La voz a la confidencia debida." *Revista de occidente* 9 (1962): 435–42.

_____. *Tres voces de Pedro Salinas.* Madrid: Josefina Betancor, 1976.

Morris, C. B. "*Visión* and *mirada* in the Poetry of Salinas, Guillén, and Dámaso Alonso." *Bulletin of Hispanic Studies* 38 (1961): 103–12.

Rogers, Daniel. "Espejo y reflejos en la poesía de Pedro Salinas." *Revista de literatura* 29 (1966): 57–87.

Vila Selma, José. *Pedro Salinas.* Madrid: Epesa, 1972.

Vicente Aleixandre

Alvarez Villar, Alfonso. "El panteísmo en la obra poética de Vicente Aleixandre." *Cuadernos hispanoamericanos* 175–76 (1964): 178–84.

Bourne, Louis M. "The Spiritualization of Matter in the Poetry of Vicente Aleixandre." *Revista de letras* 6 (1974): 166–89.

Cabrera, Vicente, and Harriet Boyer, eds. *Critical Views on Vicente Aleixandre's Poetry.* Lincoln, Neb.: Society of Spanish and Spanish American Studies, 1979.

Cano, José Luis, ed. *Vicente Aleixandre.* Madrid: Taurus, 1977.

Connell, Geoffrey. "'Posesión' and the Origins of Aleixandre's Cosmic Sensuality." *Revista de letras* 6 (1974): 204–09.

Del Villar, Arturo. "Vicente Aleixandre o el diálogo cósmico." *Arbor* 381–82 (1977): 65–72.

Fernández-Morera, Darío. "Vicente Aleixandre in the Context of Modern Poetry." *Symposium* 33 (1979): 118–41.

Galbis, Ignacio R. M. "The Scope of *Ambito*: Aleixandre's First Cosmic Vision." *Revista de letras* 6 (1974): 253–62.

Gimferrer, Pere. Prologue. *Vicente Aleixandre: Antología total.* Barcelona: Seix Barral, 1975. 9–32.

Harris, Derek. "Spanish Surrealism: The Case of Vicente Aleixandre and Rafael Alberti." *Forum for Modern Language Studies* 18 (1982): 159–71.

Herter, Hugh A. "El concepto del amor en *La destrucción o el amor* de Vicente Aleixandre." *Hispanófila* (Madrid) 32 (1968): 28–32.

Luis, Leopoldo de. *Vida y obra de Vicente Aleixandre.* Prologue by Ramón de Garciasol. Madrid: Espasa-Calpe, 1978.

Miró, Emilio. "El 'otro' en la poesía de Vicente Aleixandre." *Cuadernos hispanoamericanos* 196 (1966): 390–97.

Onís, Carlos Marcial de. "Vicente Aleixandre." *El surrealismo y cuatro poetas de la generación del 27.* Madrid: José Porrúa, 1974. 245–88.

Personneaux, Lucie. *Vicente Aleixandre o une poésie du suspens.* Montpellier: Université de Montpellier, 1980.

Valente, José Angel. "Vicente Aleixandre: La visión de la totalidad." *Indice* 17 (1963): 29–30.

Villena, Luis Antonio de. "La luna, astro fiel del 'primer Aleixandre' (algo sobre *Mundo a solas*)." *Insula* 368–69 (1977): 8, 33.

Luis Cernuda

Barnette, Douglas. "Luis Cernuda y su generación: La creación de una leyenda." *Revista de estudios hispánicos* 18 (1984): 123–32.

Barón, Emilio. "Soledad en Cernuda." *Cuadernos americanos* 231 (1980): 248:55.

Brines, Francisco. "Ante unas poesías completas." *La caña gris* 6–8 (Fall 1962): 117–53.

Cacheiro, Maximino. "La problemática del escrito en *La realidad y el deseo*." *Cuadernos hispanoamericanos* 316 (1976): 54–60.

Couso Cadhaya, J. Luis. "Búsqueda de lo absoluto en la poesía de Luis Cernuda." *Cuadernos hispanoamericanos* 316 (1976): 21–44.

Debicki, Andrew P. "Luis Cernuda: la naturaleza y la poesía en su obra lírica." *Estudios sobre poesía española contemporánea.* Madrid: Gredos, 1968. 285–306.

Goytisolo, Juan. "Cernuda y la crítica literaria española." *El furgón de cola.* Paris: Reudo Ibérico, 1967. 86–97.

Ilie, Paul. "La órbita francesa (Cernuda, Hinojosa)." *Los surrealistas españoles.* Madrid: Taurus, 1972. 293–302.

Real Ramos, César. *Luis Cernuda y la generación de 27.* Salamanca: Universidad, 1983.

Romero, Francisco. "El muro, la ventana: La 'otredad' de Luis Cernuda." *Cuadernos hispanoamericanos* 396 (1983): 545–75.

Salinas, Pedro. "Nueve o diez poetas." *Ensayos de literatura hispánica.* Madrid: Aguilar, 1961. 334–36.

Sánchez Reboredo, José. "La figura del poeta en la obra de Luis Cernuda." *Cuadernos hispanoamericanos* 316 (1976): 21–44.

Velázquez Cueto, Gerardo. "Para una lectura de *Un río, un amor* de Luis Cernuda." *Insula* 455 (1984): 3, 7.

Federico García Lorca

Aguirre, J. M. "El sonambulismo de Federico García Lorca." *Bulletin of Hispanic Studies* 44 (1967): 267–85.

Allen, Rupert. "An Analysis of Narrative and Symbol in Lorca's *Romance sonámbulo*." *Hispanic Review* 36 (1968): 338–52.

Anderson, Andrew A. "Lorca's 'New York Poems': A Contribution to the Debate." *Forum for Modern Language Studies* 17 (1982): 256–70.

———. "The Evolution of García Lorca's Poetic Projects 1929–36 and the Textual Status of *Poeta en Nueva York.*" *Bulletin of Hispanic Studies* 60 (1983): 221–46.

Andueza, María. *Once poemas comentados de Federico García Lorca.* Mexico City: Universidad Nacional Autónoma de México, 1978.

Babín, María Teresa. *Estudios lorquianos.* Universidad de Puerto Rico: Editorial Universitaria, 1976.

Bary, David. "Preciosa and the English." *Hispanic Review* 37 (1969): 510–17.

Belamich, André. *Lorca.* Paris: Gallimard, 1962.

Bosch, Rafael. "El choque de imágenes como principio creador de García Lorca." *Revista hispánica moderna* 30 (1964): 35–44.

Cannon, Calvin. "Lorca's *Llanto por Ignacio Sánchez Mejías* and the Elegiac Tradition." *Hispanic Review* 31 (1963): 229–38.

Cano Ballesta, Juan. "Utopía y rebelión contra un mundo alienante: El *Romancero gitano* de Lorca." *García Lorca Review* 6 (1978): 71–85.

Cirré, Francisco. "Vanguardia y clasicismo en la 'Oda a Salvador Dalí.'" *Estudios sobre literatura y arte dedicados al profesor Emilio Orozco Díaz.* Ed. Gallego Morell, André Soria, and Nicolás Marín. Granada: Universidad de Granada, 1979. 297–302.

Correa, Gustavo. "El simbolismo del sol en la poesía de Federico García Lorca." *Nueva revista de filología española* 14 (1960): 110–19.

Craige, Betty Jean. *Lorca's Poet in New York: The Fall into Consciousness.* Lexington: UP of Kentucky, 1977.

Crosbie, John. "Structure and Counter-Structure in Lorca's *Romancero gitano.*" *MLR* 77 (1982): 74–88.

Debicki, Andrew P. "Federico García Lorca: Estilización y visión de la poesía." *Federico García Lorca.* Ed. Ildefonso-Manuel Gil. Madrid: Gredos, 1980. 169–90.

Díaz-Plaja, Guillermo. *Federico García Lorca.* Madrid: Espasa-Calpe, 1954.

Dust, Patrick H. "Cosmic Love in Lorca and Guillén." *At Home and Beyond: New Essays on Spanish Poets of the Twenties.* Ed. Salvador Jiménez-Fajardo and John C. Wilcox. Lincoln, Neb.: Society of Spanish and Spanish American Studies, 1983. 53–68.

Eisenberg, Daniel. *The Textual Tradition of Poeta en Nueva York.* Chapel Hill: U of North Carolina P, 1978.

Feal Deibe, Carlos. "García Lorca y el psicoanálisis: Apostillas a unas apostillas." *Bulletin of Hispanic Studies* 54 (1977): 311–14.

García Lorca, Federico. *Federico y su mundo.* Ed. and with prologue by Mario Hernández. Madrid: Alianza Tres, 1980.

García-Posada, Miguel. *García Lorca.* Madrid: Edaf, 1970.

Giacovate, Bernardo. "Serenidad y conflicto en la poesía de Federico García Lorca." *Asomante* 18 (1962): 7–13.

Harris, Derek. "The Theme of the Crucifixion in Lorca's *Romancero gitano.*" *Bulletin of Hispanic Studies* 58 (1981): 329–38.

Herrero, Javier. "'La luna vino a la fragua': Lorca's Mythic Forge." *De los romances-villancico a la poesía de Claudio Rodríguez: 22 ensayos sobre las literaturas española e hispanoamericana en homenaje a Gustav*

Siebenmann. Ed. José Manuel López de Abiada and Augusta López Berna-socchi. N.p.: José Esteban, 1984. 175–97.

Josephs, Allen. "Lorca and *Duende*: Toward a Dionysian Concept of Art." *García Lorca Review* 7 (1979): 55–72.

Laguardia, Gari. "The Butterflies in Walt Whitman's Beard: Lorca's Naming of Whitman." *Neophilologus* 62 (1978): 540–54.

Lara Pozuelo, Antonio. *El adjetivo en la lírica de Federico García Lorca.* Madrid: Ariel, 1973.

Leighton, Charles H. "The Treatment of Time and Space in the *Romancero gitano.*" *Hispania* 43 (1960): 378–83.

Londré, Felicia Hardison. *Federico García Lorca.* New York: Frederick Ungar, 1984.

Maurer, Christopher. "En busca de un texto perdido: 'Imaginación, inspiración, evasión.'" *García Lorca Review* 6 (1978): 169–74.

Morris, C. B. "'Bronce y Sueño': Lorca's Gypsies." *Neophilologus* 61 (1977): 225–44.

Nunes, María Luisa. "Absence and Presence in the Six Galician Poems of García Lorca." *García Lorca Review* 9 (1981): 97–108.

Ortega, José. "García Lorca, poeta social: 'Los negros' (*Poeta en Nueva York*)." *Cuadernos hispanoamericanos* 320–21 (1977): 407–19.

Perri, Dennis. "Tension, Speaker, and Experience in *Poema del cante jondo.*" *Revista Hispánica Moderna* 39 (1976–77): 1–10.

Predmore, Richard L. "Simbolismo ambiguo en la poesía de García Lorca." *Papeles de Son Armadans* 64 (1971): 229–40.

Rodrigo, Antonina. *García Lorca, el amigo de Cataluña.* Barcelona: Edhasa, 1984.

Umbral, Francisco. *Lorca, poeta maldito.* Madrid: Biblioteca Nueva, 1968.

Vicent, Manuel. *García Lorca.* Madrid: Epesa, 1969.

Rafael Alberti

Arean, Carlos. "La imagen pictórica en la poesía de Alberti." *Cuadernos his-panoamericanos* 289–90 (1974): 198–209.

Arniz, Francisco M., ed. *Homenaje a Rafael Alberti.* Barcelona: Península, 1977.

Bayo, Manuel. *Sobre Alberti.* Madrid: CVS Ediciones, 1974.

Herrero, Javier. "The Sun against the Moon and the Birth of the Sea: Rafael Alberti's *Marinero en tierra.*" *Studia Hispanica in Honor of Rodolfo Cardona.* Madrid: Cátedra, 1981. 97–129.

Manteiga, Robert C. "Color Synthesis and Antithesis: The Parallel Construction of Color Images in Rafael Alberti's Early Works." *Crítica hispánica* 1 (1979): 75–86.

Pérez, Carlos Alberto. "Rafael Alberti: Sobre los tontos." *Revista hispánica moderna* 32 (1966): 41–77.

Rugg, Marilyn D. "*Sobre los ángeles:* The Poetic Voices of Rafael Alberti." *MLN* 98 (1983): 259–67.

Stiem, Bruce G. "Derivación léxica como recurso poético en algunas poesías de Rafael Alberti." *Cuadernos hispanoamericanos* 360 (1980): 585–92.

Winkelmann, Ana María. "Pintura y poesía en Rafael Alberti." *Papeles de Son Armadans* 30 (1963): 147–62.

Zardoya, Concha. "El mar en la poesía de Rafael Alberti." *Poesía española del siglo XX.* Vol. 3 Madrid: Gredos, 1974. 446–78. 4 vols.

Index

267

About the Author

C. Christopher Soufas grew up in Columbia, South Carolina, and was schooled in a combination of traditions that stirred his interests in art, poetry, ideology, and politics. He served in the army during the Vietnam War. He is a graduate of Emory University (B.A. 1970), the University of South Carolina (M.A. 1975), and Duke University (Ph.D. 1980), and studied at the Universidad Complutense de Madrid in 1975–76.

Soufas is associate professor of Spanish at Louisiana State University; he has taught at West Chester University and North Carolina State University. His wife, Teresa S. Soufas, is associate professor of Spanish at Tulane University. He is co-editor, with Cecilia Castro Lee, of *En torno al hombre y los monstruos: Ensayos críticos sobre la novelística de Carlos Rojas* and guest editor of *The Newist Criticisms,* a special issue of *College Literature.* He received a National Endowment for the Humanities grant in 1985. His home is in La Place, Louisiana.

About the Book

Conflict of Light and Wind is typeset in ITC Garamond, a twentieth-century typeface designed for the International Typeface Corporation in the spirit of the classic work of the sixteenth-century French type designer Claude Garamond. The book was composed by World Composition Services of Sterling, Virginia. The design is by Kachergis Book Design of Pittsboro, North Carolina.

Wesleyan University Press, 1989